The Fear That Stalks

Published in collaboration with UNDP and CEQUIN

the fear that stalks

GENDER-BASED VIOLENCE IN PUBLIC SPACES

Edited by
Sara Pilot and Lora Prabhu

zubaan

ZUBAAN
an imprint of Kali for Women
128 B Shahpur Jat, 1st floor
NEW DELHI 110 049
Email: contact@zubaanbooks.com
Website: www.zubaanbooks.com

First published by Zubaan 2012
First paperback edition 2014
Copyright © this collection Zubaan/Cequin 2012

10 9 8 7 6 5 4 3 2

ISBN 978 93 83074 72 3

Zubaan is an independent feminist publishing house based in New Delhi with a strong academic and general list. It was set up as an imprint of India's first feminist publishing house, Kali for Women, and carries forward Kali's tradition of publishing world quality books to high editorial and production standards. *Zubaan* means tongue, voice, language, speech in Hindustani. Zubaan is a non-profit publisher, working in the areas of the humanities, social sciences, as well as in fiction, general non-fiction, and books for children and young adults under its Young Zubaan imprint.

Typeset in Adobe Thai by Jojy Phillip, New Delhi 110 015
Printed at Raj Press, R-3 Inderpuri, New Delhi 110 012

Contents

✳✿✳

Foreword

❊❀❊

Despite the improved indicators in education and workforce participation can we really say that the status of women in India has improved? The declining sex ratio surely has a different story to tell.

In order to understand this story in a holistic manner we need to first understand what women's empowerment is. What does it entail? What are its critical barriers? Is there a final destination, or is it the journey and the process of attainment, that we are engaged with? These are some of the questions we grappled with while we were Programme Officers at UNIFEM (now UN Women). We set up CEQUIN, the Centre for Equity and Inclusion, in 2007 as a social laboratory, to look for answers to these questions.

Indeed, when you work for women's empowerment it is imperative to have a 360 degree approach, one that can address itself to every aspect of women's lives, including education, health and livelihoods. However, despite concerted efforts in all these areas, challenges remain. The most critical one is the continuing cycle of violence women face – physical and mental violence on the one hand and violence in the form of discrimination and exclusion on the other. This scourge of gender-based violence needs to be tackled urgently if empowerment is to happen in a meaningful way.

In India, the Domestic Violence Act 2005 was a landmark legislation, and has provided a framework to look at all forms of violence in the domestic sphere. It is hoped that the Sexual Harassment at Workplace Bill will fill the legislative gap to protect women in their workplaces. However, while addressing gender-based violence in public spaces, that is, between the domestic space and the workspace, there seems to be no cohesive approach or framework. The significance of this space is in its direct connection with women's mobility, access, and engagement with public life.

In effect, the entire process of building women's capabilities hinges on their ability to access education and skills, healthcare, markets, livelihoods and recreation. With mobility curtailed due to safety concerns, a vicious cycle of low capability is perpetuated, leading to gender discrimination. Women are unable to achieve their full capabilities because of social and cultural constraints which create violent barriers, thus impeding their effective economic and political participation. This stems from the patriarchal understanding that public spaces belong to men.

Examining gender-based violence in the notional public sphere also becomes particularly relevant in situations where such acts are condoned, ignored or actively abetted. Gender-based violence goes beyond sexual harassment. The woman's body in many instances is used as a battleground to settle scores and to assert power. The rape of Dalit women, atrocities committed by the armed forces in conflict zones, instances of 'honour' killings, moral policing, parading women naked, tonsuring, witch hunting, acid throwing and so on, are all alarming trends which urgently need to be addressed.

As we struggled to gain a clearer understanding of these issues, we felt a pressing need to initiate an informed debate; which led us at CEQUIN to approach the United Nations Development Programme (UNDP) and the National Commission for Women (NCW) to partner with us. In October 2010, CEQUIN organised a two-day conference in New Delhi entitled 'Gender-based Violence in Public Spaces: Challenges and Solutions'. Participants included activists, practitioners and policy makers from across India. Thematic papers were presented by a wide range of contributors, reflecting various concerns and perspectives. The papers commissioned for the conference included: 1) 'Gendered Claims of Citizenship and Notions of Honour and Stigma', by Flavia Agnes; 2) 'Gendered Usage of Public Spaces: A Case Study of Mumbai', by Shilpa Phadke; 3) 'Masculinity and its Role in Gender-based Violence in Public Spaces', by Sanjay Srivastava; 4) ' "Neutral" laws or "Moral" Codes Controlling and Recreating Sexualities/Intimacies', by Rukmini Sen; 5) 'Role of Media in Addressing Gender-based Violence in Public Spaces', by Mohuya Chaudhuri; 6) 'Gender-based Violence in Public Spaces: Consequences and Cost', by Nandita Bhatla; 7) 'Women and

Homelessness', by Shivani Chaudhry, Amita Joseph, and Indu Prakash Singh; 8) 'Redeeming "Honour" Through Violence: Unravelling the Concept and its Application', by Prem Chowdhry; 9) 'Gender-based Violence in Public Places: Acid Throwing', by Keerthi Bollineni; 10) 'Gender-based Violence in Conflict Zones: Case Study of Impact of Ongoing Armed Conflict, Small Arms Proliferation and Women's Response in India's Northeast', by Binalakshmi Nepram; 11) 'Police Response to Gender-based Violence in Public Places', by Suman Nalwa. (These papers can be accessed at www. cequinindia.org)

There could have been no better publisher that Zubaan to put this rich collection of papers into a compiled knowledge base for researchers and practitioners. While most of the conference papers find place in this publication, a few could not be included due to technical reasons. We would like to acknowledge the contribution of Suman Nalwa, Binalakshmi Nepram and Keerthi Bollineni. An important aspect which was not addressed during the conference discussions was the issue of trans-genders. This gap has been compensated by the inclusion of the paper – 'Gender-based Violence faced by Hijras in Public Spaces in Urban India', by Priti Prabhughate, Ernest Norhona and Alka Narang.

It is our hope that this publication will provide a framework with which to understand the nature and dimensions of gender-based violence in public spaces and that it will contribute to an informed debate on strategies to tackle this issue. It is imperative for women to assert their citizenship rights and claim their space in the public domain, thereby blurring the public-private divide which has confined women to the domestic space.

We take this opportunity to thank Girija Vyas for providing NCW's support. This project may not have seen the light of day, but for the unstinting support of Meenakshi Kathel of UNDP who constantly provided valuable guidance. We would like to thank Urvashi Butalia for her insights, as well as enthusiastically taking on the task of compiling an eclectic collection into a cohesive book, and for writing the overview chapter. We thank our distinguished writers, for their valuable contributions as well as their patience. We would also like to acknowledge the guidance and participation of Kiran Bedi, Farah Naqvi, Sohaila Kapur and Govind

Kelkar. Last but not the least we would like to thank our friends Radhika Kaul Batra, Mimi Choudhury, Nitin Panmani and the CEQUIN team for their continued support!

Sara Pilot and **Lora Prabhu**
Centre for Equity and Inclusion

The Fear That Stalks

Gender–based Violence in Public Spaces

URVASHI BUTALIA

At a recent meeting on safety in urban spaces, I asked the young men and women gathered in the room a question. How many of them felt unsafe in Delhi—the city where we were meeting—when they were out on the streets. No male hand went up. Every single female hand did. There were no surprises there. I then asked the men if they had ever felt unsafe at all in the city- and some more nuanced answers were offered. One man said the only time he had ever felt unsafe was in the presence of a baton-wielding policeman! Another said he had felt unsafe once when he had seen some hijras at a traffic light, but barring one or two such answers, men remained firmly located within their sense of male privilege.

For the women, however, it was a different story. They nodded in agreement as I spoke of why women never seemed to idle in public spaces, why they often felt the need to look busy and businesslike, and how speaking on the cellphone had become a way of establishing purpose and sending a signal that they were in communication with someone, probably a man, and could therefore call for help. They offered stories of their own: riding on the metro had made things much easier, and the fact that there was a women's compartment helped, but at the same time, many of them hated being pushed into the 'ghetto' of the women's compartment. Why can't we, they asked, ride in the general carriages freely and without restraint? Why indeed? As many of them pointed out, they were also part of the 'general'. public, and while women-only carriages made it easy for single women, they did not necessarily offer the same comfort to married women, or mothers, who would rather be with their children and/or husbands.

I was reminded of my college days and the sorts of things we had to battle with. Over three decades ago, when women of my age went to college, Delhi's buses were a different kind of animal. Rickety, old, battered, and spilling over at the seams with people desperate to get from A to B. As well, there were smaller vehicles known as mini-buses, not the RTV types that you see today, but broad, squat buses operated by private operators and which, in theory, held half the number of people an ordinary bus could hold, but in practice did quite otherwise. Those days of travel in these buses—for there was no other system of transport on offer—were sheer hell for most of us, and assault and molestation were a daily occurrence. I recall many occasions on which I would arrive home feeling soiled and violated, having spent an agonizing forty or fifty minutes feeling a strange man's hands on me and not knowing how to deal with what was happening. Eventually, we joined a battle for separate buses for women. These were called Ladies Specials, and it was these that made a difference to our lives. Most of us did not mind waiting even three hours after classes for the sheer relief of riding on a bus without having to hold your body and skin within itself. But we often asked ourselves why it had to be that way, and why we could not feel both safe and comfortable while going to and from the university. As the French say, the more things change, the more they remain the same.

The question of gender-based violence is, of course, much wider than merely the issue of safe transport in the city. Indeed the problem of gender-based violence is a deeper and more complicated one than questions of safety and comfort, although both are inherently linked to the subject. Further, when we try to locate such violence in what is known as the public space, the layers become even more complex. The very notions of what is public and what is private have, for some considerable time, been the subject of debate. Feminists in particular have argued that the division, which is also fundamentally a gendered division, with the private being equated with the home and therefore with women, and the public with the world outside and therefore with men, is inherently false. Further, such a division is also inherently class-biased in nature as it assumes that everyone has a roof over their head, a home enclosed within four walls. Yet for the hundreds of thousands of homeless people in our cities and villages, the so-called 'public' space is actually the only 'private' space they know. The street is their home, the footpath their bed and as always for women, these issues carry other, deeper implications. Clearly, inequalities of gender and class, indeed of location and caste, are built into these very concepts of public and private, and therefore they cannot be taken at face value.

Space itself is not a homogenous concept—its existence and its definitions are closely tied with other things, chief among which is a notion of entitlement and ownership. Middle class and wealthy dwellers in urban areas for example—and indeed rural as well—lay exclusionary claim to certain spaces that, in theory, are public spaces and should therefore be accessible to all. Thus a public road, a park, a shopping mall, a sports ground, any or all of these can become the preserve of the rich simply by virtue of their status and power, and they can then claim ownership and entitlement, and draw on the apparatus of the State to defend their 'rights'. In the residential area where I live for example, the local tea stall owners and roadside eateries—that served the poor and working class people who work as guards, domestics, road sweepers—have been removed from the public areas where they were located in order to make, as the welfare association claims 'the colony safer for our residents, particularly our elders, our women and children.' The assumption is that the mere presence of working class people, no matter that these same people work in the houses of the wealthy, somehow renders a public space 'unsafe', perhaps because here is where they may loiter, and therefore get up to no good.

Space is also not only a geographical description, but connotes much more, including the 'luxury' to have private time, your own space—inside your head and outside. And here too, while men can lay claim to different kinds of spaces, women do not have that luxury. In a collection of posters from the women's movement in India, that has been put together by the feminist publishing house, Zubaan, to make up an exhibition, there is one poster of a woman seated in front of a television, her feet up on a stool, a book in her hand and lying back in a relaxed position, a coffee cup by her side. She reads as the television continues to talk. The curators called this poster 'the right to leisure', making the point that this was a right women could claim as much as anyone else. The reality, however, is that this is not a right women have, whether in the home or outside.

If public spaces, particularly in cities and towns, are inherently classed, they are also, equally, inherently gendered. The convenient division of public and private into male and female, the world and the home, lends itself easily to the understanding, or indeed the interpretation, that men somehow have a right to public spaces while women do not. So, a man loitering in a park, travelling by public transport at night, hanging around at a railway station or a roadside kiosk after dark, does so because it is his 'natural' right; a woman doing the same is somehow transgressing, a transgression that then, and expectedly, takes away very many of her other rights—the right to dignity, autonomy, her body, and so on.

Rights are, of course, intrinsically linked to another key concept—that of citizenship. The Indian Constitution promises that no citizen will be discriminated against on the basis of religion, location, class, gender. Its own rules and legislations, however, routinely carry such discrimination, especially on grounds of gender with the male gender being seen as the 'norm' and the female as somehow the lesser, dependent one. Women's rights are by and large mediated through the prism of the family, the assumption being that this is also the proper place for women to be. The protective custody of the family is also said to ensure for women a kind of safety and security, which the public sphere, away from the 'benign' influence of the family, cannot offer. So the circle is then complete and the woman is once again returned to the four walls of the home.

Wherever she is, whether within the four walls of the home, or at the workplace or merely outside, in a purposeless, aimless wandering (of the kind that men often do) violence stalks her everywhere. It is pervasive and, over the years, so naturalized that it is not even noticed, or remarked upon. As many of the essayists in this book show, statistics on gender-based violence have only been growing in the last few years, and growing alarmingly. Rape, sexual assault and molestation, dowry deaths, sex selective abortion, caste and community-based killings disguised as 'honour' killings, acid attacks, and attacks on people of alternative sexualities, or on sex workers—none of these hold any surprises for us. And these are the realities we know, those that receive some measure of public attention. There are innumerable other forms of violence that we have not even begun to apprehend. How many women, for example suffer not physical, but continuing mental violence? For those who have no home, for whom the very public space of the street is the only home they have (and researchers put the number of these in the city of Delhi alone at 150,000—a conservative figure—with an estimated 10,000 of them being women (see essay in this volume)), the forms of violence are multiple, and everyday, and there is no recourse because they are barely recognized as being human, let alone having access to the rights and privileges that are the rightful due of every Indian citizen.

By and large, it is women who are the targets of gender-based violence. But it does not stop there—people of alternative sexualities, whether they are homosexual, lesbian or they inhabit the spectrum of transgender identities – are also particularly vulnerable, and violence directed at them often also carries a hatred of anything that represents 'difference', or anything that questions the status quo. Many transgender people live on the margins of our society, and are not considered worthy of rights or privileges. As well, the poorer among them often do not have shelter and therefore become targets of violence both at the hands of the police and the law keepers, as well as ordinary citizens. Anger and resentment against transgender and homosexual people is also particularly acute because of their relative openness about issues of sex, or indeed of the involvement of some of them in sex work. This makes them fair game for specific kinds of violence, and their lack of recognition and acceptance in what is known as 'normal' society, makes it that much more difficult for them to access justice.

Sexual identities are not the only ones to be thus targeted. A study of caste-based violence in four states of India (Irudayam, Mangubhai and Lee 2011) shows how women at the very bottom of the caste ladder are continually exposed to violence, both from upper caste men and indeed from their own men who, brutalized by being at the receiving end of terrible discrimination and violence themselves, take it out on their women. Such violence can take any form: refusal to provide sexual services can result in rape, sometimes even death, or public humiliation. Also known as common punishments for stepping out of line are things like enforced poverty, starvation, and others that are as bad, or worse.

There is another 'hierarchy' or 'difference' encoded in the given concepts of the public and the private that is important to address, and this is that the 'public' is, in some strange way, usually taken to mean urban—almost as if public spaces do not exist in rural areas. Perhaps the reason for this is that women in rural India do not have much access to 'public' spaces, particularly those for leisure. So, while the field and the village shop may be permissible, or a place of worship equally, the tea stall, the street corner, the open courtyard where people may gather, where theatre performances or films may be viewed, these are not so easily seen as spaces women can inhabit, unless they do so in a sheltered and protected way. Much of this is changing today, particularly with the entry of women into village level politics as a result of the 73rd and 74th Amendments to the Indian Constitution, but the issue remains. It was because she was seen as having stepped out of line that Bhanwri Devi, a worker with the Indian government's Women's Development Programme in Rajasthan, was subjected to gang rape by upper caste men of her village—by stepping out, by daring to confront men, especially upper caste men, she had violated many of the codes set for women and therefore had to be given the appropriate punishment.

Choice and desire, these are two things that are simply not permissible. In parts of northern India (not only in Haryana but also in places like Bengal) families impose strict—and usually irrational—rules on young people who are not allowed to marry within the same gotra or group. The punishment, if the young people exercising the choice to marry can be caught, is almost certain death—or murder, for which the offenders are seldom even arrested, let alone convicted. In theory, this crime takes place inside families, but in effect, its practice is very public, and widely publicly accepted, sometimes even celebrated. Not only does this give a new meaning to the notion of public, but it also raises the important and vexing question of what it is that allows people to so widely and indeed so publicly support and accept such a fundamental violation of the rights and dignity of a person or persons, and what it is within our State and our system that allows impunity to flourish thus unchecked? Why is it that a widow can be immolated on her husband's funeral pyre, that a thousand people can be witnesses, but when it comes to filing a case, or conducting an investigation, there is not a single voice that is willing to speak up? Is this fear of being targeted by 'the community' or something deeper—a fundamental acceptance of the marginality of the lives of women?

In recent years there has been considerable discussion in India, and particularly among women activists in India, about the ongoing violence of conflict, particularly in the two 'wings' of the country, in the northwest (Kashmir) and the northeast. In these two areas and along the eastern Maoist corridor, militancy and state violence have claimed many lives, among them those of women. But more, women's entry into and participation in anti-state, sub-national and people's movements, has meant that they have had to confront not only State violence—as in the rape of women by army forces in Kashmir or in continuing search and seizure operations in conflict areas—but also violence from their compatriots, something that is, in many ways, more difficult to address. In such movements, while the public becomes women's domain as much as it is men's and no one questions their right to be there, and the gun offers a kind of protection, none of this makes women any less vulnerable to sexual exploitation and abuse. While some political movements have strict codes of behaviour for men and women, others do not and for women, it becomes difficult to raise issues of gender-based violence because, in the face of the wider goals of the movement, they seem almost trivial, and no matter how political the leaders may be, because most of them are male, somewhere they too have internalized the ideology of the male/female world/home public/private division.

The list is long, and many more aspects of gender-based violence can be added to what has been detailed above (for example acid attacks, attacks on homeless women and so on). Since its beginnings in the mid-seventies until the present day, the question of violence has been a central one for the women's movement in India, and its multiple forms and manifestations have been addressed in different ways. Over the years, however, as the social, political and economic contexts have changed, so have the many forms of violence women have had to confront. Less than three decades ago, when technology was not advanced enough to be able to detect the sex of the unborn foetus, women's groups could not have imagined the scale and size of the problem that would confront them; today, one only needs to look at the statistics on sex ratio in the Census to see the wideranging and disturbing impact of sex-selective abortions. Nor was it possible then to predict the changes that would come about with globalization and the growth of the outsourcing industry and how that would make women vulnerable to different forms of violence. Today, while the forms of violence have multiplied, and the concept of the public has so radically changed, one of the encouraging signs is that there is considerable research that addresses not only the forms of violence but also its roots and history, as well as its costs—in real terms, in terms of woman days lost—to society.

The essays in this volume address various aspects of the question of gender-based violence in what are known as public spaces. In doing so they not only provide an analysis of the public and the private, but ask how the binaries of the two have come to be associated with gender, with the public being seen as a male domain and the private as the female, an opposition that also then locates women firmly within the domestic sphere and establishes any presence they may have in the 'real public' as illegitimate. As Flavia Agnes points out in her analysis of different legislations relating to violence against women particularly, the consensus on the nature of public/private, on issues of violence and justice, is a consensus that is implicit between the State and communities and families, represented usually by men. The negotiations that then take place between State, community and family on questions of women's rights, are important markers for determining the citizenship claims of women and they lead, inevitably, to a gendered notion of citizenship. Because such an understanding then locates women firmly within the familial sphere and sees them as passive and lacking in agency, patriarchal authority seems then to be both natural and desirable and a woman's need for a public identity somehow illegitimate. On the part of women, however, their demand for safety in public places can be read as a demand for their citizenship rights, and yet, the family and State in many ways collude to deny them this, subjecting them to violence both from without—as markers of the identity and honour of the community—and from within, at the hands of the family and community who see the need to discipline them if they so much as step outside the bounds set for them.

What, one might then ask, makes men behave the way they do? Sanjay Srivastava explores the concept of masculinity, a socially produced but embodied way of being male whose manifestations include manners of speech, behaviours, gestures, social interactions and the division of tasks considered proper for women and men. Such a discourse, Srivastava tells us, so naturalises masculinity and establishes it as superior that it sets the tone and forms the bedrock of so much violence against those who are then seen as 'weak'—whether women, or effeminate men, or transgender people. Thus masculinity possesses both external (as relating to women) and internal (as relating to other, 'different' men) characteristics, and enables and legitimizes particular forms of behaviour.

While these two essays form the conceptual and general basis for the explorations in this book, others deal with more specific forms and their particular contexts. Historian Prem Chowdhry traverses a terrain that is familiar to her, that of family and caste in urban and rural Haryana and Punjab, looking at how customary law and so-called 'traditional' practices target both women and men who are seen to step out of line. Often, this results in the deaths of the young couples, and the impunity and social acceptance that such structures have—they build on the accepted ideals of masculinity—means that communities and sometimes families literally get away with murder. Once again, the unwillingness of the State to 'tamper' with what is seen as accepted custom, but what in actuality are the structures of power and privilege that State bodies do not wish to alienate, means that women, and men, those who defy the codes of what are legitimate relationships and what are not, have to pay with their lives.

Rukmini Sen takes the discussion on law further by addressing herself to some key 'incidents' that have taken place across the country in recent years. She looks at how sexualties and intimacies have become a part of social science discussion in ways that establish heterosexual familial relationships as normative, and identify certain types of sexual behaviour as deviant, which then legitimizes the need for laws to sanction 'correct' codes of behaviour. Her examination of specific examples leads her to a discussion of the women's movement's perspectives on sexuality, the response of the public sphere to contemporary issues relating to sexuality and an examination of legal provisions and their silences in relation to sexuality.

Shilpa Phadke, a researcher who has spent long years working on urban safety in Mumbai, takes a somewhat different tack. Women, she says, inhabit a city differently from men Women spatially inhabit a city differently, they perceive it differently, they carry different mind maps in their heads and they negotiate it differently. Using this basic premise and on the basis of empirical research, she looks at the conceptual categories and the ideological context which influence urban planning as well as the policies that impact women's capacity to be in public space. In particular women's access to public space is examined in the context of citizenship, civic and sexual safety and risk and respectability.

Two papers (by Indu Prakash Singh, Amita Joseph, and Shivani Chaudhry on homelessness and Priti Prabhughate, Ernest Norhona and Alka Narang on transgenders) address hitherto relatively untouched aspects—that of homelessness, looking particularly at the city of Delhi, and of transgender people, in particular hijras. Among the large numbers of the homeless in Delhi, a considerable percentage is made up of women, and yet, there is only one home for homeless women in the city. In their case, the easy binaries of home and the world, the private and the public, break down for the public is in fact the private, precisely because they are homeless. What then are the guarantees of safety or justice that they can claim? Anyone can abuse or molest them, they are fair game because they sleep on the roads, if they are raped and try to report they are not believed, if they become pregnant and wish to abort they are shunned, indeed fear and danger stalks them at every step. While homeless women face particular problems, people of indeterminate sexualities are also extremely vulnerable as many of them are 'people of the streets' so to speak and if they are not, they are engaged in professions—such as singing and dancing, offering blessings, sex work, begging—that locate them in the public space. Socially marginalized, they also have to face the exclusion from citizenship rights and access that comes from being seen as somehow 'not normal', and therefore, to put it crudely, not deserving of citizenship rights and privileges.

While the situation on the ground therefore does not offer much to be positive about, it is worth examining the role of another major social actor, the media. In earlier days, staunch supporters of the causes espoused by the women's movement, the media in recent days have undergone radical and wide-ranging change. Mohuya Chaudhuri describes how the proliferation of news channels, the tyranny of the 24x7 wheel where new content has to be generated virtually non-stop, the desperation to be the first, have all pushed media into acting first and thinking or indeed regretting, later. In the process a great deal is lost, and much damage is done. While recognizing the occasional positive input by the media, it is this kind of flattening out or harmful effect that we need to be alert to. While many issues have benefited from the coverage they have received, in others the media has acted as trial court, judge and juror, condemning women particularly, even before the facts of the case are known, and flouting every single guideline on reportage and ethics that exists. Is the media then ally or foe? There are no easy answers to this.

Every essay in this volume addresses itself to one basic question: what kind of policy interventions can be made to deal with the many aspects of gender-based violence in public spaces. An analysis of the problem, specific in some cases and general in others, leads to some key recommendations for policy and planning. It is in this connection that Nandita Bhatia offers an important approach when she suggests that one way of getting society and policy makers to take the question of gender-based violence seriously is to estimate its costs to society as empirical evidence alone may not be sufficient to press for policy changes. Calculating the costs of violence in economic and social terms, as well as individually and collectively, and indeed calculating them more specifically in monetary terms (that is, by measuring and quantifying the consequences that households and national economies experience), can, crucially, help to demonstrate impact and therefore serve as an advocacy tool to influence policy decisions as well as draw attention to the need for political action.

Together these essays not only draw attention to the many forms of gender-based violence in public spaces, but also question the contradictions and hierarchies that lie at the heart of the division of spheres into the public and the private, showing not only how the two overlap and blur into each other, but how these divisions are inherently class and gender biased and work against women. No single collection on a subject that is so multi-dimensional and that has such a long and troubled history can hope to cover every aspect of it, but it is our hope that in drawing attention particularly to the need for policy changes, and in tracing the historical and ideological basis of gender-based violence, this collection of essays will make a small, but significant, beginning in addressing this pervasive problem, and suggesting how we may begin to deal with it.

References

Irudayam, Aloysius S.J., Jayshree P. Mangubhai and Joel G. Lee (2011). *Dalit Women Speak Out: Violence Against Dalit Women in India*. New Delhi: Zubaan.

Masculinity and its Role in Gender-based Violence in Public Spaces

Introduction

This essay reflects the position that in order to comprehend the nature of gender inequalities we must closely interrogate the *relationship* between gender identities in their various social, cultural, economic and political contexts. For, as Rosalind O'Hanlon points out:

A proper understanding of the field of power in which women have lived their lives demands that we look at men as gendered beings too: at what psychic and social investments sustain their sense of themselves as men, at what networks and commonalities bring men together on the basis of shared gender identity, and what hierarchies and exclusions set them apart. (O'Hanlon 1997: 1)

Hence, the study of feminine, masculine and trans-gender identities concerns the exploration of *power relationships* within the contemporary gender landscape, where certain dominant ideals of manhood impact on women, different ways of being men, as well those identities that may not fit either gender category. This way of engaging with 'gender' is an exploration into the naturalisation of the category 'man' through which men have come to be regarded as un-gendered and as the 'universal subject of human history' (O'Hanlon 1997: 1).

Masculinity refers to the *socially produced but embodied ways of being male*. Its manifestations include manners of speech, behaviour, gestures, social interaction, a division of tasks 'proper' to men and women ('men work in offices, women do housework'), and an overall narrative that positions it as superior to its perceived antithesis, femininity. The discourse of masculinity as a dominant and 'superior' gender position is produced at a number of sites and has specific consequences for women as well as those men who may not fit into the dominant and valorised models of masculinity. These sites include: customary laws and regulations, the state and its mechanisms, the family, religious norms and sanctions, popular culture, and the media.

In order to stand in a relationship of superiority to feminine identity, masculinity must be represented as possessing characteristics that are the binary opposite of (actual or imagined) feminine identity. However, this is not all. Dominant masculinity stands in a relationship not just to femininity but *also to those ways of being male* that are seen to deviate from the ideal. It is in this sense that masculinity possesses both external (relating to women) as well as an internal (relating to 'other' men) characteristics. Both these contexts assist in bolstering what scholars have referred to as 'hegemonic' masculine identity (Connell 2005). So, the heterosexual, white-collar married male who is the 'breadwinner' is a useful (if somewhat caricatured) type to think about hegemonic masculinity. For, embedded in this representation is an entire inventory of the behaviours and roles that have been historically valorised as becoming of ideal masculinity. Hence, the dominant modes of being men could be said to be manufactured out of discourses on sexual orientation (heteronormativity), class, race, conjugality, the 'protective' function of males and women as recipients of protection, and the place of emotions in the lives of men and women.

What, however, is the difference between the linked concepts of 'patriarchy' and 'masculinity'? Patriarchy refers to a *system* of social organisation which is fundamentally organised around the idea of men's superiority to women. Within this system, even those who may not approximate to the male ideal (such as homosexual men) still stand to benefit from the privileges attached to being a man. So, as a parallel, we might think of the situation during the apartheid era South Africa where all whites—those who supported apartheid and those who opposed it—were potential beneficiaries of the institutionalised privileges of being white. Though it is difficult to posit simple definitions of 'patriarchy' and 'masculinity', we might say that patriarchy refers to the systemic relationship of power between men and women, whereas masculinity concerns both inter- and intra-gender relationships. And, while it can not be argued that under patriarchy *all* forms of masculinity are equally valorised, there is nevertheless an overwhelming consensus regarding the superiority of men over women. Patriarchy 'makes' men superior, whereas masculinity is the process of producing superior men.

The ideas of 'making' and 'producing' are crucial to the study of gender identities, for they point to their historical and social nature. The various discourses of 'proper' masculine behaviour—in novels, films, advertisements and folk-advice—would clearly be unnecessary if it was a naturally endowed characteristic. The very fact that masculinity must consistently be reinforced—'if you buy this motor-cycle you'll be a real man'—says something about the tenuous and fragile nature of gender identities; they *must* continually be reinforced. Following from this, we might also say that masculinity is *enacted* rather than expressed. For, when we say that something is 'expressed', we subscribe to the idea that it 'already exists', and gender identities in particular do not *already* exist (say, biologically). They involve an entire task of building and rebuilding, consolidation, representation and enforcement; in other words we must think of gender identities as works in progress. 'Deep masculinity' is the realm of uncritical 'men's studies' that proceeds from the assumptions of essential masculine identity that needs to be either maintained or recovered. In any case, it can not be part of a project that seeks to critically analyse the contours of the gendered power and its effect of proscribing a diversity of male and female identities. This does not of course imply that existing formations of masculinity do not also contain instances of men's deviation from the dominant mode (see, for example, Chopra 2003), rather that we still need to be attuned to whether such deviations disrupt existing frameworks or, in fact, find ways of operating within them.

As should be clear, a crucial task is to foreground the *social* nature of gender identities. This approach moves away from the biologism that has historically afflicted the study of gender and sexual identities. More importantly, to imagine identities and behaviours as socially and historically constituted is also to imagine the possibility of effecting change in a desired direction. For, if masculine identities vary across time and space—appear in different forms at different times and are different across societies—therein lies the possibility of formulating appropriate policy measures to influence the contexts within which gender inequalities persist.

It is important, then, to be clear about what is meant by 'biologism', for it continues—through naturalizing social categories and processes—to be a significant context through which gendered operations of power unfold. A significant part of the modern history of the study of gender and sexual cultures is the history of biologism. So, in the accounts of European sexologists such as Richard Freiherr von Krafft-Ebing (1840–1902) and Havelock Ellis (1859–1939), and others such as Sigmund Freud (1856–1939), even the defence of 'abnormal' sexual behaviour and gender identities was couched through the reasoning that these are 'natural' identities and hence should be tolerated. Biologism is the idea that identities derive from a 'deep source' within the self. Hence, the notion that we 'express' our gendered and sexual selves, rather than *enact* it. Enactment contains within it the idea of learning and performing, whereas 'expressing' embodies the notion of an essence that, no matter what, will come tumbling out.

Biologism, then, is the thinking that suggests that gender and sexual identities:

- are biologically derived;
- have been historically stable (i.e., the same since the 'dawn of time');
- are 'essentially' about our 'private' lives; and,
- are 'basically' the same across different cultures;
- are normative.

The view that gender identities are fixed is—as scholars who work in cross-cultural contexts know—a highly suspect one. The social and contextual nature of gender is nowhere better explained than in the case of 'women marriages' in many African societies where:

...an infertile woman or a woman who had no sons herself married a younger woman who would then bear sons for her husband in the name of the female-husband. The female-husband could then be wife to her husband and mother to their children, and husband to her wife and father to the children of that wife. (Morgan and Wieringa 2005: 300)

Notwithstanding the abundant nature of evidence of the malleability of human identity, it is often suggested—as a clinching argument to demonstrate the significance of biology—that one can not bring up sons to be daughters and daughters to be sons. This confuses biological attributes with social learning. Indeed, it is possible for *biological* male children to be brought up as *culturally* female. Consider the case of a family in Samoa where 'a mother has no young daughters and can not adopt a young girl to help with the housework':

In such a case, a son may be recruited by the mother to fill the role of a young girl in helping the mother manage the household. In such cases, when the boy continues to adopt the female gender role into adolescence and perhaps adulthood, the name *fa'afafine is applied*. A *fa'afafine* may marry and have children but continues to play a female role in the family and the village. (Bindon 2003: 935)

Male-ness and female-ness are, then, social attributes which we learn, and are taught. Further, and as already mentioned, if these were natural attributes then we would surely not need all the advertising that tells us what the appropriate behaviour is for men and women; we would simply know. The view that men-are-the-way-they-are-because-they-are-'hardwired'-that way is corollary to the positioning of men as 'universal subject'. That is, categories such as 'citizen', 'worker', 'intellectual' and 'the active agent of history' come implicitly to be understood as those occupied by men.

The above paragraph leads to two specific perspectives on 'culture'. First, our attempts to understand the ideologies and norms of gender that affect the lives of men and women in different ways should be premised on an understanding of broader cultural, social and political contexts—the family, educational systems, religious beliefs, ideas regarding human biology, sexuality, etc.—that produce and maintain these ideologies and norms. And, second, we must comprehend that cultures are always in flux and have a hybrid character (that is, made up of a number of different cultures).

History, Gender Identities and Norms

Gender norms and categories are directly related to the distribution of power among genders, and hence to issues of social justice, equity and human rights. 'Power', in turn, relates to the control over both symbolic as well as material goods. That is, the *ideas* we hold about men and women—their 'appropriate' roles, capacities and characteristics—along with the access they enjoy to *material resources* go towards determining their positions with respect to each other. Hence, both symbolic and material processes are of crucial importance when we plan upon affecting changes in oppressive social structures and conditions. *All* social contexts are gendered, and the gendered nature of social contexts 'means that neither male nor female power can be examined entirely in isolation' (Malhotra and Mather 1997: 603). 'Gender' is, therefore, a *relationship*, and in this paper even when the discussion is solely focussed upon one gender, it is the relationship between genders—their relative location in structures of hierarchy—that is implicitly under investigation.

In all cultures, including the European, a wide variety of conceptions of gender and sexuality existed before the advent of the modern era. Many forms of expression—body appearance, gestures, voice, and so on—were seen to be part of maleness and femaleness. In fact, some theorists now argue for a strong connection between modernity and the currently dominant form of masculinity. It has been suggested that the modern era ushered a way of thinking which *rigidly* defined how men and women should behave; that there emerged ways of thinking which implied that *a)* gender identity could be divided into two categories, that is, male and female, and that *b)* each of these two categories could be understood in terms of their 'essential' being. Hence, the *binarism* and essentialism of modern thought that colonised diverse fields of activity also had a strong influence upon ideas of gender identity. This was manifested in a 'separation of reason from nature [which] works to divide men from their emotions and feelings which become threatening to [their] identities as men.... [men were exhorted to] disdain emotions and feelings as signs of weakness and so as potentially compromising [their] sense of male identity' (Seidler 1994: x–xi).

The colonial era was particularly important in the historical development of the career of modern masculinity. Hence, as Edward Said (1979) has famously suggested, an entire corpus of writing and other material—literature, poetry, philosophical tracts, government reports, picture postcards, travelogues, 'scientific' reports, religious commentary, etc.—represented the Orient in specific ways. 'Orientalism' refers to the processes and sites of 'producing' a space called the Orient for western consumption, such that the 'West' and the 'Orient' come to be in a relation of superiority-inferiority. Western religious, aesthetic, philosophical, kinship, literary, scientific and ontological traditions come to be established as superior to their Oriental counterparts. And, hence, colonialism becomes justifiable as the 'civilising mission' of a superior 'race'. Most significantly for our purposes, Orientalism also established the dominant meanings of masculinity through 'feminising' entire populations who came to be represented as unfit for self-rule. So, the 'cunning Arab', the 'inscrutable Chinese', and the 'effeminate Bengali' were simultaneously stereotypes of gendered behaviour: they were, compared to western men, 'womanly'. This way of thinking proceeds, of course, from the premise that women are inferior to men. Hence, the idea that western men were superior to non-western men was based on the notion that 'masculine traits' were superior to 'feminine' ones. The career of Orientalism is, then, inseparable from that of gender stereotypes.

It can be argued that Orientalist and colonial discourses consolidated specific images and discourses of being a man to the exclusion of others. They combined the valorisation of science, the 'feminisation' of non-European people and biologism to produce specific images of ideal masculine types. These, in turn, were internalised by the colonial intelligentsia to 'produce a self-image of effeteness' (Rosselli 1980) and led to attempts by the latter to 'overcome' such 'shortcomings'. In many ways, then, colonialism becomes an expression of the masculine ideal which had been developing in Europe through the 17th and 18th centuries.

The impact of colonialism can not simply be understood to imply that colonial powers single-handedly 'invented' certain types of masculine cultures and introduced them into the culture of the colonies; and that certain ideas that came to be associated with masculinity—such as being 'war-like'—simply did not exist before colonialism. As one historian has argued, 'martial masculinity' (O'Hanlon 1997: 17) was an important aspect of pre-colonial life in India, one which the colonisers might, in fact, have built upon and incorporated into the discourses of colonial masculinity.

Nevertheless, it is important to understand the *intensification* of certain forms of discourses around masculinity that occurred during colonialism in different parts of the Asia-Pacific and continue to circulate during our own time. When we think of the present, it is important to reflect upon the ways in which 'the boundaries of race and gender were negotiated, policed, and reinforced in an age of colonial modernity... [an aspect that points to the] processes that increasingly undermined the flexibility and fluidity that characterised many earlier social formations' (Ballantyne and Burton 2005: 6). Further in this context, while 'women and colonialism' form an important topic of research, not nearly as much attention has been paid to the making of colonial masculine cultures. So, 'colonial projects and their processes were frequently believed to throw white male bodies into crisis... and the supposed "femininity" of colonised men was frequently used as a political tool to justify their exclusion from positions of power and as a means of justifying their colonization in the first place' (ibid: 7). Within the discourse of 'colonial masculinity' (Sinha 1997), non-European men were represented as incapable of self-government due to their 'effeminacy' (this discourse already incorporates, of course, the inferiority of women in general). Hence kingdoms were annexed (for the sake of 'better' governance), and natives were denied positions in local bureaucracies. Much more generally, non-European cultures were also 'effeminised', being represented as 'otherworldly', 'un-focused', 'unscientific', etc. A connected process was the emergence of colonial stereotypes such as the inscrutable Oriental, the mysterious Oriental, etc. Various descriptive terms also came to be attached to 'womanhood' as mysterious, and threatening (to malehood: hence the importance of an all-male school atmosphere for 'real' men to be nurtured in [Mangan and Walvin 1987]). However, whilst some natives were feminised, others were represented as 'martial' races (the Gurkhas of Nepal) (Omissi 1991) and hence worthy of some respect, though not the equals of the colonisers since they did not possess sufficient intellectual prowess. Most frequently, the 'martial races' were infantilised, that is, treated on par with children.

Masculinities, Public Spaces and their Cultures

A significant manner of understanding social relationships—class, gender, ethnicity, sexuality, etc.—is through exploring the relationship between social identity and space. For, our everyday lives—played out through a variety of freedoms and constraints—unfold upon and through specific spaces. Further, spaces have a dual identity: they are both sites upon which different social identities play out in different ways, as well as sites for the formation and consolidation of identities. That is to say, spaces are both objects as well as processes. So, for example, the home is commonly understood to be the domain of women, but it is also the space that defines the kinds of activities women may take part in. Similar arguments can be made for other spaces such as streets, parks, offices, bazaars, shopping malls, schools and university campuses.

It is in this context that we need to focus upon the significance of two relatively recent ideas in human history, viz., the 'public' and the 'private'. Whether or not the public/private categorisation has existed in all societies across time, it is certainly true that the idea that each gender has a separate sphere to which it 'naturally' adapts has become part of modern 'common sense'. Increasingly, through a number of processes of modernity, there has come to be a convergence between the different-spheres-for-different-genders perspective, and the public/private distinction.

Scholarship on the topic has approached the issue in different ways. However, given the historical specificity of the Indian situation—our systems of distinction and hierarchies, the colonial experience and the interplay between the two, for example—it is unlikely that writings that address the European experience (Arendt 1951, Habermas 1989, Sennett 1976) can capture local complexities. Also, in 'classical' discussions on the topic, the role of gender has tended to be sidestepped (Fraser 1992, Pateman 1989). So, both in terms of the dimensions of historical and contemporary specificity and gender, we should formulate our understanding of the Indian situation in terms other than those that might have been true of the European case, while nevertheless borrowing from scholarship on these contexts.

Let us begin with the idea that the categories of public and private play an important role in the beliefs we hold about how society 'works', and *should* work. So, it is commonplace to understand certain spaces (say, the street) as public, and others (say, the home) as private. There is also the belief that spaces thus categorised have their own characteristics in terms of behaviours expected of those located in those spaces, as well as the 'natural' claims of certain groups to them (say, men against women). The idea of 'publicness' clearly invokes its putative opposite, that is, 'privateness'. However, are the 'public' and the 'private' simple opposites of each other? Here, it will be suggested that the two should *not* be understood as mere opposites, each with its own independent set of characteristics. And that it is only if we understand the public and the private as *complementary*—rather than oppositional—spheres that we will be able to understand the ways in which masculine and patriarchal power operates in society.

Following the discussion in the sections above, if we remember that the public sphere has historically been defined as that of men and the private as that of women, then it becomes easier to understand why the two operate as complements to bolster gendered power. So, if the public is presented as the domain of action, 'rationality', 'educated opinion', and a realm where important matters of social life can be discussed among the rightful claims to the public sphere—men—then the private is imagined as that sphere where men can find relief from the 'difficult' tasks of engaging and forming the public sphere. The private is represented as the 'soft' sphere where other kinds of—'feminine'—sensibilities come into play. Here, women rule as they are supposedly endowed with those qualities that are best suited to the domestic sphere: capacity for maternal care and emotional response, lack of ability for 'rational' and 'scientific' thinking and capacity for thinking about concrete matters such as the state, and abstract matters such as philosophy. However, according to this line of thought, the private sphere is a necessary complement to the public as it provides relief from the pressures of the public: the private is then in a *binary* relation to the public in as much as it demonstrates why the public is a superior realm. Without the notion of the private, the public would not carry the connotations of a superior realm that it does. It is in this sense that the two are complementary. It is also here that we can understand the hostility that women face should they choose to place themselves in the imagined public sphere: masculine anxiety and hostility guards the public as a realm of men. What we have, in effect, are masculinised public spheres.

Another significant point relating to the public/private distinction has to do with the fact that we need to make a further distinction between 'private' and 'domestic'. For, a woman may well have autonomy over a private space (say, a single woman who can afford to rent her own flat), but not over the domestic (in as much as this is the space shared with the husband and, possibly, an extended family). While these terms will be used interchangeably in this essay, the distinction is important to remember.

Notwithstanding the above perspective on the public and the private, it is also important to remember that the distinction has itself been questioned by feminists. An important ground for the feminist objection pertains to the fact that, in addition to its 'women's sphere' connotations, the 'private' has come to denote the sphere that is immune to 'outside' intervention. An important corollary of this is the belief that domestic violence is an 'internal' matter and the state, or other non-state bodies, should stay out of the matters of private (family) life. These notions of the inner and the outer aspects of social life are significant contributors to the overall debate that relates to masculinities and public and private spaces. Finally, in this context, we should also remember that while we may come across greater instances of violence against women—both actual and symbolic—in public spaces, it is not as if the incidence was lower in the past. The relative lack of attention to the topic in past years may be due to a situation where men had a more undisputed relationship to so-called public spaces. And that in the present time, there are more women who seek to occupy—or find themselves—in public spaces as a result of a number of social, cultural and economic changes.

The historic division of social life as 'public' and 'private' has simultaneously entailed a division of *institutions* as public and private. And, along with this, there has developed a logic of the gender of such institutions. According to this logic, public institutions have been understood to be the 'natural' preserve of men and hence have tended to operate according to a variety of masculinist ideologies. One example of this is the manner in which the media quite often provides accounts of public women (say parliamentarians) by describing what they wear or how many children they have; women's primary identity continues to be defined through an implicit understanding that public institutions possess (and should possess) a masculine identity. Beyond this, there are even more serious issues, such as the denial of equal opportunities to women through masculinity: notions of what men can do and what women are capable of. It becomes important, therefore, to explore the gender of our institutions in order to devise strategies for change.

Hence, there are a number of other issues we need to keep in mind as a background to any discussion on the relationship between the public and private spheres, gender relations and the unfolding of gendered power. These include: How is gender power consolidated through civic associations such as clubs and societies that, either implicitly or explicitly, base themselves upon masculinist ideologies? And, how are the conjoined contexts of patriarchal privilege and masculinist ideals normalised through institutions such as state bureaucracies, schools, the legal system and the police? That is to say, there are significant linkages between discourses and ideologies formulated at institutional sites (whether public or private) and behaviours and expectations at non-institutional spaces such as streets and parks. Hence, if we are to address violence against women in specific instances (say, at a bus stop or in a park), then a proper understanding of the issues that underpin such violence requires a focus on those other *institutional* sites where ideas on the nature of the public/private dichotomy are formulated, discussed and promulgated.

Following from the above, the idea that the public sphere is a 'masculinised' one is the starting point for exploring the relationship between gender and publicness. The kinds of issues we need to explore within this context have already been alluded to above. These throw light upon the causes and nature of gender-based violence in public spaces, and the new emerging issues in urban and semi-urban contexts that are leading to such violence.

One of the first things we might say about violence against women in public spaces—and other groups, such as non-heterosexual people—is that it relates to ideas of 'natural' claims to such spaces. That is to say that once the 'private' is defined as the (inferior) complement to the 'public', some people are seen to more 'properly' belong to public spaces than others. The most straightforward way of elaborating upon this is to say that heterosexual men are seen to have a greater (if not exclusive) claim upon public space. But, of course, it is not as simple as that and a more nuanced understanding is required. So, in order to introduce a level of complexity into our understanding, we might say, for example, that upper caste middle-class heterosexual men are likely to have greater sway over public spaces as compared to women, lower caste non-middle class men and non-heterosexual men (in as much as the latter category is easier to 'identify'). Linked to this is the popular perception that there are specific conditions under which men and women may access public spaces. Hence, while it is generally understood that men's access to public spaces need not be tied to a 'purpose' (that is, carrying out specific tasks), the idea of women loitering in such spaces becomes both incomprehensible and condemnable. A recent study carried out in Mumbai that asked respondents to indicate how men and women use space summarises its findings as follows:

...it is always men who are found occupying public space at rest.... Women, on the other hand are rarely found standing or waiting in public spaces—they move across space from one point to another in a purposeful movement.... Women occupy public space essentially as a transit between one private space and another. (Ranade 2007: 1521)

The idea of the necessity of purposeful activity by women is one that emanates from many sites of which the domestic is one of the most powerful. It is, perhaps, also the most stringent in its enforcement of the rule of 'purpose'. And, just as significantly, we should be mindful of how—in addition to gender—different kinds of social attributes come into play in restricting or permitting physical mobility. A recent study by the School of Women's

Studies at Jadhavpur University (SWSJU) points out that while there exist different restrictions on women's mobility outside the home among various caste and class groups, 'restrictions over time are completely absent in the case of upper-caste men. The only condition for men is that they should inform a family member in case of delay, indicating a gendered ideology at play' (SWSJU 2010: 30). Further, the discourse of women and purpose is reinforced by a complimentary formulation that refers to the 'balance' a working woman must achieve between her paid work and household responsibilities. So, a woman's 'paid work was not objectionable, provided she took good care of her household responsibilities' (ibid.: 38). In order to achieve this 'balance', however, it becomes imperative that women spend only that time in the public sphere that serves the purpose of carrying out the responsibilities of paid work, thereafter retreating to the home for other duties. In their interviews with a wide cross-section of men and women in Kolkata, the SWSJU researchers were told that should a woman be found wanting in her abilities to balance work and home life, she must get back to where she belongs—the home' (ibid.).

Spaces, therefore, are not 'natural' in their attributes, and, following from the above, have a *social* character. Hence, when thinking about relationships among human beings—that, after all, unfold in specific spaces—we must consider the character of spaces in terms of a number of social categories such as class, caste, ethnicity, and, of course, gender. The freedoms and constraints that confront us as human beings are crucially determined by our social attributes, of which gender is a significant aspect.

Frequently, the gendered discourse of public spaces also represents them as sites where women may both be allowed and afforded security of movement *as long as they behave as women should* (more on this ahead). So, for example, women at nightclubs who wear 'revealing' western clothing are often regarded as having forfeited the right to (male) protection and regard. This aspect most directly bears upon notions of female sexuality and the idea that 'to deliberately titillate men is a fault in a woman and the responsibility for its consequences ought not to be placed upon men' (ibid.: 28). This also relates to an understanding of masculinity in biological terms: that men possess sexual drives that are both uncontrollable and easily stoked.

Female sexuality and the discourse of public women come together in another way. An example from contemporary Kerala will be helpful. During the 1990s, several scholars have pointed out an increasingly strident debate that indexes 'augmented public fears about sexual transgression' (Devika 2009: 33) by women. Hence, 'visions of dystopia in public discussion in Kerala in the 1990s' is 'painted heavily with the horrors of "sexuality unleashed"' (ibid.). Significantly, young women who had been subject to sexual crimes were often portrayed not as victims, but those whose 'worldliness' was to blame for the crimes they suffered. So, a High Court judgment on the so-called Vithura case of 2000 involving the serial rape of a teenage girl noted that she was a '"lascivious strumpet" who, as the days passed by... became more and more coquettish and voluptuous by availing the services of beauty parlours' (Sreekumar 2001, quoted in ibid.). As Devika points out, the 'fixation with the sexualisation of female bodies is... telling of how misogyny forms a sizable part of elitist cultural panic' (ibid.: 34). Women in public spaces not conforming to masculine rules of 'modesty' are frequently the source of a great deal of masculine (and patriarchal) anxiety regarding the 'decline of society'. The 'decline' perspective appears to have been particularly salient in an era of globalisation, where women are seen to be affected by the cultural and social changes in a manner not 'befitting' models of 'feminine honour' and respectability.

Finally, in this context, it is *male* notions of what constitutes 'violence' that frequently guide women's recognition of it. So, a woman who has faced harassment may choose to overlook it if, say, her father suggests that it is too 'trivial' a matter, or that 'girls must learn to live with a certain degree of harassment'. This may happen in those instances where the man feels unable to act to redress the 'insult' to 'family honour', and it seems better to not do anything rather than risk further humiliation. What comes into play in such instances is not so much a consideration of the feelings of the woman but, rather, various contexts of male honour.

Masculinised Public Spheres and Institutional Discourses

In order to grasp the relationship between violence, public spaces and masculinity, it is important to understand how the cultures of gender play out across various contexts of civil society and agencies of the state. This will further allow us to make the linkages between the home and the world. Scholarship on the state-civil society interface suggests that there is an inescapable and complex relationship between the two. This interweave is the crucial first step in exploring the dynamic of this relationship. And, given this, cultures of gender have to be understood as practices that transit across various agencies of the state and institutions of civil society.

Feminist interrogations of the dichotomy between the 'public' and the 'private' have alerted us to the significance of insisting that there is an intimate relationship between the two spheres. So, feminist analyses have shown us that men and women's participation in one or the other of these spheres is influenced by the ways in which ideas regarding gender circulate within them, as well as intersect. So, for example, if Parliament is imagined as the realm of men and home as that of women, then each gender comes to be established as having its 'proper' realm of operation (Fraser 1992, Pateman 1989). This, in turn, has significant consequences for the freedoms and constraints accorded each gender. It is in this context that this section explores the ways in which a 'masculinized public sphere' (Moon 2002) comes to be established through both private and public discourses of gender. When we speak of the masculinisation of the public sphere, we refer to the combination of a number of discourses—such as religious, statist and, in some cases, militaristic—that combine to gender space, including the private.

Clubs, Societies, Leisure and Civic Associations

How is gender power consolidated through civic associations such as clubs and societies that, either implicitly or explicitly, base themselves upon masculinist ideologies? How are the conjoined contexts of patriarchal privilege and masculinist ideals normalised through associations? Let us consider the case of 'traditional-modern' masculinity as propagated by the Samarth Vyamshala Mandir (SVM), a club for 'physical exercise' for young people located on the grounds of the famous Shivaji Park in the suburb of Dadar in Mumbai.[1] SVM was founded in 1925, and its establishment expressed a certain tendency within Indian nationalism whereby rejuvenation of the subjugated (upper caste, primarily male) body was understood as the precursor to regaining Swarajya (self-rule). It is one of many such clubs and leisure societies that have been instrumental in the propagation of specific notions of masculinity through representing them as part and parcel of 'nation-building' and 'character-building'.

At the time when SVM was founded, it was frequently argued that the depths to which a 'glorious' and 'ancient' civilisation had fallen could only be remedied through strict attention to the physical condition of the body through allegiance to a disciplinary mechanism which had become alien to it. The theme of physical exercise, masculinity and the task of 'nation-building' was, of course, a common one in late 19th and early 20th centuries in a variety of discourses in India.

In the contemporary period, SVM makes a special claim towards preserving and promoting the 'ancient' physical culture of *malkhamb*, the name given to both a wooden pole and a series of exercises built around it. SVM activities follow a set pattern, routinised through the practice of many years: children lined up in their various groups (*malkhamb, kho-kho* [an Indian game], gymnastics, basketball, and a 'general' category), the raising of the (Hindu) saffron flag, children saluting the flag and then dispersing to their activities, etc. At the end of each day's sessions, the participants line up again for the flag lowering ceremony and, with the nationalist hymn *Vande Mataram* playing in the background, salute the flag and with a shout of *Jai Hind* ('Long Live India!') disperse (*visarjan*).

Both boys and girls participate in the various 'physical culture' activities of SVM, and though the girls are able to take part in almost all the activities, they do *not* perform on the pole *malkhamb*; their routines being confined to the 'rope *malkhamb*', and other exercises such as gymnastics. The proponents of *malkhamb* point out that 'certain exercises similar to *mallkhamb*, can also be traced in the 12th century classic, *Mansolha* written by Chalukkya (A.D. 1135). In modern times, its history can also be interpreted as tied to the emergence of Marathi Hindu male identity. *Malkhamb* was 'revived' as an organised activity through the efforts of Kale Guru. With its strong turn-of-the-century Marathi upper-caste milieu, the suburb of Dadar was fertile territory for the mandir's establishment. And, though SVM does not have explicit affiliations to any political or religious organisations, it has been an important site for the advocacy and elaboration of upper-caste Hindu masculinity. Here, in myriad ways, the Hindu male body and society—'Indian tradition'—are imagined as one.

For the past thirty years or so, the central figure at SVM has been Ramesh Kulkarni (name changed), a government employee whose life outside office hours has been spent in nurturing an institution that is run on a shoestring budget and attracts a great deal of support from the local area. Kulkarni is a very particular kind of masculine figure which has an important place in the cultural imagination of the post-liberalisation economy: the *modern* renouncer engaged in the task of 'improving' society, a task seen to be undertaken at great personal cost and sacrifice. Kulkarni's day begins around 5 a.m., when he leaves his house for the SVM premises in order to supervise the morning session of exercises. At the conclusion of the morning session, he leaves for work from the SVM premises itself. Then, at the end of work, he returns to the SVM, only going back home around 10 p.m., after attending to all the SVM business. This is his routine for the entire week. When asked what his wife thinks of this routine, he responds saying 'she was informed of this before we got married', and is now 'used to it'. Needless to say, for more than twenty years or so of married life, his wife has taken on the role of housekeeper, cook, budget manager and educator of their children; Ramesh Kulkarni is, as he puts it, free to work towards the 'good' of a society that is increasingly caught in the vices of modernity and is unceasingly attentive to its material needs at the cost of the spiritual. The positioning of Hindu masculinity and the male 'improver'—an embodiment of *tyag* (renunciation)—within the matrices of class, caste, and politics of the 'domestic' needs to be noted here. For, quite clearly, the burden of doing 'social good' that is carried by Kulkarni's wife is largely obliterated through the close association of the social—and 'Indian tradition'—with *male* agency. In middle-class contexts at least, such as the one exemplified by SVM, we can see an outline of 'traditional-modernity' in a time of rapid social change. Among other things, it serves the very real purpose of consolidating a discourse of masculinity that seeks preservation of male privileges that in many spheres of life are being brought into question.

Hence, in order that *men* do public good, women must take care of the private sphere; once again, the *complementary* nature of the public and the private. The man's public *tyag*, is dependent upon the proper conduct of female domestic responsibility.

SVM also has some women officials, and one of these is Kulkarni's second-in-command, Meera Tendulkar (name changed). Tendulkar has been associated with SVM since the age of eight, and thirty years later is very much a veteran and respected senior member of the institution. She narrates how during the 1980s she performed on the cane *malkhamb* wearing gymnast's clothes which was quite a 'daring' thing to do, in addition to travelling to various parts of the country to perform. The only gap in her participation in SVM's activities was when for four years after the birth of her son, she was an infrequent visitor. One of the 'adjustments' her family has made is that she is at SVM premises every evening from 6.30 to 8. Initially, there was some concern in her kin circles, but now her relatives have 'adjusted their visits according to this'. She has managed, she points out, to combine the roles of housewife, teacher (she is a college lecturer in psychology) and deputy to Kulkarni 'without much effort'. So, here the 'female modernity' that is permissible is that of someone who learns to combine, rather than have the option of opting out of 'feminine tasks'. It is important to remember that even where clubs and societies do not exclude women from membership, they may still be sites for the propagation of patriarchal and masculinist gender politics.

Educational Institutions and Processes of Identity Formation

Let us now consider the relationship between education processes and gender. There are two key issues we need to explore when we think about the link between education and gender. First, how does formal education at the earliest periods of life—schooling—inculcate normative gendered values and behaviours? That is to say, how do schools teach boys to be 'boys' and girls to be 'girls'? The school marks the first link between the pedagogic programmes of the family and that of the state and, often (though not always), such programmes replicate patriarchal values. Second, while on the one hand schooling may be complicit in reproducing dominant values, it is also important to inquire about the ways in which it empowers those whom it educates. That is, *how* does schooling equip the schooled to effect changes in their material and social circumstances?

A great deal of scholarly analysis that assumes an automatic connection between education and paid work and an improvement in women's position in non-western countries has been influenced by similar assumptions in feminist scholarship that has dealt with the historical experience of *western* societies. This has also proved to be a popular perspective within policy contexts. To zero in upon schooling and work as productive policy measures of women's 'empowerment' has seemed to be an easier task than incorporating the seemingly abstract and complicated nature of cultural factors that influence gender power. Notwithstanding this, it is important to explore the ways in which gendered power—the relationship between men and women within the household, for example—operates to stymie the best laid plans for gender equity. Education is but one factor towards addressing gender equity; it can not itself stand as proxy for 'empowerment'. In other words, we need to engage with the larger social context that the 'educated' and employed woman encounters that can act as a counterweight to the quest for empowerment. While an educated woman may find paid employment, who decides how she spends her income? How do norms and discourses of sexuality, marriage and deference to 'tradition' constrain everyday lives of the supposedly empowered—educated and employed— women? The fundamental aspect is to understand the extent to which women have control over decision-making processes that affect their lives. This is something that can not simply be understood through talking of education itself as a sufficient indicator of empowerment.

Malhotra and Mather (1997) provide a valuable corrective to the notion—widely prevalent in both academic and policy literature—that education and employment are powerful indicators of the social positions enjoyed by women. First, it is important to remember that 'access to resources is distinct from control over them, and only the latter can be considered an indicator of power' (ibid.: 604). However, even in those situations where women exercise power over a particular sphere, say in financial decision-making within the household, it is not necessary that they will have a similar say in social and organisational matters; so, an educated young woman in paid employment may well be able to decide whether to purchase consumer goods or not, but this does not translate into her ability to dictate whom she may marry. This is because power is 'multilocational': it operates in different spheres—social, domestic, political and economic—in different ways. Hence, if a woman has a say over social issues within the household (perhaps because she is an older woman), this does not necessarily translate into an ability to exercise autonomy outside it. In considering women's abilities to take decisions about their lives it is fundamental to consider the broader social and political spheres within which their lives unfold. Hence, as Malhotra and Mather point out, 'the relevance of schooling and paid work in determining domestic power depends on the social context under consideration' (ibid.: 607).

Further, if we focus too narrowly on what makes for women's empowerment—through an excessive reliance on the access-to-education framework—then we are likely to miss the dynamics of how the different spheres of which women are part interact with each other, in turn either constraining or promoting women's advancement as social beings. Hence, taking the Sri Lankan case as focus, Malhotra and Mather point out that 'women's control over their earnings allows them a role in some spheres of domestic decision-making, but not others' (ibid.: 609). What, then, might be the broader social contexts we need to keep in mind in order to fully comprehend issues of constraint or facilitation? Even in those societies, such as Sri Lanka, where women are subject to fewer constraints than in other parts of South Asia, women's domestic power will depend upon the manner in which patriarchal and masculinist definitions make meanings in the domains of 'class and ethnic differences, the nature and dynamic of productive work, a woman's life course, and the structure and composition of the household' (ibid.: 607). Hence, middle- and upper-class women are more likely to have more say in family matters, even though women from lower socio-economic categories may actually contribute a greater percentage of household income; women from certain ethnic backgrounds tend to face greater constraints as decision makers in financial and social issues; not just current work status, but also experience of past work is likely to secure a

considerable level of authority for many women; life cycle contexts such as
motherhood and age can be significant factors in determining how much
of a say a woman has in different decision-making contexts; and, in some
cases, if women live away from in-laws they may be able to exercise greater
independence, whereas in others, this may be achieved through residence
with natal kin who will support them in personal and financial matters.
Finally, after a point education may not matter: so it isn't as if a woman who
is educated above the 12th standard is likely to have greater say in how to
conduct her life—and that of her family—as compared to someone with
only an 11th standard level of education.

It is important, then, to remember that 'even independent of educational
and work issues, there are clearly defined cultural norms regarding the
power women wield over household matters among ethnic groups and
social classes' (ibid.: 623).

The most significant lesson we might draw from the above is that
formal educational levels in themselves are inadequate indicators of both
women's capacity to protect themselves from violence and men's attitude
towards it. While education is a necessary condition of empowerment, it
is not sufficient. Educated women do not necessarily possess the means of
deflecting violence within the household and hence—given the intrinsic
connection between the home and the world—continue to be subject to
the violence of public spaces. What is required is not simply a diploma or
a degree, but specific understanding (by women) of their rights as humans
and citizens.

The Home and the World: Women and Work

The world of work is of great significance when we seek to explore both
the contexts and causes of violence against women in public places. We
need, first, to begin with certain ideas regarding work itself. Particularly,
the idea of 'men's work' and 'women's work' has been important in the
structuring relationships between men and women. Of course, what gets
defined as 'women's work' is itself the consequence of a number of historical
and social factors. So, for example, in the Kumaon Himalayan region of
northwest India, the identification of 'harvesting fuel, fodder, roots, herbs

and berries' (Gururani 2002: 235) as women's work has much to do with the long history of male out-migration from the region which led to a 'process in which the burden of livelihood... came slowly but surely to rest on women' (ibid.: 235). It is interesting to note the ways in which the gendering process operates in those contexts where both men and women work. So, in the Kumaon Himalayas, when men do go to the forest to collect firewood or other produce, their representation of this activity is couched in the ideals of dominant masculinity. So, men speak of how they were able to bring back 'in one night' what it took women six months to collect. Hence, 'men's trips to the forest were an assertion of their strength and ability, which helped to reinscribe patriarchal relations of power and inequality' (ibid: 239).

Recent changes in social and economic spheres—including 'globalisation'—have led to important developments in urban contexts. In particular, this relates to the significant increases in the demand for workers in new as well as older professions—some which were historically women-centred, and some not—that has led to greater visibility of women in public spaces. So, there has been a visible increase in the number of women workers in industries such as media and communication, new technologies (including call-centre work), service industries (such as bar-hostesses and check-out operators), travel and hospitality, and banking and insurance. The increase has been cumulative rather than sudden. So, writing in the mid-1990s, one observer pointed out:

The last decade has seen a systematic rise in the employment of women in the banking and finance sector. The result of a multiplicity of factors, including: profound social changes taking place in India regarding women's education and employment; the changing policies of management, especially after the nationalization and reorganization of the LIC and of major banks; the policies of the Indian government; international changes in banking and finance and, not least, the technological changes being effected in the industry.

[...]

These all have a specific impact on women employees, who are being recruited in large numbers in the banking and finance sector, mainly in the clerical category. Women employees are increasingly looking at their work in terms of career prospects and are keen on learning new skills and advancing in their careers, despite severe limitations. They are organizing themselves into unions and separate women's caucuses within and outside unions. (Gothoskar 1995: 174)

So, there is increasing visibility of (non-elite) women in public work spaces. However, notwithstanding the above, it is important to remember that although economic growth in India has created greater employment opportunities for women, it nowhere—at least in the formal sector of the cities—matches the rate of increase of male employment. 'In the era of globalisation', a recent report on urbanisation and women's employment points out, 'it has become commonplace to argue that trade openness in particular generates processes that encourage the increased employment of women' (Chandrasekhar and Ghosh 2007: 1). However, as Chandrasekhar and Ghosh go on to suggest, 'rather than the much cited' sectors such as information technology and finance, 'the greatest labour market dynamism has been evident in the realm of domestic labour' (p. 5).

Hence the problem of sexual harassment is a problem that, though it affects white-collar women workers, has significant consequences for poorer women. For, '92 per cent of working women are in the informal, unorganised sector, where they don't get any statutory protection' (Patel 2007: 109). Keeping in mind this caveat, we need to take account of the fact that the increasing visibility of women in the *public* workplace attracts a male hostility in terms of the changing nature of popularly held opinions regarding the 'proper' spaces of men and women. The irony is that in keeping with the economic demands of globalisation—where increasing consumerist aspirations require an additional earning member in the family—the 'working wife' is a common male expectation, but she also raises male anxieties.

There is a further aspect to consider with regard to the place of women in service and hospitality industries. In a deeply hierarchical society such as ours, the providers of services that enhance bodily comfort have traditionally enjoyed a very low status. This attitude finds a place among the processes of the contemporary era. So, it is not uncommon for, say, air hostesses and those who work in bars, to face the double jeopardy of male attitudes towards women in public places *and* traditional attitudes towards service providers. Such women are also, thanks in no small measure to the culture of Indian cinema, imagined as 'loose' women who do not mind—if not welcome—male attention. For, the argument goes, by both their demeanour and dress—'friendliness' and western wear—they lack the signs of respectability and modesty that characterise the 'traditional' Indian woman. Men's engagement with women in such professions seems to carry the baggage of a relatively recent fascination with western (white) women, a fascination that is structured in equal parts through desire and fear. In cinematic terms, this fascination may be thought of through the screen persona of Helen, Bollywood's Anglo-Indian 'vamp' and, before that, the Australian-born actor Mary Evans, famous for her role as Fearless Nadia in a number of films made in the 1930s and 1940s (Thomas 2005). Contemporary forces of globalisation and their impact on women's employment are, then, the site of a complex set of male responses that hover between desire, anxiety and hostility.

Spaces of Leisure and Consumption

Feminist scholarship has usefully suggested that the discourse of 'safety' that is companion to the issue of women's access to public spaces is mired both in patriarchal and masculinist notions of 'protecting' women (and hence men's honour), as well as classed notions of urban threats to 'respectable' women (Phadke 2007). The offer of 'safety' seeks to guard women's 'reputation', and hence brings with it, among other restrictions, a 'desexualised version of public visibility' (ibid.). It is desexualised in the sense that women—unlike men—are prohibited from public expressions of sexuality. The choice is clear-cut: women should be safe in public spaces, but this also entails 'proper' conduct on their part.

It is in this regard that we need to consider some newer contexts that relate to women's access to public spaces and masculine reactions to it.

The rise of a new consumer culture that includes a larger section of the population than before has entailed the production of both new spaces as well as new identities. In terms of the former, they include new spaces of residence, leisure and shopping, and with regard to the latter, the relatively recent figure of the 'consuming woman'. The hectic construction activity that relates to gated residential communities and shopping malls are important to consider in this context. An extraordinary range of large and small cities across the country—with equally mind-boggling inventory of land area under construction, or completed—constitute sites of such activity. So, the Lucknow-based Sahara corporation has plans for the 'world's largest chain of well-planned self sufficient high quality townships across 217 cities in the country' (Ahmedabad: 104 acres; Coimbatore, Kerala: 103 acres; Lucknow: 200 acres); it has already constructed the Amby Valley township near the city of Pune in Maharashtra on 10,000 acres which is described as 'independent India's first planned, self contained, aspirational city, remarkable for its unsurpassed grandeur and plush signature features'. In the Rajasthan township of Bhiwadi, some 60 kilometres from Delhi, no less than eleven real estate companies are reported to have launched *gated* residential projects in different price ranges, hoping to cash in on the proposed development of a number of 'Export Processing Zones' and 'Special Economic Zones' by large corporations such as Reliance and Omaxe.[2] The Omaxe group has residential projects in twenty-two cities across nine states in north and central India. These include the Omaxe Riviera (Rudrapur, Uttarakhand) and Omaxe Park Woods in Baddi (Himachal Pradesh), a township that is 'home to some of the top industries like Nicolas Piramal, Bajaj Consumer Care, Ranbaxy, Dr. Reddy's Lab, Torrent Pharmaceuticals, TVS Motors, Colgate Palmolive, Dabur India, Cipla, Cadbury's, Wipro, Wockhardt, Procter & Gamble, Marc Enterprises etc.'[3] The Omaxe Heights in Lucknow offers an 'in-house club with swimming pool and wave pool, tennis court, basketball court, banquet/community hall, squash court, steam room, jacuzzi, gymnasium and television lounge'.

While the numbers of operational shopping malls in India are not comparable to North America, it is not for want of local ambitions. So, before the economic downturn of the past few years, retail operators and mall entrepreneurs had predicted there would be around 700 malls in India by end of 2010 (Goswami 2010). At present, there are 172 malls already operating in India that 'offer 52 million square feet of space' (ibid.: 12), and by the first quarter of 2011, this number is expected to rise to 350. At present, North India has seventy-nine malls, western India fifty-six, the eastern region sixteen, and south India twenty-one. South India is expected to treble the number of malls (to seventy-two) by this time, registering the fastest rate of growth. The National Capital Region has the most number of malls in the northern region, with Gurgaon home to eleven (compared to Jaipur's five and Lucknow's three).

The promises of spatial modernity held out by gated communities and malls have important consequences for our thinking on the relationship between space and gender. A significant aspect of the spatial narrative of consumerism is the concurrent one of the 'consuming woman'. And, while the consuming woman is usually imagined as a middle-class figure, the aspiration to be one is not limited to the traditional middle classes. Indeed, for many younger women from lower socio-economic backgrounds, the idea of being 'middle class' (which itself is a complex notion in the Indian context) is tightly bound up with being able to take part in the new consumerism (see, for example, SWSJU 2010). Further, the consuming woman is an object of great interest and research among marketing and advertising companies (Srivastava 2007).

The most significant social characteristic of the new spaces of consumerism is their invitation to *all* consumers to participate equally in the *public* life of such spaces. A 'consumerist democracy' is the key to both profitability and an implicit justification for an activity that, historically, has been looked at with suspicion. However, it is also the site for male anxiety regarding the consuming woman. For, the consuming woman is one who spends upon herself, rather than necessarily furthering the interests and welfare of the family (and particularly the males among them). 'Professional women', as Tanika Sarkar points out, now 'have access to unprecedented self-reliance, [but] even housewives, faced with the ad culture and the shopping arcades, seek out things that are specially meant for themselves' (Sarkar 1995: 212–13). Contemporary economic and cultural changes pose an interesting challenge to masculine notions of the self: consumption is a good thing and none should be excluded, but what about the consuming woman who appears to 'spend like a man'? So, at the present time, the idea of the 'public woman' (viewed with suspicion if we recall the earlier discussion on the masculinised public sphere) has become entwined with that of the consuming woman.

In some instances, the potential 'threat' of the consuming public woman is resolved through the notion of the traditional-modern woman, where the woman as consumer is, nevertheless, positioned (or positions herself) as being able to strike a 'balance' between her public activities and her 'responsibilities' towards the home. Hence, the modern woman can, when required, come back to being a good housewife. In other cases, certain spaces such as gated communities are able, through strict control over space, to produce a 'safe' realm for women. However, given the male dominated nature of the Residents Welfare Associations (RWAs) of the gated communities that are responsible for safety and 'security', the rules of protection referred to in the opening paragraph of this section apply. Also, while in gated communities women residents are afforded 'protection', the same may not apply to the female domestic workers who serve the households: both within the compound and between the spaces of their homes and the gated community, female domestic workers may be subject to harassment.

The development of privatised 'public spaces' such as gated communities and shopping malls are often looked upon with favour inasmuch as they are positioned alongside the 'dangers' of the street and the bazaar. And, further, gated residential enclaves work towards producing a sense of the public through organising a variety of activities—religious and non-religious—that imitate the activities of the street. What makes possible the ersatz pell-mell of the street within the gated enclave is the directed circulation of the discourse of consumerist choice and intent that is, in fact, *uninterrupted* by the 'distractions' of the street such as the need for constant vigilance against putative others. It is within this crucible—where the street is not the street, but, for precisely that reason, intensely engaged with—that 'public' women of the gated community can be both the guardians of tradition *and* take part in the sexualised presentations of the self; the morning after elaborately dressed women have performed the rituals of *Karva-Chauth* (to ensure their husbands' well-being), they pace the condominium grounds on their exercise rounds dressed in skin-hugging clothing. And, unlike the constraint placed on women at street celebrations of the spring festival of Holi (that can also involve a sexual economy of 'fun' [Cohen 1995]), at corporate-sponsored Holi melas (fairs) in many gated communities, men *and* women dance together to Bollywood songs on an open-air stage. The broader context of this is, as already suggested, a particular kind of gender politics that relates to the perceived ability to move between the worlds of 'tradition' and modernity (see Srivastava 2007) by exercising choice. Through the notion of choice, consumerist modernity and its spaces appear to offer women the possibility of both maintaining their 'reputation' and taking part in 'disreputable' activities denied by the open street. It is in this sense that contemporary middle-class notions of urban citizenship—with its specific configuration of a manageably hybrid modernity—reformulates the 'fraternal social contract' (Pateman 1989) within its own terms to include the consuming woman within its remit. Hence, the female consumer-citizen takes on a significant role in the RWA discourses of the making of the 'global' city and its inhabitants.

There is an additional issue connected with the making of such 'public' spaces: they tend to promote the ideas of a Hinduised public sphere. The public acts that simulate the street are almost exclusively in the nature of a Hindu world of beliefs and rituals. Here, masculinity, religion and the public sphere converge.

However, more significantly, it is clear that a very large number of women who wish to take part in the processes of contemporary modernity—including consumerism—do not have access to the 'safety' of the gated community. Their everyday lives as public women—as workers, commuters, leisure seekers, shoppers, etc.—unfold in places where they are open to male hostilities that target the putative threat of the public-consuming woman. It is the park, the bus stand, the street, the footpath, and the tourist monument that more properly needs to be 'secured'. However, safety and security can not, simultaneously, be 'offered' to women as part of the bargain of 'protection'. Finally, in this context, it is also inadequate to assume that what is needed are better urban planning visions in order to design spaces where women will not face the dangers of violence. For, bricks and mortar do not prevent violence against women, people and their attitudes do (see also Vishwanath and Tandon-Mehrotra 2007). Delhi's public spaces—where crowds gather to watch rather than intervene—provide adequate evidence of this. This way of casting the issue allows us to remember that while most women face potential violence in the masculinised public sphere, the level and frequency of the threat nevertheless varies according to an individual's social standing. Some women are more able than others to deflect menace; instead of catching a bus, they can go by private transport.

'Custom', Globalisation and the Masculinised Public Sphere

A recurrent feature in the Indian context is the perceived contest between 'indigenous traditions' and 'foreign modernity'. This is a particularly important context with respect to a variety of debates—cultural, political, legislative, etc.—that relate to 'women's issues'. A significant way in which this debate unfolds is through casting women as the bearers of 'local traditions'. And, since traditions are generally seen to be fixed, the argument usually runs that in order to protect 'our' traditions from 'foreign' influence 'our' women must be also be shielded from change. In certain countries within the region (particularly in South Asia), this was a common theme in colonial debates on women's issues (Chatterjee 1993). The 'local tradition versus foreign modernity' debate plays an important role in the making of masculinised public spheres as well in violence against women within these spheres.

Debates about 'our traditions' (and how to protect them) often sit alongside expressions of ethno-nationalism based on the forging of a homogeneous cultural identity. That is to say, cultural identities are sought to be defined in terms of a consensus that primarily derives from a power hierarchy where men's interests are placed above those of women as a group. Here, the 'honour' of the community becomes coeval with that of men, and while both men and women might be punished for disobeying honour codes, it is women who bear the greatest burden of upholding community honour. The 'khap panchayats' provide a particularly gory example in this regard.

Expressions of ethnic nationalism—expressed through notions of honour, shame, valour, etc.—are commonly based upon appeals to mythic and masculinised histories. In this mythic past, men and women—and hence the society of which they were a part—lived harmoniously since, the argument goes, they followed the rules of tradition and each knew his/her organic relation to the other; each acted in a way that was 'proper' to it, biological imperatives having solidified into social norms to produce a well-ordered social machinery. According to such narratives, social dysfunction comes about as a result of different genders (and, in particular, women) not knowing their pre-ordained roles. Hence, in these ways the politics of the household that oversees the quotidian relationships between genders becomes linked with national-level formulations of gender politics. The domestic, then, both draws upon and contributes to broader debates about gender and its manifestations. Ethno-nationalist movements and their gender politics are, therefore, significant sites of discourses on gender power. For example, ethno-nationalist movements frequently demand the implementation of 'customary' laws that have particularly deleterious effects on the position of women in society. Such movements also contain within them both seeds and justifications of violence against women—frequently organised around notions of honour and shame—as well as non-dominant ethnic groupings.

The combination of shared identities formed through religion and cultures of masculinity is a prevalent feature of Indian society. Religious solidarities are often mobilised through appeals to a shared masculinity. Here, rituals, both religious and secular, play a crucial role as storehouses of masculine cultures. There are specific connections between globalisation, religion, religious violence and gender norms that need to be understood. For example, 'globalisation' is often seen as a threat to existing religious values, leading, in turn, to stricter reinforcement of putatively religious rules that particularly affect women's rights as equal citizens. Further, desires for a pure community of believers may lead to textual understanding of belief, and subsequent discrimination against women (as well as religious minorities).

In some instances, an attempt to reinforce imagined religious norms also forms the basis of restrictions upon women in public spaces. I have deliberately used the word 'imagined' in order to emphasise the frequent application of justifications based upon 'religious values' to justify gendered power. Consider, for example, attempts by members of the religious Right to both disrupt Valentine Day celebrations, as well as publicly humiliate young people who take part in them. Here, 'Indian values' and 'Hindu values' become intertwined to be represented as one, and particularly the women who take part in Valentine's Day activities come to be regarded as transgressing both national and religious values. Implicitly, the guardians of such putative national and religious cultures are men; once again, a masculinised public sphere.

Ethno-nationalism and the idea that 'ethnicity' is a fixed essence can reinforce gender power through the emphasis on the *stability* of identity. That is to say, ethnic identities tend to be built around the idea that what is typical of a particular group is so because of certain behaviours that can be expected of its men and women, the old and the young, the rich and the poor, etc. And that the identity of a group crucially depends on its members following its cultural rules which are usually understood to have been passed down from time immemorial. The idea that ethnic identities are fixed and have been so 'from time immemorial' is, as a great deal of scholarship has pointed out, simply false. All identities are constantly in the process of change and flux and, in as much as ethnicities are understood to be fixed and certain behaviours are expected of women and men (lest 'time-honoured' cultural rules be violated), they are part of the system of maintaining certain power hierarchies, including those of gender. When men come to be defined as possessing certain qualities, women too are attributed their own 'essence' and deviations from these become liable to punishment.

'Custom' often comes into play in situations of intense change. So, the rapid urbanisation taking place in India has pointed to a significant dimension of gender politics. In January 2009, newspapers reported that a gang of ten young men had raped a young woman in the Delhi National Capital Region. Press reports indicated that the men had come upon their victim as she sat in a relatively isolated spot with a man, perhaps her boyfriend. The gang had been returning from a match-winning performance in a cricket tournament. This is how the *Hindustan Times* newspaper reported the issue:

With malls and university campuses crawling closer to the villages at a steady pace, sometimes even entering them, boundary walls can no longer prevent some common spaces where the villagers and the city residents meet. [A student at one such institute of higher education noted that] 'We have studied in co-ed institutions from the beginning and being friends with a girl is not uncommon. But it is an issue in these villages. If I go out with a girl, local boys make it a point to harass us'.

However, the report went on to say, 'women from the village [from where the perpetrators are reported to have come] blame it on city girls. "In our village, the women cover themselves up. Our girls do not make boy friends. City girls come to lonely stretches around the villages and indulge in obscene acts. Late night culture of the city has spoiled the girls", said Asarfi Devi, an octogenarian from the village'. There is a wider context to this than the somewhat simplistic 'modern city person' vs. the 'backward villager' angle. As one villager pointed out, 'part of the reason was also the effort to keep villagers out. "Residents want boundary walls to keep out villagers. Are villagers untouchables? If you respect the villagers, they will respect you"'.

Masculinities and the Virtual Public Space: The Media Sphere

The media should also be considered a virtual public sphere that contributes to attitudes and behaviours towards women in physical public spheres. We might frame this discussion in terms of the symbolic violence that the media public sphere may inflict upon women.

In India, media images of women are most frequently inspired by debates between 'tradition' and 'modernity'. Hence, as one observer points out, 'perhaps the most important role that television is playing at present is the conflation of television programming with new, globally constructed versions of "modernity" and the changing dimension of the role of community in contemporary civil society. And women are the focal point of both these changes' (Gupta 2000: 61). A key question in media representations and debates is the following: How modern should the non-European woman be and yet maintain her 'local' identity? In other words, the non-western woman (and, this is usually assumed to be a monolithic category) is implicitly assumed to be the bearer of 'tradition', such that the most crucial battles over the maintenance of tradition in the face of perceived attacks upon it by 'external' forces are fought around representations of women. A contemporary representation of women within this context concerns that of the 'new woman' (Birch et al. 2001: 135). The 'modern woman' can most be found 'in the pages of glossy magazines which cater to the emerging and relatively prosperous urban middle and upper-middle classes' (ibid.), as well as in television advertising and regular programming. As Sunder Rajan (1993) points out, the new woman is usually portrayed as 'attractive, educated, hard-working, and socially aware' (p. 131). The modern woman is also represented as independent in the decisions she makes, as well as ambitious and seeking a career path for herself. And, being a working woman, she is also a consumer. From jewellery advertising to those that promote household goods, the modern woman is ubiquitous.

While the selling of products is a crucial reason for the presence of the modern woman in advertising, the purely commercial aspect is inadequate for an understanding of the changing nature of gender representations in the media. 'The representation of the new woman', it has been suggested, 'are also a way of reformulating masculinist ideologies which domesticate political assertions for equality by women' (Birch et al., 2001: 137). For, the most significant aspect of such representations is that the woman's primary role is defined as the self-sacrificing mother and the nurturer of the family. Hence, in an advertisement for a brand of contraceptive pills in an Indian magazine, a woman is the key figure. However, it is what she says that is interesting: 'I am mindful of all the needs of my family, no matter how small'.[4] Hence, simultaneously as female desire is foregrounded—through de-linking sex from reproduction—the act of using contraception is represented as responsible behaviour towards the family: one must not place a burden upon the family's resources through having more children. The possibilities of female desire are thus domesticated through pointing to her 'primary' role.

Conclusion

A significant body of theorisation has tended to proceed from the perspective that violence towards women occurs as a *consequence* of social disorganisation. However, as another strand of scholarship has pointed out, violence towards women—whether in public or private spaces—can be better understood as an attempt to *maintain* the existing structures of gender power, rather than a breakdown in the social order. Hence, feminists increasingly suggest that 'we need to see violence as bound up with the very constitution of cultural forms' (Cribb and Barnett 1999: 51). We may, similarly, position our discussion about violence, women, masculinity and public spaces within this framework: it acts as an attempt to maintain existing structures of power in a time of change.

Second, the public and the private are not unconnected spheres, and the ways in which women are treated in either of them forms a mutually reinforcing process. So, if a judge says that though rape is a crime, 'the woman may have acted or behaved in a manner so as to incite the man', and discourses within the household reiterate the perspective that women must not 'loiter' in public spaces, then these combine to produce discourses about women in public spaces and the modes of behaviour 'proper' to them.

Finally, there is the issue of 'cultural values': many women may not like to assert their autonomy lest this be seen as 'disturbing social codes and stepping outside the bounds of the cultural definitions of femininity. Therefore, such cultural stereotypes may result in reluctance by women to question traditional values' (ibid.: 61) that lead to violence against women in public spaces. The issue is to demystify 'our' culture so that that it is not treated as the repository of all that is good. Rather, the point is to see it as a contested field where different positions of power seek to normalise asymmetries as natural and inevitable. And, that cultures are not stable and fixed and, therefore, are open to change.

Notes

1. This discussion is based upon original fieldwork by the author as part of ongoing research on masculine cultures in India.
2. www.indiarealitynews.com. Last accessed 15 August 2009.
3. www.omaxe.com. Last accessed 11 July 2009.
4. An advertisement for an oral contraceptive in *Meri Saheli* magazine, January 1999.

References

Arendt, Hannah (1951). *The Origins of Totalitarianism*, New York: Harcourt Brace.

Ballantyne, Tony and Antoinette Burton (2005). 'Introduction: Bodies, Empires and World Histories', in Tony Ballantyne and Antoinette Burton (eds), *Bodies in Contact. Rethinking Colonial Empires in World History*, London and Durham: Duke University Press.

Bindon, James R. (2003). 'Samoa', in Carol R. Ember and Melvin Ember (eds), *Encyclopedia of Medical Anthropology. Health and Illness in World Cultures*, Vol. 2, New York: Plenum Publishing Corporation.

Birch, David, Tony Schirato and Sanjay Srivastava (2001). *Asia. Cultural Politics in the Global Age*, Sydney: Allen and Unwin.

Chandrasekhar, C.P. and Jayati Ghosh (2007). 'Women Workers in Urban India', www.macroscan.org. Last accessed 12 December 2008.

Chatterjee, Partha (1993). 'The Nationalist Resolution of the Women's Question', in K. Sangari and S. Vaid (eds), *Recasting Women. Essays in Colonial History*, New Delhi: Kali for Women.

Chopra, Radhika (2003). *From Violence to Supportive Practices. Families, Gender and Masculinities in India*, New Delhi: UNIFEM.

Cohen, Lawrence (1995). 'Holi in Banaras and the *Mahaland* of Modernity', *GLQ*, vol. 2, pp. 399–424.

Connell, Robert W. (2005). *Masculinities*, Cambridge: Polity Press.

Cribb, Jo and Ross Barnett (1999). 'Being Bashed: Western Samoa Women's Response to Domestic Violence in Western Samoa and New Zealand', *Gender, Place and Culture*, vol. 6, no. 1, pp. 49–65.

Devika, J. (2009). 'Bodies Gone Awry: The Abjection of Sexuality in Development Discourse in Contemporary Kerala', *Indian Journal of Gender Studies*, vol. 16, no. 1, pp. 21–46.

Fraser, Nancy (1992). 'Rethinking the Public Sphere: A Contribution to the Critique of Actually Existing Democracy', in C. Calhoun (ed.), *Habermas and the Public Sphere*, Cambridge: MIT Press.

Gothoskar, Sujata (1995). 'Computerization and Women's Employment in India's banking Sector', in Swasti Mitter and Sheila Rowbotham (eds), *Women Encounter Technology. Changing Patterns of Employment in he Third World*, New York and London: Routledge.

Goswami, Joydeep (2010) 'India's Rich Diversity', in *Malls of India*, New Delhi: Mallsnext.

Gupta, Nilanjana (2000). '*Just Switch Off!* Television: Creating the "Modern" Woman', *Social Scientist*, vol. 28, nos 3–4, pp. 61–70.

Gururani, Shubhra (2002). 'Forests of Pleasure and Pain: Gendered Practices of Labour and Livelihood in the Forests of the Kumaon Himalayas, India,' *Gender, Place and Culture*, vol. 9, no. 3, pp. 229–43.

Habermas, Jurgen (1989). *The Structural Transformation of the Public Sphere. An Inquiry into a Category of Bourgeois Society*, Cambridge Mass.: MIT Press.

Malhotra, Anju and Mark Mather (1997). 'Do Schooling and Work Empower Women in Developing Countries? Gender and Domestic Decisions in Sri Lanka', *Sociological Forum*, vol. 12, no. 4, pp. 599–630.

Mangan, J.A. and J. Walvin (eds) (1987). *Manliness and Morality: Middle-class Masculinity in Britain and America, 1800–1940*, New York: St. Martin's Press.

Moon, Seungsook (2002) 'Carving out Space: Civil Society and the Women's Movement in South Korea', *Journal of Asian Studies*, vol. 61, no. 2, pp. 473–500.

Morgan, Ruth and Saskia Wieringa (eds) (2005). *Tommy Boys, Lesbian Men, and Ancestral Wives: Female Same-Sex Practices in Africa*, Johannesburg: Jacanda media.

O'Hanlon, Rosalind (1997). 'Issues of Masculinity in North India History', *Indian Journal of Gender Studies*, vol. 4, pp. 1–19.

Omissi, David (1991). '"Martial Races": Ethnicity and Security in Colonial India 1858–1939', *War and Society*, vol. 9, no. 1, pp. 1–27.

Pateman, Carol (1989). *The Disorder of Women: Democracy, Feminism and Political Discourse*, Cambridge: Polity Press.

Patel, Vibhuti (2007). 'Sexual Harassment at the Work Place', in Rehana Ghadially (ed.), *Urban Women in Contemporary India: A Reader*, New Delhi: Sage Publications.

Phadke, Shilpa (2007). 'Dangerous Liaisons: Women and Men, Risk and Reputation in Mumbai', *Economic and Political Weekly*, vol. xlii, no. 17, pp. 1510–18.

Ranade, Shilpa (2007). 'The Way She Moves. Mapping the Everyday Production of Gender-space', *Economic and Political Weekly*, vol. xlii, no. 17, pp. 1519–26.

Rosselli, John (1980). 'The Self-image of Effeteness: Physical Education and Nationalism in Nineteenth-century Bengal', *Past and Present*, vol. 86: 121–48.

Said, Edward (1979). *Orientalism*, New York: Vintage Books.

Sarkar, Tanika (1995). 'Heroic Women, Mother Goddesses: Family and Organisation in Hindutva Politics', in Tanika Sarkar and Urvashi Butalia (eds), *Women and the Hindu Right: A Collection of Essays*, New Delhi: Kali for Women.

School of Women's Studies Jadhavpur University (SWSJU) (2010). *Re-Negotiating Gender Relations in Marriage: Family, Class and Community in Kolkata in an Era of Globalisation*, Kolkata: Jadhavpur University.

Seidler, Victor (1994). *Unreasonable Men. Masculinity and Social Theory*, London: Routledge.

Sennett, Richard (1976). *The Fall of Public Man*, New York: Knopf.

Sinha Mrinalini (1997). *Colonial Masculinity: The 'Manly Englishman' and the 'Effeminate Bengali' in the Late Nineteenth Century*, New Delhi: Kali for Women

Srivastava, Sanjay (2007). *Passionate Modernity. Sexuality, Consumption, and Class in India*, New Delhi: Routledge.

Sunder Rajan, Rajeshwari (1993). *Real and Imagined Women*, London: Routledge.

Thomas, Rosie (2005). 'Not Quite (Pearl) White: Fearless Nadia, Queen of the Stunts', in Raminder Kaur and Ajay J. Sinha (eds), *Bollyworld*, New Delhi: Sage Publications.

Vishwanath, Kalpana and Surabhi Tandon Mehrotra (2007). '"Shall We Go Out?" Women's Safety in Public paces in Delhi', *Economic and Political Weekly*, vol. 42, no. 17, pp. 1542–48.

Gendered Usage of Public Spaces
A Case Study of Mumbai

SHILPA PHADKE

Women spatially inhabit a city differently from men. They/we not only negotiate the city differently but also perceive it differently. This difference lies in the strategies women use to produce safety as also in the mind-maps that women carry in their heads of the city.

Gender and safety have been discussed in relation to each other in a variety of contexts. Feminist scholars in diverse settings have pointed out that urban narratives often construct the city as a space of danger for women and point out the ways in which these contribute to excluding women, particularly from public space (Andrews 2000, Garber 2000, Grosz 1995, McDowell 1999, Massey 1994, Parsons 2000, Rose 1999, Walkowitz 1992, Wilson 1991). Many of these narratives have also pointed out that women's class affiliations mediate significantly in enhancing or diminishing access to public space (Domosh and Seager 2001, Wilson 1991, 2001). Apart from class, other factors among them caste, community, age and physical ability also significantly impact women's access to public spaces. These intersect to enhance or restrict such access.

This essay draws substantially on insights and findings of the research conducted by the Gender & Space project under the aegis of PUKAR, an urban research collective in Mumbai. This collaborative project[1] sought to examine women's access to public space in relation to questions of citizenship, civic safety and sexual safety, risk and respectability. In this research, over a period of three years, we studied fourteen different localities in the city across geographical location, class, religious and linguistic affiliations, and usage. Segments of these localities were also mapped architecturally. We also conducted ethnographic observations at five suburban railway stations, four parks, three shopping malls and four coffee shops. These were studied largely through in-depth and structured interviews and focus group discussions. In addition, during this time we conducted three long courses and a number of short workshops and the discussions in these pedagogic contexts also contributed to our research. Though this research was conducted in Mumbai, its insights are likely to be relevant to other similar mega-cities as well.

In this essay I also draw substantially on my own previously published work (Phadke 2005, 2007a, 2007b), in relation to the conceptual and ideological terrain I engage with as many of the discussions and insights in those papers as are relevant to exploring policy concerns in relation to gendered concerns in public space. I have not previously attempted to explore policy issues in relation to public space in any detail and this is the new arena I venture into here.

This essay tries to lay out the broad terrain within which women's access to public space is located, examining the conceptual categories and the ideological context which influence the discourses of planning and the policies which in turn impact women's capacity to be in public space. My aim here is to suggest some practical ways in which women's access to public space may be enhanced.

The essay first examines some key concepts that are central to a discussion of gendered space. These include public space, gendered space, the notion of the private and the public, safety and risk. I then lay out the ideological contexts within which women access public space, and go on to interrogate some of the ways in which planning and the provision (or lack thereof) of infrastructure impact women's access to public space. Finally, I very briefly explore the policy implications of this research.

Examining Concepts

Public Space and Gendered Space: Spaces, both private and public, are hierarchically ordered through various inclusions and exclusions, and as important markers of segregation they reinforce social power structures.

Here the term, *'space'* refers to a complex construction and production of an environment – both real and imagined; influenced by socio-political processes, cultural norms and institutional arrangements which provoke different ways of being, belonging and inhabiting. This space simultaneously also impacts and shapes the social relations that contributed to its creation.[2] Feminist analyses of the 'production of space' have pointed out the ways in which gender mediates in the production and structuring of space. Their work raises a host of questions pertaining to how gender relations are manifested in space and in turn how spatial relations influence the construction of gender.[3] (Phadke 2007b)

It is also important to clarify that public space is only a part of the larger construct of public sphere. Public sphere includes not only public spaces but also public institutions, roles and positions produced over time, transforming the economy and polity and in turn getting transformed in significant ways. Public space in this essay includes sites like: streets, public toilets (in neighbourhoods, on streets, and railway stations), market places (bazaars and malls), recreational areas (parks, *maidans*, restaurants, cinema houses) and modes of public transport (which include buses, trains, taxis and rickshaws) as well as sites like bus-stops and railway stations. In this sense, I use public space in a narrower sense, though any discussion of public space is intrinsically linked to the larger concept of the public sphere.

Drawing on the work of several feminist scholars of space, I use the term 'gendered spaces' to refer to the socially constructed geographical and architectural arrangements around space which regulate and restrict women's access to those spaces which are connected to the production of power and privilege in any given context. (Phadke 2007b)

Public and Private Space: One cannot but engage with various binaries, especially those of public and private, even as one attempts to disrupt them and demonstrate the fluidity of space. The effort is at every point to see the public and private as fluid continuous categories that move in complex ways between one and the other and I would like to underscore my awareness that these are not watertight categories. However, narratives around public space are often conducted in very strong binaries of boundaries, especially those between public and private and it is difficult to avoid using these terminologies. Nonetheless it is important to state at the outset that one uses these categories fully cognisant of their limitations.

Public spaces have historically tended to be the preserve of men; a position that reinforces male control and authority over women and their access to public space. Women's restricted access to public space is connected to what one might call a notion of *defilability* – of both spaces and women themselves. This implies that women's presence in particular privileged spaces, usually public, may threaten the sanctity of these spaces; at the same time, women themselves face the threat of being defiled in public spaces, especially at particular times of the day.[4]

The public-private dichotomy has constructed the female body as fragile and lacking in strength. Various attacks on women: molestation, sexual assault and rape reinforce beliefs about the vulnerable female body.[5] Ideas of *Izzat*/honour, inscribed on the female body, create the anxieties of possible *defilement* particularly in public spaces. The false binary of public (read dangerous) versus private (read safe) hides the fact of domestic violence and sexual assault by family and neighbours. The suggestion that women are safe inside their homes erases reports in regard to the violence faced by women in their own homes. Safety then is only from the outsider or the stranger, but protection from the insider is not just unavailable it is also, more significantly, considered irrelevant. Secondly, it ignores the fact that the flip side of a protection that comes from belonging and familiarity is surveillance.

Despite the various markers that cite women as outsiders to public space, in the public sphere in urban India, women have become more visible than ever before. In the political arena, the 73rd and 74th Constitutional Amendments were passed by Parliament in 1992. The Bills, ratified by all states in 1993, guaranteed the reservation of 33 per cent of seats for women in panchayats and municipal bodies. As a result women corporators have become more visible in Mumbai as in other cities, and despite the common perception that they are proxies for men, have gained a certain amount of recognition. In the economic arena, women have become visible as white-collar workers in a variety of fields, some even reaching top management levels and being publicly lauded. Unfortunately, these changes do not

However, this effort towards augmenting lighting in order to increase women's sense of safety is not to suggest that lighting is the only factor influencing perceptions of safety. Other factors like visibility and access act in tandem with illumination. A comparison between two *maidans* in the city – Shivaji Park and The Oval – with similar lighting levels, reveals this. The low wall and 24-hour open access of Shivaji Park creates an environment that invites public participation in contrast to the high grills and gated somewhat threatening space of the Oval.[19]

Making Safer Places: The other interesting initiative is a project in Britain called 'Making Safer Places' which involves three cities – Manchester, Bristol and London – and started in November 2002. Making Safer Places is a three-year pilot project run by the Women's Design Service. There were two project areas in each of the three cities. It involved carrying out Women's Community Safety Audit Training with groups of local women to explore how the built environment impacts upon women's perceptions of safety. It involved local women in auditing their area and developing recommendations for improving their locality in relation to safety. It was also specifically targeted at older women, disabled women and women from black and minority ethnic communities.[20]

Since the 1980s, there has been a significant increase in the study of women and environments by feminists in the fields of cultural and urban geography, architecture, planning, anthropology and sociology. Feminist architects and planners have also reclaimed the faith in the built environment by making proposals to re-design streets, parks, cities, neighbourhoods and homes.

In London, a group called the Women's Design Service, was constituted in 1987 by women architects, designers and planners with a vision for 'a future where all... buildings, transport systems, streets, parks and open spaces are designed to incorporate the needs of women'.[21] Through design consultancy on public and private projects, educational programmes and research into various areas of concern, the group aims to help women's groups access the skills needed for creating an equitable built environment. Among the recurring concerns of women they have identified over almost two decades of work are toilets, nappy changing, crèches, housing design, parks, pavements, safety and transport.

Safer Cities Programme: There are also other programmes towards safe cities that are underway. For instance, UN Habitat Safer Cities Programme, in collaboration with other UN agencies (UNDP, UNICEF, UNESCO), focuses on urban safety issues and the prevention of violence of all kinds by facilitating exchange of expertise between cities and regions and collaborations of various kinds. UN Habitat Safer Cities Projects are ongoing in the following cities: Greater Johannesburg and Durban, South Africa; Dar es Salaam, Tanzania; Adjame, Yopougon, Treichville (Abidjan), Cote D'ivoire; Antananarivo, Madagascar; Dakar, Senegal; Nairobi, Kenya; and Yaounde, Cameroon.[22] These, however, have a more diffused scope and are targeted at a more general idea of violence.

In May 2002, an International Seminar on Women's Safety was held in Montreal, Canada. Among the ideas discussed at this seminar was the notion that safety must be approached through an 'empowerment approach' that focuses on autonomy and freedom rather than a 'paternalistic approach' that focuses on safety through dependence and restrictions. The 'empowerment approach' is based on the notions of women's rights of access to public space and also the right to make choices and judgements about their own lives. It is based on a recognition of the legitimacy of women's fear, and places women at the centre of the dialogue focusing on the importance of supporting each woman's choice while providing her with support.

Questions have been raised about the capacity of 'safety audits' to move beyond proposing policy-related technical solutions and changes to actually challenge conventional ideas about boundaries and about women's place in the city in order to assert women's rights to the city and to an unconstrained use of urban space at all times. Like most planning tools, safety audits depend on the kind of social forces that propel them, the tools used and the kinds of political participation that occur. The success of safety audits depends on who controls the process – women or women's groups, municipal governments (or other such bodies) or professionals (the experts in the shape of planners, lighting engineers or architects). In the latter two cases, women are located as clients, as the subjects of political action rather than as political actors in their own right. Solutions here tend to focus on technology and the aim is reassurance and the idea that greater safety is possible but it is the experts who make the decisions and have the answers. In contrast, where women or women's groups lead the safety audit processes, lived experience is the basis of participation and women who use urban space and understand how power functions in this context to exclude women are at the centre of the dialogue and decision-making. Such a dialogue also underlines how notions of 'safe' and 'unsafe' spaces are socially constructed. Solutions to restructure urban space are sought in ways that not only provide women a greater access to urban space but do it by asserting a need for a more equitable citizenship where women are political actors (Andrews 2000).

The situations of inadequate infrastructure, as in the case of toilets and urban violence against women, described above only serve to underscore the fact that women are at best marginal citizens and at worst invisible or transgressive and an illegitimate presence in public space in the perception of state, legal and infrastructural machinery. Available data in these areas, even if inadequate, still allows us to make a strong case for changes in urban policy to address the needs of women in public space.

However, at this point, one must caution that while it is important to put in place several policy measures to address the infrastructural lacunae in the urban context making it safer and friendlier for women to be part of public spaces, at the same time the strategic efficacy of these interventions is limited. The limitations of such external interventions are best explained by the distinction between 'strategic gender interests' and 'practical gender interests' proposed by Maxine Molyneux (1985: 233). 'Strategic gender interests' for women are derived from the analysis of women's subordination and the formulation of strategic objectives to overcome the subordination.[23] 'Practical gender interests' arise from the concrete conditions of women's location within the gender division of labour and are a response to immediately perceived needs. 'They do not entail generally a strategic goal such as women's emancipation or gender equality ... nor do they challenge the prevailing forms of subordination even though they arise directly out of them.' Strategic concerns must be located around questions of the politics of public space and citizenship rights must be seen as the basis for any arguments being made in regard to women's rights of access to public space.[24]

Yet while the impact of social structure on built space has been extensively studied, there is not enough theoretical understanding of how the built environment affects the users, not just in terms of their immediate behaviour within it, but in the way the built environment reinforces, contradicts, and transforms social structures.

Conclusion

In navigating the complex and nuanced terrain of gendered access to public space, I have attempted to argue that public spaces reflect the city's attitude to its citizens and the presence of sensitively planned infrastructure and welcoming well-designed public spaces are a measure of its inclusiveness.

Infrastructure that privileges the needs of one group reinforces the status-quo and promotes a lop-sided hierarchy. Infrastructural provisions that discriminate against some groups not only create everyday problems of accessibility for them but are also concrete markers of their marginalized position in the social order. When groups are denied access to public space this actually leads to a double discrimination since they are rendered invisible, reducing opportunities to publicly lobby for change. The provision of infrastructure plays a significant role in making a space more inviting to women and may even discourage situations where women get harassed. Similarly while design by itself might not be able to create an equitable and welcoming public space for women and other marginal citizens, it can create the situation for change to happen and reinforce it when it does.

As I have argued elsewhere, the claims of women to the city cannot be seen separately from those of other maginal citizens. Though it is a difficult proposition to make a city friendly to its diverse populations the attempt must be made. And some simple strategies would go a long way in making a difference. For instance, better street lighting, lower steps for buses, paved sidewalks, broad, un-chipped steps on foot-over-bridges and usable public toilets would not just benefit children, the physically challenged and other women, but also all men.

The provision of more and better infrastructure for women and other marginal groups, the disabled and children among them, would be an important statement of the recognition that they *belong* and have *rights* as citizens. An articulation of a public discourse around public facilities has significance beyond questions of infrastructure; it has implications for the ways in which people perceive themselves and envision a politics of citizenship and belonging.

Notes

1. With Shilpa Ranade and Sameera Khan.
2. For a discussion on the multiple concepts and constructions of space see among others: De Certeau (1984), Lefebvre (1991), Sennett (1994).
3. See for instance, Massey (1994), Spain (1992), Rose (1993) and Grosz (1995) among others.
4. In the Indian context the distinction between public and private got articulated during the colonial period. Partha Chatterjee, for instance, makes the argument that the bourgeois leadership of the nationalist movement chose to define the public sphere as the area for contestation where they sought to establish their equality with the colonial masters. The private sphere then was the inner domain of subjectivity where they perceived themselves as sovereign and refused to negotiate with the colonial state and which then allowed them to justify practices discriminatory to women. See Chatterjee (1997).
5. It is interesting to see how this image of 'fragility' co-exists with the reality of the back-breaking work that women do in rural contexts, walking miles to fetch heavy loads of water and fuel and in urban contexts on construction sites and in an everyday sense by performing the demanding dual roles of worker and home-manager. These images have implications particularly for an analysis of how class and caste hierarchies work in tandem with gender inequality to create an apparent rationality conveniently ignoring or erasing the contradictions.
6. On 21 July 2005, the Bill to ban the dance bars in Maharashtra was passed unanimously. The ban was enforced on 15 August last year by amending the Bombay Police (Amendment) Act 2005. This bill prohibited all dance performances in dance bars, but exempted 3-star and above graded hotels. Public interest petitions by bar owners, bar girls, activists and NGOs were

filed challenging the government legislation. The two-judge division bench of the Bombay High Court, comprising Justice F.I. Rebello and Justice Roshan Dalvi, in a 260-page ruling this week, quashed the Maharashtra government's law banning dance bars on grounds of discrimination under Article 14 of the Constitution of India. The court ruled that the ban violated the fundamental rights and constitutional right to equality of bar dancers and bar owners. However, the dance bars have not yet re-started and the Government of Maharashtra has moved the Supreme Court on the issue (*Times of India*, 14 April 2006).

7.   Safety that is linked to the sexual control of women in families and communities has even more adverse implications for those women whose communities are under threat or surveillance themselves. See Khan (2007) for a detailed discussion of Muslim women in Mumbai.

8.   Dongri is a Muslim-dominated neighbourhood in southern Mumbai.

9.   Kala Chowki is an old working class area in central Mumbai and its architectural form is a mix of industrial and residential. This area is now in the process of transformation with a number of high rises and up-market shopping centres coming up. Kala Chowki is interesting because though it is surrounded by these changes, at the time of the study, the mills in this area had not yet begun being converted and so it retains its old built form though there is an air of decay and disillusion.

10.   This is not however to suggest that heterogeneous spaces by themselves are adequate to facilitate women's access to public space. Elsewhere I have argued that despite the fact that heterogeneous space promotes women's access to public space facilitated by anonymity, this does not in any way further women's claims to public space as citizens. I suggested that the potential longer term risk of seeking anonymity rather than making a political claim to public space could well mean that women will continue to be seen as outsiders to public space (Phadke 2005).

11.   Edwards and McKie point out that research shows that women on average take twice as long as men to urinate. Research conducted in various parts of the world between 1957 and 1991, collated by Kira (1994), record the time taken measured in seconds from entering to exiting a toilet. There are eight studies on men's urination times showing averages of between 32 to 47 seconds and six studies on women showing averages of between 80 and 97 seconds. All these studies have been conducted largely in Western countries with the exception of the inclusion of Japan. See A. Kira (1994), 'Culture and

Behaviour of Public Toilet Users', paper delivered to International Symposium on Public Toilets, Hong Kong, cited in Edwards and McKie (1997).

12. *Hindustan Times*, 12 December 2011.

13. Reetika Subramanian , 'Bus travel: Not the BEST', *Hindustan Times*, 13 December 2011.

14. *Business Today*, November 23, 2003.

15. METRAC (The Metropolitan Toronto Action Committee on Violence Against Women and Children) is a community-based organisation that works towards eliminating all forms of violence against women and children. METRAC began in 1982 when there were a number of brutal sexual assaults and murders of women in Toronto. A group of Toronto women organised themselves as 'The Toronto Pink Ribbon Committee' to demand that something be done to stop the violence. This grew into a taskforce and eventually the establishment of METRAC. See http://www.metrac.org

16. For instance, in one study conducted in Canada, 63 per cent of women said that darkness and poor lighting made them feel unsafe and/or uncomfortable (METRAC 1990). Another study in Liverpool, UK, cited poor lighting as the top reason women felt unsafe in railway station areas (see Safe Women Project 1994, *Ask Any Woman: A report of a phone-in on women and safety in Liverpool local government area*).

17. It is interesting to note that women's definitions of what constitutes 'late in the night' differed significantly. For some women 9 pm would be considered late for others it was not late till midnight.

18. The survey was conducted between August 2004 and January 2005 by research assistants to the project, Abhinandita Mathur and Sonal Makhija, with some help from the author.

19. It is true that the Shivaji Park area is more residential than The Oval, but even the front near the Art Deco buildings of The Oval is not friendly.

20. More information about the Making Safer Places Project can be found on www.wds.org.uk/.

21. As mentioned on the Women's Design Service homepage, http://www.wds.org.uk.

22. For more information see UN Habitat website: http://www.unhabitat.org/.

23. These would include among other objectives, 'the abolition of the sexual division of labour; the alleviation of the burden of domestic labour and child care; the removal of institutionalised forms of discrimination such as rights to own land or property, or access to credit; the establishment of

political equality; freedom of choice over child bearing; and the adoption of adequate measures against male violence and control over women' (Molyneux 1985).

24. The focus on women's rights to citizenship is here neither a denial of women's heterogeneous location nor of the need to articulate similar rights of citizenship premised on questions of access for other marginal groups. In the 1990s, citizenship in Mumbai has been increasingly articulated and organised around middle class lives and concerns with 'citizens groups' demanding of the city administration more regulated and policed services, infrastructure and public spaces. These demands are premised on a perception of the city being encroached on and polluted by those who are not rightful citizens and are articulated in a voice that reclaims the city for its rightful middle class, tax paying citizens. For a broader discussion of this see, for instance, Chatterjee (2003).

References and Additional Reading

Andrews, Caroline (2000). 'Resisting Boundaries; Using Safety Audits for Women', in Kristine B. Miranna and Alma H. Young (eds), *Gendering the City: Women, Boundaries and Visions of Urban Life*, Lanham: Rowman and Littlefield, pp. 157–68.

Chatterjee, Partha (1997). 'The Nationalist Resolution of the Women's Question', in Kumkum Sangari and Sudesh Vaid (eds), *Recasting Women: Essays in Colonial History*, New Delhi: Kali for Women, 1997 edition, pp. 233-53.

——— (2003). 'Are Indian Cities becoming Bourgeois at Last?', in Indira Chandrasekhar and Peter C. Seel (eds), *Body.City: Siting Contemporary Culture in India*, Delhi & Berlin: Tullika Books & The House of World Cultures, pp. 170–85.

Corteen, Karen, Paul Tyrer and Les Morgan (2000). *Violence, Sexuality and Space*, http://les1.man.ac.uk/sociology/vssrp/researchsummary.html. Last accessed June 2005.

de Certeau, Michael (1984). *The Practice of Everyday Life*, Berkley: University of California Press.

Domosh, Mona and Joni Seager (2001). *Putting Women in Place: Feminist Geographers make Sense of the World*, New York: The Guildford Press.

Edwards, Julie and Linda McKie (1997). 'Women's Public Toilets: A Serious Issue for the Body Politic', in Kathy Davis (ed.), *Embodied Practices: Feminist Perspectives on the Body*, London: Sage Publications, pp. 135–49.

Garber, Judith A. (2000). "Not Named or Identified': Politics and the Search for Anonymity in the City' in Kristine B. Miranna and Alma H. Young (eds), *Gendering the City: Women, Boundaries and Visions of Urban Life*, Lanham: Rowman and Littlefield, pp. 19–40.

Grosz, Elizabeth (1995). *Space, Time and Perversion*, New York: Routledge.

JAGORI (2010). *Making Delhi Safe for Women*, 5 July 2005. Available at http://www.jagori.org/wp-content/uploads/2006/02/SAFE%20CITY%20 NOTE%20FOR%20HDR.pdf. Last accessed on 3 October 2010.

Kannabiran, Kalpana (2006). 'Introduction' in Kalpana Kannabiran (ed.), *The Violence of Normal Times: Essays on Women's Lived Realities*, New Delhi: Women Unlimited, pp. 1–45.

Khan, Sameera (2007). 'Negotiating the Mohalla: Exclusion, Identity and Muslim Women in Mumbai', Review of Women's Studies, *Economic & Political Weekly*, vol. 42, no. 17, pp. 1527–33.

Lefebvre, Henri (1991). *The Production of Space*, Oxford, Blackwell.

Massey, Doreen (1994). *Space, Place and Gender*, Minneapolis: University of Minnesota Press.

McDowell, Linda (1999). *Gender, Identity and Place: Understanding Feminist Geographies*, Minneapolis: University of Minnesota Press.

METRAC (1990). 'Women Taking Space', *Women and Environments*, vol. 12, no. 1, March/April.

Meyer, Esther da Costa (1996). 'La Donna è Mobile: Agoraphobia, Women and Urban Space' in Diana Agrest et al (eds), *The Sex of Architecture*, New York: Harry N Abrams, pp. 141–56.

Mitchell, Don (2000). 'Public and Private: Gendered Divisions of Space', in *Cultural Geography: A Critical Introduction*, Oxford: Blackwell, pp. 201–23.

Molyneux, Maxine (1985). 'Mobilization without emancipation? Women's Interests, State and Revolution in Nicaragua', *Feminist Studies*, vol. 11, no. 2, 227–54.

Nair, Janaki (2005). *The Promise of the Metropolis: Bangalore's Twentieth Century*, Delhi: Oxford University Press.

Parsons, Deborah (2000). *Streetwalking the Metropolis: Women, the City and Modernity*, Oxford: Oxford University Press.

Phadke, Shilpa (2005). 'You Can be Lonely in a Crowd: The Production of Safety in Mumbai' *Indian Journal of Gender Studies*, vol. 12, no. 1, pp. 41–62.

_____. 2007a. 'Dangerous Liaisons: Women and Men; Risk and Reputation in Mumbai', in Review of Women's Studies, *Economic & Political Weekly*, vol. 42, no. 17, 1510–18.

———. 2007b. 'Re-mapping the Public: Gendered Spaces in Mumbai' in Madhavi Desai (ed.) *Gender and the Built Environment,* New Delhi: Zubaan.

Phadke, Shilpa, Sameera Khan and Shilpa Ranade (2006). *Women in Public: Safety in Mumbai,* Unpublished Report submitted to the Indo Dutch Programme on Alternatives in Development (IDPAD).

Phadke, Shilpa, Shilpa Ranade and Sameera Khan (2009). 'Why Loiter? Radical Possibilities for Gendered Dissent', in Melissa Butcher and Selvaraj Velayutham (eds), *Dissent and Cultural Resistance in Asia's Cities,* L

Phadke, Shilpa, Sameera Khan and Shilpa Ranade (2011). *Why Loiter: Women and Risk on Mumbai Streets,* New Delhi: Penguin.

Gendered Claims of Citizenship and Notions of Honour and Stigma

FLAVIA AGNES

Citizenship Claims of Women

The negotiations between state, community and family which take place in the context of women's rights are important markers for determining the citizenship claims of women. These negotiations lead to a gendered notion of citizenship. The 'gendering' of citizenship has arisen due to the creation of the public-private divide, where the male is perceived to belong to the public sphere and the female to the private (Roy 2005: 28). In this formulation, women are perceived as passive or dependent citizens confined within the private domain of the home and family. The assumption that a woman's primary location is the private sphere, where she is placed under the patriarchal authority of her father or husband, has historically prevailed under most legal regimes. A woman's need for a public identity and a legal relationship directly with the state has not been adequately addressed within the citizenship discourse and hence women's claims to citizenship are mediated through the male heads of families and through the interventions of the community.[1]

Women had to wage a sustained struggle to enter the public domain and forge their claims of equal citizenship under modern constitutions worldwide. It is only through these struggles that women were able to secure their rights of equality, political participation, to vote and to bodily integrity.

In India, women's struggles to enter the public domain started in the 18th century with a struggle for basic literacy, and later in the 19th century for professional education. In the early 20th century, the setting up of organisations such as the All India Women's Conference (AIWC) and women's participation in the nationalist struggle resulted in their being granted the right of equality along with men and the right to vote within the new Constitution. Through these milestones there was an acceptance of formal equality within the political sphere. However, despite these gains, the patriarchal control to which women are subjected within the private domain of the home constantly gets reproduced in a convoluted, fragmented and distorted manner in the public domain which results in brutal violence against women.

An exploration into the realm of violence against women in public places must start with the violence unleashed upon women at the dawn of nationhood. While ushering in a new Constitution with its guarantees of Fundamental Rights to life, liberty and freedom, the state also had to deal with the aftermath of the violence that was unleashed at the time of Partition. The partition of a composite colonial political unit into two postcolonial nation-states and the re-drawing of political boundaries resulted in the displacement of a huge population. While entire communities suffered in this process, women were subjected to brutal sexual violence, inflicted upon them as bearers of their community's identity. Apart from killing and maiming, women were also raped, brutally violated and abducted (Butalia 2000, Das 1995, Menon and Bhasin 1998). In order to save the community 'honour', the families urged women to commit mass suicides when faced with the threat of sexual violence. Later, the abducted women who had settled with their abductors and had children through these relationships were located and branded 'citizens' of their original host nation-state and had to be retrieved even against their own wishes. The entire debate on the recovery of abducted women and children in the post-independence period was a debate among men in the Indian Constituent Assembly and Parliament. It was a debate about what was happening to 'their' honour, 'their' women and 'their' children. The abducted women symbolised the shame of the nation as mother, and hence the honour of the nation had to be restored (Butalia 2000: 191). It is within this formulation of 'our women' and 'nation's honour' that the gendered genealogy of citizenship of a postcolonial nation-state was constructed. The citizenship claims of women were encaptured within two conflicting frames—one of equality and dignity and the other as custodians of the nation's honour.

This saga of rape, mutilation, abduction and retrieval sheds some light on the complex and layered relationship between the nation-state and 'its' women. At one level, women staked their claim for equality with men, for 'sameness' of treatment in the public domain and for equal rights, opportunities and protection. At another level, their claims were negotiated through other mediums such as tradition, culture, religion, community and family, and were framed by notions of 'honour' and 'stigma'. This leads to the construction not just of a uni-dimensional gendered citizen in opposition to men, but a multi-dimensional one, and compels women to negotiate their citizenship with the state through a kaleidoscope of identities resulting in layered, fragmented, hierarchical and, at times, overlapping claims. It is in this interface between family, community and state that women negotiate their rights. It is also within this interface that much of the violence suffered by women, both within the private sphere of the home as well as the public domain, is located.

The notions of honour and control, shame and stigma govern the violence that takes place in the public domain. When we examine the communal violence (or rather genocide) that took place in Gujarat in 2002, fifty years after partition, we can see a similar pattern of violence where bodies of women from the minority Muslim community were subjected to extreme sexual brutality in order to humiliate an entire community. The incident at Khairlanji, where Dalit women were raped and killed, is yet another stark reminder of the manner in which women become the markers of their community honour and their violation becomes the primary weapon to wreak vengeance upon an entire community.

This essay seeks to outline the various public locations of violence against women, examine the social and political frameworks within which it occurs and lay out the statutory provisions that are meant to offer the possibility of redress and the lacuna therein as well as the judicial framing of these issues. Categorising broadly into four themes—rape and sexual crimes, caste- and community-based violence, violence in workplace-related situations and violence by the family and the community—the essay provides a historical context and examines the contemporary debates around a wide range of issues which lead to violence against women in public places. While conceding that this is not an exhaustive list of the type of violence which women are subjected to within the public domain, it provides a fair sampling of incidents which can be addressed within the rubric of 'violence in public places'. The style of analysis that has been adopted is socio-legal with due emphasis on statutory laws, court verdicts and proposed legislative reforms.

Rape and Sexual Crimes

The Anti-rape Campaign of the Eighties

Rape forms the central pivot around which other sexual crimes against women are constructed. This is a crime which may occur both in the privacy of the home as well as the public domain, though within the domestic sphere it continues to be shrouded in secrecy. It has continuously made headlines through its public manifestations. Notions of female sexuality embedded in the discourse on rape are important to our understanding of this crime. While the violent physical act is degrading and dehumanising, its social implications result in deep emotional scars because of the notions of shame and stigma that transform the victim into a vile and evil schemer and the accused into an innocent man who has been 'framed'.

During the early eighties, rape became the central theme in campaigns in the Indian women's movement. The shame and stigma attached to the offence had resulted in a deep silence about it, and most cases of rape and sexual assault remained unreported. But even in the rare case that was reported, it was the victim who had to bear the brunt of humiliation and justice remained elusive.

The catalyst for the anti-rape campaign launched by women's organisations was the Supreme Court judgement in the Mathura rape case.[2] Mathura, a sixteen-year old, illiterate, orphan, tribal girl was raped by two policemen, while they were on duty. The rape took place inside the police station; a stark incidence of public and custodial violence against a young girl. But since the young girl had eloped with her boyfriend and was brought to the police station on a complaint filed by her own brother, she was viewed as a woman of loose moral character. Since there were no marks of injury on her body, the court termed Mathura a liar. Her evidence regarding the rape was disbelieved. The Supreme Court set aside the Bombay High Court decision and acquitted the policemen.

The judgment shocked some legal academics, who wrote an open letter to the Chief Justice of India condemning it. They were of the view that such a judgment would snuff out all hopes of justice for millions of Mathuras in the country and they questioned 'whether the illiterate, labouring, politically mute Mathuras of India [should] be continually condemned to their pre-constitutional Indian fate' (Baxi et al (1979) 4 SCC (Jour) 17. Also see 2008: 271). This open letter was the trigger for the anti-rape campaign which received wide media coverage, something that helped to build public pressure and ultimately resulted in changes in the rape laws. This was a path breaking victory, as rape laws had remained unchanged for over a century.

Box 1   **The Salient Features of the 1983 Rape Law Amendments and its Impact**

Shifting of Burden of Proof: In selective cases of custodial rape—in police lockups, prisons, hospitals, rescue homes, remand homes, etc.—the burden of proving consent, once sexual intercourse was proved, shifted to the accused.

Minimum Mandatory Punishment: The amendment prescribed a mandatory minimum punishment of seven years for ordinary rapes and ten years for rapes of aggravated nature—gang rapes, custodial rapes, rape of children under the age of twelve years, rape of pregnant women, etc.

Consensual Intercourse in Custodial Situations: To deal with the issue of sex with consent (as made out in the Mathura rape case), the amendments introduced a new offence and made consensual sexual intercourse in certain custodial situations culpable.

Initially there was considerable hope that the amended law would ensure a greater number of convictions and, more importantly, the dignity of women would not be violated during rape trials. Further, it was believed that the increase in punishment would act as a deterrent. However, the subsequent events in the years following the amendment belie these aspirations.

In the following years, sexual assault continued to dominate the public discourse as the country witnessed a steady increase in reported cases. The National Crime Record Bureau (NCRB), Ministry of Home Affairs, in its annual publication *Crime in India*, provided us with the following official statistics of reported cases of rapes in India, over the years:

TABLE 1   Reported Cases of Rapes in India

1990	1994	1995	1996	1997	1998	2000	2005	2007	2008
9,518	12,351	13,754	14,846	15,330	15,031	16,496	18,359	20,737	21,467

In 1980, the year in which the anti-rape campaign was launched, there were 5,023 reported cases of rape. Statistics for rape were compiled only from 1971 and in that year the number of reported cases of rape was 2,487. As we can observe, by 1980 the figures had doubled. During the decade 1988–98, there was an increase of over 65 per cent in reported cases of rapes. (The figures for 1988 were 9,099.) The 2008 report of NCRB comments that from 1971 to 2008 there was an alarming increase of 763.2 per cent in reported cases of rape. Even more alarming is the fact that these figures reflect only the tip of the iceberg as a large number of cases remain unreported due to the stigma attached to the crime as well as the ordeal of facing a criminal trial. There were also several instances where the family and the community pressurised the rapist to marry the victim as she was deemed to be tainted and unworthy to be married off to another man (Bhattacharjee 2008: 9–52).

Despite the positive stipulations within the amended rape laws, most cases ended in acquittals.[3] But periodically, the Supreme Court and the High Courts laid down procedural norms and issued strictures against a lax and corrupt investigative machinery and a gender-biased lower judiciary for their hostile attitude and suspicious approach towards a rape victim.

The Credibility of the Victim

The relevance of the victim's moral character and sexual history was another contentious point, and rape trials continued to be traumatic for the victim-survivor. Despite the demand from the women's movement for its deletion during the anti-rape campaign of the early eighties, the stipulation that a victim's past sexual history can be used as a defence for the accused had been retained.[4] This continued to provide scope for the defence lawyers to humiliate the victim. Only by shaming the complainant in a packed courtroom through crude and vulgar cross-examination could a criminal lawyer display his legal acumen and obtain an acquittal for his client, or so it seemed. The offending section was finally deleted in 2002.[5]

Despite this, the practice of using the 'finger test' to ascertain the girl's 'chastity' continues in our public hospitals and this medical evidence is then used by defence lawyers to secure acquittals for the accused, as the following cases reveal. If two fingers pass easily into a woman's vagina, it is assumed that she is habituated to sexual intercourse and hence her testimony is unreliable.[6] In *Hare Krishna Das v State of Bihar*,[7] the Patna High Court, while acquitting the accused, placed great weightage on the medical examination that the survivor was habituated to sex. In view of this, the court ruled that the testimony of the victim (prosecutrix) was not reliable.

In cases wherein two fingers have passed easily, the doctors have used this information against the rape survivors. In the case of *Gokul and Atmaram v State of Madhya Pradesh*,[8] the court held that the prosecution had failed to show that the rupture of the vagina was fresh. On the contrary, the evidence that 'two fingers could easily enter in the vagina' was relied upon. The High Court held: 'If the version given by the prosecutrix[9] was unsupported by any medical evidence and the surrounding circumstances were improbable, the court should not act on the solitary evidence of the prosecutrix.'

In *Government of NCT Delhi v Sant Ram*,[10] the court acquitted the accused on the ground that the medical examination of the hymen revealed that two fingers could easily be inserted into the vagina and hence the prosecutrix was habituated to sexual intercourse and her testimony was not reliable. In this case there was also a delay of four days in filing the FIR.

In the context of rape, the two most prevalent social myths, which often translate into dominant legal discourse, are that when a woman says 'no' she means 'yes' and that jilted lovers turn around and accuse their boyfriends of 'rape'. The extension of this myth is that when a woman or her family wants to 'frame' a man, due to spite or vengeance, she/they will file a case of rape against an 'innocent' man.

Medical textbooks reinforce the myths that women frequently dream, hallucinate and even derive pleasure from the act of sexual violation, as also the myth that women lie, fabricate and manipulate evidence of rape; that women would go to the extent of rubbing chilli powder on the vagina of children to fake evidence of rape. Through this supposedly 'scientific' discourse, the myth of the woman who 'cries rape' is granted legitimacy. For instance, *Modi's Medical Jurisprudence and Toxicology*, a standard textbook on forensic medicine states:

False charges of rape are not uncommon in India. Occasionally parents may introduce chillies into the vagina of their female child to cause irritation and inflammation or may injure her genitals for the purpose of substantiating a false charge of rape brought against an individual with a view to take revenge or extort money from him. And may tutor their child to tell a circumstantial story of a rape. Modi saw a case in which the father thrust his thumb forcibly into the vagina of his daughter, six years old, in order to bring a false charge of rape against his neighbour, who was his enemy, and lacerated the posterior part of the hymen, the posterior part of the vagina and the posterior commissure. At times, the parents inflict injuries on the private parts of their female child and then kill her by strangulation or suffocation in order to bring a false accusation of rape and murder against their enemy. (Subrahmanyam 2002: 506)

The above passage, which might have been present in one of the book's early editions of the pre-independence era, continues to be mindlessly reproduced and is found in the 22nd edition published in 2002, despite two decades of the anti-rape movement in India. The sole concern of the medical profession, as reflected in this passage, seems to be for the man 'falsely accused of rape' and not for the occurrence of incest, child sexual abuse and murder of the girl child by their own families! Where does the medical profession, with its primary concern for healing and curing, place this little girl who has been brought with evidence of sexual abuse? The same passage then continues and goes on to express the most widely prevalent bias against rape victims, that women are fickle minded, that they are liars, and that they have much to gain by hoisting a false case of rape.[11] It is little wonder that medical students fed on this dogma become highly suspicious of a woman/child brought in for examination on a complaint of sexual abuse (Agnes 2005).

Leniency to the Accused

One of the most important ingredients of the 1983 amendment is the clause regarding the minimum punishment of ten years in cases of custodial rapes and child rapes. But it appears that this clause had no bearing on conviction patterns in the post-amendment period, as courts continue to award token punishments even in the few cases which result in convictions. The provision of mandatory minimum punishment is in direct contrast to the progressive legal theory of leniency towards offenders.

Usually, in child molestation cases, the offenders are young men. This brings about a clash between two diagonally opposite legal theories regarding conviction, that is, minimum punishment of ten years in cases of rape of girl children and leniency towards youth offenders. In such a situation, since our criminal jurisprudence grants all advantages to the accused, leniency towards youth offenders will prevail. Hence the statutory provision of a mandatory minimum sentence is sidetracked. Below I provide a sampling of some rulings delivered soon after the 1983 amendment.

In a case reported in 1984, a seven-year-old girl was raped by a boy of eighteen. She was severely injured and was left in a pit by the roadside in an unconscious condition. The Sessions Court convicted the accused to five years rigorous imprisonment. The appeal to enhance the sentence was dismissed on the following ground: 'Although rape warrants a more severe sentence, considering that the accused was only 18 years of age, it would not be in the interest of justice to enhance the sentence of five years imposed by the trial court.'[12]

In another case of 1987, an eleven-year-old girl was raped by a youth in a field while another kept her pinned down to the ground and gagged her with her sari. The Sessions Court convicted the accused with five years' imprisonment. In an appeal to enhance the sentence, the Madhya Pradesh High Court went to the extent of holding: 'Increasing cases of personal violence and crime rate cannot justify a severe sentence on youth offenders'.[13]

Notions of Shame and Stigma

The rare positive judgments are those where young girls were brutally attacked and had received multiple injuries. So there was not much difficulty in proving the case beyond reasonable doubt as is required under the criminal jurisprudence. Since the girls were very young, the issue of their consent was an irrelevant factor at the trial. But even in such cases, the court did not concern itself with the trauma suffered by a minor girl and the extent of her injuries. The concern of the judiciary was confined to the loss of virginity and prospects of marriage, as the following case reveals. A young girl was dragged into the forest, kept there the whole night and was raped. She received severe injuries and bled profusely. While upholding the conviction by the Sessions Court, the High Court held: 'The girl was a virgin upto the time of rape. It is difficult to imagine that an unmarried girl would willingly surrender her virtue. Virginity is the most precious possession of an Indian girl and she would never willingly part with this proud and precious possession'.[14]

In the *Suman Rani* rape case,[15] the Supreme Court reduced the mandatory minimum punishment of ten years awarded to two policemen on the following ground: 'The peculiar facts and circumstances of this case coupled with the conduct of the victim girl, do not warrant the minimum mandatory punishment'. This was yet another case of custodial rape of a young girl who had been abducted. A complaint could be filed only when she reached her village and hence there was delay. Despite this, the lower courts had awarded the mandatory minimum punishment of ten years. The 'peculiar facts and circumstances' of the case and the 'conduct' of the girl, which led to the reduction of the sentence were: there were no marks of injury on her body, she was habituated to sexual intercourse and there was delay in filing the FIR. Due to the countrywide agitation against these comments, the Supreme Court subsequently clarified:

Application of conduct has not been referred to the character or reputation of the victim. Character, reputation or status of a raped victim is not a relevant factor for consideration by the court while awarding the sentence to a rapist.[16]

While these comments made good 'case law' (or in other words, legal precedent) which could be relied upon in subsequent cases, it did not lead to the enhancement of sentence in this particular case.

The cases discussed in this section which are randomly selected from law journals highlight the fact that the amendments to rape laws brought about in 1983 did not result in dislodging the patriarchal contentions regarding the rape survivor and the sympathies of the courts continue to be with the accused. The hope that an increase in punishment would act as a deterrent in reducing the incidents of rape in the country also did not materialise. Rape trials continue to revolve around issues such as the character, conduct and credibility of the rape victim.

Gurmit Singh: A Rare Instance of Judicial Sensitivity

Viewed against this backdrop, the Gurmit Singh judgment becomes an important marker of judicial sensitivity.[17] The highly sensitive comments in this landmark judgment are grounded in the realities of women's lives:

In sexual offences delay in the lodging of the FIR can be due to variety of reasons particularly the reluctance of the victim or her family members to go to the police and complain about the incident which concerns the reputation of the girl and the honour of her family. ... Even if there was some delay in lodging an FIR, if it is properly explained and the explanation is natural in the facts and circumstances of the case, such delay would not matter.

Except in some cases where there is acceptable material on record to show that the victim was habituated to sexual intercourse, no such inference like the victim is a girl of "loose moral character" is permissible to be drawn from that circumstance alone.

It is the accused and not the victim of sex crime who is in trial in the court. ... Why should the evidence of a girl or a woman who complains of rape ... be viewed, with doubt, disbelief or suspicion? ... The evidence of a victim of a sexual offence is entitled to great weight, absence of corroboration notwithstanding.

The case concerned the rape of a schoolgirl while she was appearing for her Class X examination. She was kidnapped after her exam, was taken to a lonely spot and was gang raped. Next morning she was left outside the school entrance. The girl did not disclose the incident to her teachers or classmates. She even appeared for her exam, a behaviour which is in direct conflict with the notion that 'rape is worse than death'. For this first generation literate girl, the exam was of paramount importance. Only upon reaching home, did she narrate the incident to her mother. The lower courts had viewed this behaviour as 'highly suspicious' and on the presumption that the girl was of 'loose moral character' acquitted the accused. But the Supreme Court viewed the conduct of the girl as natural and declared that her evidence could not be disbelieved on grounds that she did not disclose the incident to the first person she came across.

Redefining the Crime

During the subsequent decades the need to widen the definition of 'rape' which hinged on the patriarchal premise of peno-vaginal sexual act became evident. The three different concerns which came into the public domain in the subsequent decades were—the need to widen the definition of sexual assault and bring within its purview a wide range of sexual violations, the need to include issues concerning sexual abuse of male children, and the need to recognise and redress violence suffered by people of different sexual orientations.

A major concern was the sexual abuse of male children in state-run orphanages for children and cases of paedophilia and sex tourism by foreign tourists on the beaches of Goa. Sheela Barse, a child rights activist, was among the first to pierce the shroud of silence and question the rigid demarcations of the gender divide within rape laws while following up some path-breaking cases such as the one concerning a doctor, Freddie Petes.[18]

Since these offences could not be made culpable under the conventional construction of peno-vaginal violations, an archaic law formulated to regulate the moral behaviour by penalising unconventional sexual acts under the title 'unnatural offences' had to be invoked to punish the offenders.[19]

Another dimension was the sexual abuse of children within their own homes which shattered the myth that rape occurs only in dark alleys, outside the intimate domains of a loving and nurturing home. Cases of sexual abuse by fathers, uncles, brothers, cousins and grandfathers, through blatant and vulgar usurpation of patriarchal power, started spilling out in the public domain. The concern over the legal lacunae in cases of incest and child abuse was articulated before the Delhi High Court in what is popularly known as the 'Jhaku case'.[20] A high-ranking government official was charged with sexually abusing his six-year-old daughter. The acts included finger penetration and oral sex. Since the police had refused to charge the father with rape, a Writ Petition was filed by the mother before the Delhi High Court. On her behalf it was argued that when a male penetrates a female with any part of his body or shoves any foreign object such as a stick or a bottle into a woman's vagina without her consent, it would amount to rape within the meaning of Section 376, Indian Penal Code (IPC).

The court rejected this argument and held that insertion of a bottle into the vagina would amount only to 'violation of modesty', which stipulates a maximum punishment of two years imprisonment.[21] While the judge expressed his inability to expand the scope of S.376 beyond its prescribed confines, he suggested that there is a need to redefine the crime of rape. This judgment paved the way for advancing the argument of gender neutrality.

This judgment marks a shift in the debate over rape law amendments in India with its plea of complete gender neutrality both for the victim and the violator. There was a presumption here that if women can be framed as violators then the trauma of rape for women as victims would be reduced and the stigma attached to the offence would automatically peel off. Underlying this recommendation is a presumption that, by the stroke of a pen, the offence of rape will be desexualised. By rewriting a sexual crime located within a phalocentric culture, the social norms and values of a predominantly heterosexual society will automatically change.

Even while disagreeing with this comment, one must concede that it had become evident that there was a need to redefine the offence of rape to include the emerging concerns of a vulnerable section of male children, which had remained unarticulated in the first phase of the campaign.

In 1993, the National Commission for Women (NCW) had drafted a bill titled 'Sexual Violence Against Women and Children Bill', which advocated deletion of Sections 354 (violating modesty), 375 (rape), 376 (punishment for rape) and 377 (unnatural offences) of the IPC and brought them under the broad banner of 'sexual assault'. In its 'Statement of Objects and Reasons', the NCW stated that the existing definitions of rape and molestation do not adequately address the range of sexual violations nor do they sufficiently recognise the gender-specific nature of such crimes and that the law had become outdated, in terms of language and intent. The unique character of the offence of sexual assault and its effects upon the lives of women and children and violation of their fundamental principles of human rights was specifically set out.

Despite its best intentions, the Bill did not proceed much further. In 2000, in a case filed by an NGO,[22] after the verdict in the Jhaku case discussed above, the Supreme Court issued interim directions to the government to frame a new law on sexual abuse and, more specifically, to address issues of child sexual abuse. In response, the Law Commission of India in its 172nd report, while suggesting sweeping reforms in the rape laws, also recommended that the rape law should be gender neutral.

The recent ruling of the Delhi High Court in the case filed by a Delhi-based NGO, the Naz Foundation, has served to further problematise the issue of sexual assault upon vulnerable groups and the manner in which power structures within society are invoked to unleash violence upon them. The judgment served to decriminalise consensual sexual intercourse between same sex people in private, an offence defined under Section 377 of the IPC.[23]

After this ruling, there was a need to bring in non-consensual sex between same sex people within the purview of the law of rape and sexual assault. More importantly, the violence and abuse suffered by people of different sexual orientation—gays, lesbians and the hijra community, etc.—needed to be addressed. In response to this, the government once again announced that it would enact a gender neutral law of sexual assault. This announcement alarmed several women's rights groups. But it also highlighted the need for a wider definition of sexual assault. Several special interest groups—women's groups, child rights groups and gay, lesbian, bi-sexual and transgender (LGBT) groups worked together to campaign for a nuanced law which would take into account the concerns of all these different segments. After many rounds of deliberations, a draft for a new law on sexual assault was submitted to the home ministry and to the law minister in July 2010.

> **Box 2   Salient Features of the Proposed Criminal Law Amendment Bill, 2010**
>
> The Bill seeks to place all provisions relating to sexual violence—Sections 375, 376, 377, 354 and 509 of the IPC—within a single chapter, in an attempt to provide a comprehensive framework for protecting women, children and all other persons who on account of their sexual, gender or other identities suffer from sexual violence and abuse.
>
> The proposed definition of sexual assault moves away from the penetrative reproductive logic to a more nuanced understanding of sexual assault redefined as sexual violence; that which takes into account a range of violations perpetrated against persons, with or without the use of criminal force. These include acts ranging from sexual harassment to the gravest forms of sexual assault.
>
> The Bill includes within its scope sexual assault on men in custodial situations and otherwise, on transgender persons and on children. There is by now a realisation that while sexual assault against women continues to be a major concern, children, men and transgender persons also face sexual abuse—children by family members and strangers; men in custody by police; and gays and transgender persons due to their different sexual orientation by both police and members of civil society.
>
> In view of the fact that prosecution depends heavily on the question of consent, the Bill introduces a comprehensive definition of consent to guide the prosecution and the judiciary.
>
> The Bill provides for effective and speedy procedures. Protective measures such as safe havens, counselling, rehabilitation and support services, witness protection, compensation to victims of sexual crimes have been included.

Violence Against Women as Markers of their Caste and Community

The gendering of citizenship renders women unequal citizens, not just in opposition to men within the binaries of the public and private domains, but also within the hierarchical order of class, caste, and community. In order to understand this dynamic we need to examine the violence that is unleashed upon women in the public space and the manner in which the state and judiciary respond to it. Here the woman's identity, her caste, class and community positions seem to play an important role. The intersection of multiple marginalities renders women from these sections even more vulnerable to rape and sexual assault. This section examines the different ways in which women from minority communities are targeted during mass violence. It also exposes the manner in which women from marginalised sections are viewed within the official and judicial discourse.

The significance of the anti-rape campaign of the eighties lies not just in focusing upon sexual violence but also in addressing theories of dominance and subordination and the construction of gender within wider social parameters. Women carry the honour of their communities on their bodies and raping them is one of the surest ways of defiling the entire community. Rape, as a weapon of terror and subjugation in situations of caste, class and communal conflicts, custodial and state sponsored rape by police, armed forces and the para-military have all been concerns, both in theoretical debates and ground level interventions. Rape has been one of the means through which the social hierarchy of power relationships is maintained and nurtured in a gendered society.

The comments by judges while deciding cases of rape concerning women from lower castes and marginalised communities reveal how the class and caste hierarchies get conflated within the discourse on rape.

In 1988, a group of policemen entered Pararia village in Deogarh district of Bihar, ransacked homes, beat the villagers and committed mass rapes upon the village women. There was a public uproar against this incident. As a response, the then Chief Minister Bhagwat Singh Azad ordered Rs 1000 as compensation for the victims to rebuild the huts which were demolished by policemen on the rampage. In 1989 while acquitting the eight policemen and six chowkidars who were accused of rape, the District and Sessions Judge O.P. Sinha commented: "It cannot be ruled out that these ladies might speak falsehood for a sum of Rs 1000 which was a huge sum for them ... these women cannot be equated with such ladies who hail from decent and respectable society; they were engaged in menial work and were of questionable character ...I do not rule out misbehaviour, molestation and assault. But I am convinced that there was no rape. Rape can take place only in exceptional circumstances and not when a group of assorted men in the age group of 25 to 68 are together. Will a sub-inspector ever open his pants in the presence of a constable?'[24]

In another incident reported in a law journal in 1992, which concerned the rape of a tribal girl, the High Court reduced the sentence on the ground that sexual morals of the tribe to which the girl belonged are to be taken into consideration to assess the seriousness of the crime. In this case, two persons had entered her house in her father's absence, dragged her by her hair, forcibly taken her to a nearby jungle and raped her. The sessions court awarded four years for the offence of rape (while the minimum punishment is seven years) and another four years for kidnapping. In appeal the High court held that the girl was not a minor and hence the charge of kidnapping and abduction cannot be sustained. The conviction for rape was upheld but the sentence was reduced to the period of imprisonment already undergone by the accused i.e. two months and 24 days on the ground that as per the norms of the tribe the rape did not cause her much stigma.[25]

While deciding rape cases of women belonging to upper castes, a statement often made is that "no woman of honour will accuse another of rape and thereby sacrifice what is dearest to her", implying thereby, that women who do not belong to this caste/class are capable of making false accusations of rape since they do not possess 'honour'.

The comments in the Bhanwari Devi rape case bring out the judicial bias even more starkly: "It is beyond doubt that teenagers of the same age can commit gang-rape. But it is beyond comprehension that those who live in a rural culture would, in this manner, commit a rape, particularly in collusion with someone who is 40 years of age and another, a Brahmin, who is 70 years of age, during broad daylight, in the presence of other men. Indian culture has not fallen to such low depths that someone who is brought up in it, an innocent rustic man, will turn into a man of evil conduct who disregards caste and age differences and becomes animal enough to assault a woman (read *'of a lower caste'*)." These comments were made by the Sessions Judge, Jaipur, Jagpal Singh in his judgement delivered on 15th November, 1995, while acquitting the five upper caste men who were accused of gang-raping the lower caste woman. The rape had occurred three years earlier and had received wide media publicity. The acquittal was based on a presumption that an upper caste man will not rape a lower caste (untouchable) woman since it is not permissible as per the caste dictates to touch a lower class woman.

Bhanwari Devi was raped while working on a government programme and while campaigning against child marriage among the upper caste influential Thakores. Through this she had crossed her caste boundaries and had to be taught a lesson. One hears of several such examples of maintaining the social hierarchy of gendered citizenship. While the Constitution empowered women through reservations to local panchayats by enacting the 73rd and 74th amendments to the Constitution, through which lower caste women could participate and win elections, newspapers continued to carry reports of Dalit women sarpanches (panchayat heads) being paraded naked and humiliated for holding these positions.[26] The rape of Dalit women continues to be a common occurrence with around 1172 Dalit women having been raped during the year 2005, as reflected in the statistics compiled by the National Crime Record Bureau.[27] The landmark cases of rape around which the women's movement built its anti-rape campaigns, Mathura, Rameeza Bee and Bhanwari Devi, were poor, tribal, Muslim or Dalit women (Agnes 1995; Kannabiran 2008). Rape, murder, and maiming of Dalit women by upper caste men, as a retaliation for aspirations of the community for economic and social progress, still continues in villages and towns of independent India. While most of these violations go unchecked, the gruesome killing of a Dalit woman along with her seventeen-year old daughter and two sons, in Khairlanji village in Buldhana district of Maharashtra in September 2006, made national headlines when six people were convicted and given the death penalty and two with a sentence of life imprisonment.[28] But they were acquitted of charges under the Prevention of Atrocities (POA) Act. Dalit and human rights activists felt that this glossed over the atrocities committed upon citizens solely due to their caste positions.[29] This ruling served to highlight the lacuna within the (POA) Act. As most crimes of this nature are committed by a large mob or several persons it becomes almost impossible to pin the responsibility on specific individuals. This results in acquittals or inadequate punishment. In an appeal filed against the verdict of the sessions court, on 14th July, 2010 Justices A.M. Lavande and R.C. Chavan reduced the death penalty to life imprisonment.[30] The central argument here is not for or against the death penalty but to question the manner in which gendered violence against women from lower castes is made culpable within the criminal legal system.

This lacuna was further highlighted in the Gujarat carnage of 2002 wherein women were threatened with a life and death situation, while being chased by bloodthirsty and sexually debased mobs. The women's bodies became a site of almost inexhaustible violence, with infinitely plural and innovative forms of torture. Women's sexual and reproductive organs were attacked with a special savagery. Their children born and unborn, also became the targets of violence and were killed before their eyes.[31]

There are myriad ways in which the seemingly innocuous laws of rape, murder, and fundamental rights such as the right to life tend to get subverted within the complex terrain of social hierarchies. The violators and the prosecutors merge together and form one consolidated identity mocking the Constitutional provisions of separation of powers. Due to civil society interventions and the initiative of the National Human Rights Commission, the Bilkis Bano case was shifted out of Gujarat through a direction of the Supreme Court and was prosecuted in Maharashtra. It was necessary to override the mandate of a criminal trial as laid out in the Code of Criminal Procedure in defence of a fair and just trial. Only through this was it possible to secure a conviction. Bilkis Bano was raped when she was three months pregnant. Her mother and sisters were also raped before they were burnt to death. A sessions court in Gujarat had acquitted the accused. But in a subsequent retrial held in Mumbai 11 rioters were given life imprisonment.[32]

The Gujarat carnage of 2002 serves to highlight the fact that when the constitutional machinery breaks down, when the political and executive powers work along with the majority community (civil society) and when even the judiciary fails in its duty of protecting the most basic of all civil and fundamental rights—the right to life and liberty—minorities are left with no avenues of safety and protection. At the time of Partition, the violence that took place was within the situation of political chaos when the national boundaries had not yet been drawn and in the context of heightened communal strife. It was also a time when the Constitution of India with its clear mandate of protecting fundamental rights had not come into existence. The Gujarat violence which took place fifty years after the enactment of the Constitution serves to ring a warning bell and brings to the fore the need for additional measures to protect the rights of minority communities and more particularly women citizen's right to life, liberty and dignity. It is in this context that there is a demand from secular and human rights organisations for a special law to deal with Communal Violence (which is discussed later in this section).

Another recent instance of women being victims of violence as a result of communal aggression was during the communal violence unleashed upon Christian tribals in 2008 in Kandhamal, Orissa. Houses were burnt, churches were destroyed, priests and nuns were publicly molested and humiliated.[33] Under further threats of violence thousands fled from their village hamlets and have been living in deplorable conditions in transit camps with very little help from the government for rescue, rehabilitation and reparation. While most of these trials are still in progress, the reports of witnesses constantly turning hostile are disturbing.[34] This, once again raises the very important issue of culpability during mob violence. After the violence and displacement, there have been several instances of young girls missing from their temporary rehabilitation centres and subsequently some of these girls were found in trafficking rackets and had been located in brothels in Andhra Pradesh and Delhi.[35]

Sex crimes committed by armed forces are another major concern for women in conflict zones such as Kashmir and the North East. The nation woke up to the atrocities committed by the army in the north east by the protest of women in Imphal, Manipur against the rape and murder of 32 year old Thangjam Manorama Devi, allegedly a member of Manipur's banned People's Liberation Army (PLA) by the Armed Forces, the Assam Rifles. Manorama's bullet-ridden body was found near her home in Imphal marked with signs of torture and rape. Five days later, as a mark of extraordinary outrage, and in order to get the attention of the country to the plight of Manipuri women, on July 15, 2004, around 30 women, between the ages of 45 and 73, walked naked through the streets of Imphal to the Assam Rifles bastion at Kangla. '*Indian Army, rape us too,*' they screamed, '*we are all Manorama's mothers*'. They were ordinary women. None had met Manorama, but her torture and the Government's silence horrified them. How can a civilised nation keep quiet about something like this, they queried. The women narrated that to hide her rape, the Assam Rifles had stuffed cloth in her vagina and shot bullets through her body. When they were done, her body looked like a blood stained battlefield.[36] It is interesting to note here, that the sexualised female body which is constantly violated and humiliated gets transformed into a weapon of retaliation and causing humiliation for the masculine state power.

Equally poignant are the stories from Kashmir where women have been caught in the crossfire between the Indian armed forces and the local militant insurgencies. Since the insurgency began in the late eighties, a large number of women have been subjected to sexual violence. Their number surpasses that of women in other conflict areas such as Sierra Leone, Chechnya and Srilanka. The disputed stakes of national boundaries rupture their daily lives but over the years, living at the edge, they have learnt to live their lives, despite the ruptures and horrors that await them at every bend of the road.

It has now become evident that provisions of IPC and criminal laws are inadequate in addressing issues of mass crimes as the criminal law focuses on crimes against individuals and not crimes against a group or a collective. Hence if mass crimes are treated as common crimes, it negates the possibility of justice to the victim-survivors. Applying definitions that were intended for crimes against individuals in the context of mass crimes results in injustice as the context in which the crime was committed, the state complicity and communal hostilities that get built up prior to the outbreak of violence are not taken into account at the time of the trial. Therefore, sexual violence against women in certain specific situations of conflict where they are targeted by reason of their identity including community, ethnicity, caste, religion and language, merits special recognition

Inclusion of Sexual Violence within the Proposed Communal Violence Bill

In an effort to bring in a law to deal with communal violence, in 2005 a bill was drafted titled, Communal Violence (Prevention, Control and Rehabilitation of Victims) Bill, 2005. But due to severe opposition from minority groups and secular organisations who feared that it could be used against vulnerable groups and would also enhance executive powers in districts and states it was referred to a Joint Select Committee of Parliament. Subsequently, it was redrafted as the Communal Violence (Prevention, Control and Rehabilitation of Victims) Bill, 2009. But even this redrafted Bill did not suggest any radical departure from the earlier one. The basic objection pertained to an unbridled authority granted to the police and administrative officers under the Bill which would lead to curtailment of civic rights and therefore result in untold misery to the vulnerable sections, more specifically the Muslim community which has always suffered the most during any riot.[37] A memorandum was submitted to the Government of India on 17 November 2009 by various secular organisations who demanded that the Bill should be revised along the lines of the constructive suggestions made by various civil society and anti-communalism groups in the country.[38] The salient points of this memorandum are stated here:

- It must create new crimes/offences, definitions and new rules of procedure and evidence.
- There should be a provision for Command Responsibility, to pin responsibility on political and military powers who fail to curb communal violence.
- There should be accountability of public officials who at present enjoy immunity from prosecution.

- It should specifically provide for gender-based crimes.
- It should provide for setting up of an independent National Authority to ensure effective compliance with the law.
- Reparations and Witness Protection clauses must be clearly set out and these must include rescue, relief, compensation, restitution, rehabilitation and reconstruction of places of worship destroyed during the violence.

The most important recommendation relates to gender-based violence. Special recommendations were made for redefining the crime of rape and to bring it within the purview of sexual assault in the context of the sexual crimes that have been committed during communal, caste and ethnic violence in recent years. The increasing centrality of sexual violence to mass crimes warrants an urgent legal response. The prevailing provisions of the IPC regarding rape are extremely inadequate and do not incorporate within its scope the range of sexual violations perpetrated in contexts of mass crimes, or the gravity of such crimes. Therefore in conformity with international standards, a range of sexual offences have been sought to be included within the purview of the Bill to give recognition to ground level experiences of victim-survivors. These include rape, mutilation, indecent sexual exposure, sexual slavery, forced nudity, forced pregnancy and enforced sterilisation. The following special evidentiary rules have also been recommended:

- All investigations should be conducted in a gender-sensitive manner.
- Delays in reporting should be condoned in view of the extraordinary circumstances and no adverse inference should be drawn for this delay.
- Medical evidence should not be insisted upon as corroborative evidence.
- Uncorroborated victim's testimony can form the basis for conviction provided it inspires the confidence of the court.
- Delay in lodging an FIR should not impact the case in any manner.
- Consent to the sexual act as a defence to the perpetrator should be specifically excluded.

- Admission of evidence of prior or subsequent sexual conduct of a victim of sexual violence should be explicitly prohibited.
- Sexual violence in a communal situation should be equated to custodial rape as mobs exercise complete control and are in a position of authority.
- Hence, the Bill should, as in cases of custodial rape, provide for enhanced punishment and also shift the burden of proof from the victim to the perpetrator.
- Victim/witness protection measures should be introduced for survivors of sexual violence.
- Special efforts should be made to conduct the trial in a gender sensitive environment to ensure that the consequent trauma is diminished

More recently, in August 2010, the work of redrafting the Bill along the lines of the recommendations has been assigned to a special committee constituted under the National Advisory Council.[39]

Workplace-related Violence against Women

Landmark Rulings Protecting the Rights of Women at the Workplace

The Indian Constitution guarantees equality, freedom and liberty to its citizens including women citizens. The relevant provisions of the Constitution are reproduced below for easy reference.

Box 3   Constitutional Provisions to Safeguard Women's Rights to Equality

Article 14:	Equality before law and equal protection of laws.
Article 15(1):	Non discrimination on grounds of sex
Article 15(3):	Special provisions to protect women and children
Article 16(1):	Equal opportunities to women in employment
Article 16(2):	Non discrimination in respect of employment
Article 16(3):	Special provisions to protect women in terms of employment.

Of these, Article 16(1) and (2) which guarantee equal opportunities to women in terms of employment and prohibit discrimination against them are of special relevance for our discussion on women's rights as workers. In addition, Article 16(3) provides for additional safeguards and confers power on Parliament to make special provisions to protect women in terms of employment. This move facilitated the enactment of legislation meant especially to strengthen and protect women, beyond the confines of formal equality.

However, for nearly three decades after the Constitution came into effect, even the provisions of formal equality, such as equal conditions of employment or equal pay for equal work, remained at the level of empty proclamations until the judiciary stepped in to breathe life into them. In several landmark rulings, the Supreme Court and various High Courts were called upon to examine contested claims of women to legal equality.

The transition of Indian women from the private to the public domain and their struggle to redefine traditional gender-based, stereotypical roles of wife and mother and acquire a new identity for themselves, and the resistance to this change from the patriarchal social and economic order, led to several challenges to the constitutional claims of equality. Positive rulings in these cases have served to bring in a culture of women's rights in the public domain.

In the early post-Independence years women's primary identity was defined by their role as homemakers, and their entry into the workforce was considered to be temporary and therefore not to be taken seriously. They were not respected as workers and if their role in the public was at odds with their domestic duties, they had to resign. From cases such as *C.B. Muthamma*[40] and *Nergesh Meerza*,[41] where women workers had to fight for their right to enter into marriage, to cases such as *Neera Mathur*,[42] where women raised concerns regarding privacy, dignity and discrimination, it has been a long and sustained struggle. The *C.B. Muthamma* case concerned the right of married women to enter the Indian Foreign Service. The *Nergesh Meerza* case, also known as the Air Hostess case, struck down the government ruling which prescribed that air hostesses must resign at the time of their first pregnancy on the ground that as they get older, they lose their charm and sex appeal.[43]

In *Neera Mathur v Life Insurance Corporation of India,*[44] the Supreme Court addressed the issue of the right to privacy and dignity of working women. In this case, the services of a probationer were terminated on the ground that she had falsely stated in her application the last date of her menstruation and had conveyed an impression that she was not pregnant at the time of filling the application. The Supreme Court struck down the termination and directed the Corporation to delete the questions included in the application form, which were not only extremely personal but also offensive. The Supreme Court held that such questions are awkward and infringe the right of privacy under Article 21 of the Constitution.

More recently, in *Anuj Garg v Hotel Association of India,*[45] the Supreme Court upheld the Delhi High Court ruling which had struck down Section 30 of the Punjab Excise Act, 1914, which prohibited employment of 'any man under the age of 25 years' or 'any woman' in any part of such premises in which liquor or intoxicating drug is consumed by the public. The court held that the provision is violative of Articles 14, 15 and 19(1)(g).[46] This ruling opened up the scope for women to seek employment in bars serving liquor.

Despite the constitutional assurances, it has been a long and sustained struggle for women to achieve a measure of equality at the workplace. Gains achieved by a few women who staked their claims and sought the intervention of courts in defence of their rights, helped in the advancement of rights of a multitude of women workers in the organised sector. But this segment is comparatively small as compared to women workers in the unorganised sector who continue to work without basic protection under exploitative conditions.

Sexual Harassment at the Workplace: The Vishaka Guidelines

The public campaign around the gang rape of Banwari Devi (also referred to as Bhanwari Devi) who was rapid while working on a government-sponsored development programme raised the issue of workplace safety for women. Despite her repeated complaints she received no support from her superiors. The district administration, including the police, tried to cover up the case by making the woman worker accountable for the incident. Many more cases of sexual harassment at workplaces were being reported from different parts of the country. Leading social activists filed a Writ Petition in the Supreme Court of India demanding protection of women workers which resulted in the landmark ruling *Vishaka* v *State of Rajasthan*.[47]

The ruling amounted to judicial law making. The Division Bench of the Supreme Court, speaking through Chief Justice J.S. Verma, laid down a number of guidelines remedying the legislative vacuum on the subject of sexual harassment of women at their workplace. Taking into consideration the definition of women's rights contained in Section 2(d) of the Protection of Human Rights Act, 1993, the court defined 'sexual harassment' in the following words:

Definition of Sexual Harassment

Any unwelcome, sexually determined behaviour, whether directly or by implication, like physical contact and advances, a demand or request for sexual favours, sexually-coloured remarks, showing pornography, and any other unwelcome physical, verbal, or non-verbal conduct of sexual nature.

The Supreme Court referred to the Committee on the Elimination of Discrimination Against Women (CEDAW) and the violation of gender equality as enshrined in Articles 14 and 15 and the right to life and personal liberty of women under Article 21 of the Constitution. As a result of this judgment, any woman employee who is subjected to sexual harassment of any kind at the workplace can take recourse to initiating criminal proceedings and/or disciplinary action and can also seek compensation from the guilty employer and other persons responsible for the harassment. The court further directed that the guidelines laid down in this case should be followed until the legislature enacts a statute in this regard.

The guidelines are unique as they recognise that sexual harassment at the workplace is a reality which is experienced by a large number of women workers and it cuts across professions, social strata and levels of skill. The focus is on the impact of harassment rather than the intent of the harasser.

In the case of *Apparel Export Promotion Council v A.K. Chopra*,[48] the Supreme Court applied for the first time the law laid down in *Vishaka* and upheld the dismissal of a superior officer of the Apparel Export Promotion Council who was found guilty of sexual harassment of a subordinate female employee on the ground that it violated her fundamental right to life and personal liberty as guaranteed under Article 21 of the Constitution. In this case, the Supreme Court laid down that physical contact is not essential to constitute sexual harassment and lewd remarks and overtures would suffice to constitute the offence.

In another significant case, *Medha Kotwal Lele v Union of India* (WP (Crl.) Nos. 173–177/1999, decided on 26 April 2004), the Supreme Court tried to resolve the conflict between the verdicts of a complaints committee and a departmental enquiry. Until then, the decisions of the complaints committee had to be reaffirmed through a departmental enquiry before they could be brought into effect which led to a dual procedure and caused a great deal of harassment to the victim-survivor and her witnesses. The Medha Kotwal Lele ruling resolved this. The Apex Court held: 'Complaints Committee as envisaged by the Supreme Court in its judgment in the Vishakha case,[49] will be deemed to be an inquiry authority for the purpose of Central Civil Services (Conduct) Rules, 1964'. This ruling dispensed with the necessity of conducting dual enquiries, first by a complaints committee and subsequently through a departmental enquiry, before the punishment could be enforced.

In another case of sexual harassment, a senior IAS officer, Rupan Bajaj, was slapped on the posterior by the then Police Chief of Punjab, K.P.S. Gill, at a dinner party in 1988. Rupan Bajaj filed a suit against him in spite of an attempt by senior IAS officers to suppress the issue. K.P.S. Gill was fined Rs 2.5 lacs by the Supreme Court in lieu of three months rigorous imprisonment under Sections 294 and 509 of the IPC.[50]

Following the Vishaka ruling, a large number of private and public sector undertakings, including academic institutions, have put in place policies for sexual harassment and have constituted grievance cells (complaint committees). To ensure fair and transparent procedures and reduce bias, most complaints committees have at least one external member from a non-governmental organisation (NGO). Subsequent to the Vishaka guidelines, conduct rules and services rules of several public sector undertakings were amended to include sexual harassment as unfair labour practice.

Situation of Women in the Unorganised Sector

However, the most unfortunate part of this campaign is that, so far, the women most affected, the class of women who Banwari Devi represented, the women outside the purview of the organised sector have not benefited from the guidelines. Though the judgment can be considered a milestone in many aspects, only women employed in white collar jobs have been its beneficiaries.

The situation of women in the unorganised sector, where the bulk of the female workforce is located, continues to be exploitative. Here, women are made to labour in extremely difficult conditions, devoid of the constitutional guarantees and protective legislation. They do not even have the minimum protection that the labour law offers, such as maternity benefits, crèche facilities, health care, education of children, and even minimum wages. For many women in the unorganised sector, their workplace itself is a public place. Construction workers, agricultural workers, menial labourers, street vendors and sex workers function in public and open spaces and are subjected to extreme violations of their rights, particularly in the shape of sexual crimes. Their own supervisors, the contractors, the police and the public—all contribute towards creating exploitative and sexually abusive work conditions for these women.

In order to bring these women within the scope of the sexual harassment guidelines, which are now applicable to the public sector, the government has proposed a new Bill on sexual harassment at the workplace. The salient features of the proposed Bill are summarised below.

- **A wider definition of sexual harassment:** The Bill broadens the definition of 'sexual harassment' provided by the Supreme Court in *Vishaka v State of Rajasthan*[51] to include any implied or overt promise or threat of preferential or detrimental treatment in her employment or future employment status, conduct of any person which interferes with her work or creates an intimidating, offensive or hostile work environment and humiliating conduct constituting health and safety problems for her.

- **A wider definition of 'workplace':** It provides for a very wide definition of 'workplace' and brings within its purview the private sector, society, trust, NGO, hospital or nursing home and any place visited either by air, land, rail or sea by the employee arising out of, or during and in the course of, employment.

- **A wider definition of 'employee':** It defines 'employee' as any person employed at a workplace for work on a regular, temporary, ad-hoc or daily wage basis, either by an agent or a contractor, whether for remuneration or voluntary, whether the terms of employment are express or implied and includes a co-worker, a contract worker, probationer, trainee, or apprentice.

- **Protection to women from the unorganised sector:** The Bill brings within its purview women employed in the 'unorganised sector' and defines this sector as an enterprise owned by individuals or self-employed workers and engaged in the production or sale of goods or providing a service wherein the number of workers employed is less than ten.

- **Local Complaints Committees:**
    o   To bring redressal to women in the private sector and the unorganised sector, it provides for the constitution of Local Complaints Committees to be constituted by the District Officer (either a District Magistrate or Additional District Magistrate or the Collector or Deputy Collector as appointed by the Government) when the constitution of the Internal Complaints Committee is not feasible due to the employment of less than ten persons or where the complaint is against the employer himself. This is in addition to the Internal Complaints Committees which are already in existence after the Vishaka Guidelines.
    o   The members of the Local Complaints Committee are to be nominated by the District Officer and comprise a chairperson from

among eminent women in the field of social work and committed to the cause of women, one member from amongst women working in the block, *taluka* or *tehsil* or ward or municipality in the district, two members, of whom at least one shall be a woman, from local NGOs or the protection officer appointed under the PWDVA in the district. At least one-half of the total members must be women.

o The aggrieved woman is given a choice to either approach the Internal Committee or the Local Committee.

- **Settlements:** It provides for a settlement through conciliation before initiating an enquiry.

- **Powers of the Committees:**

  o The Committee has been awarded the same powers that are vested in a civil court under the CPC while investigating a complaint. The employer or the District Officer has been mandated to act on the recommendations made in the Enquiry Report within sixty days of its receipt. Where the allegation has been proved the Committee shall recommend action in accordance with the service rules. If there are no service rules the committee shall deduct from the salary or wages of the Respondent such sum that should be paid to the aggrieved woman as compensation. Where such deduction is not possible due to his being absent from duty or cessation of employment it may direct to the Respondent to pay such compensation to the aggrieved woman.

  o While determining compensation the Committee shall have regard to the mental trauma, pain, suffering, emotional distress caused to the aggrieved woman, the loss of career opportunity, medical expenses, the income and financial status of the respondent and feasibility of such payment in lump sum or in instalments.

  o The Bill provides for penalty for the employers for non-compliance of its provisions. Further, it provides for the prohibition and penalty for making known contents of complaint and enquiry proceedings, name of the victim, respondent, etc.

It is hoped that when enacted, the Bill will provide solace and redressal to a large segment of women workers from the unorganised sector. By laying down clear guidelines, it will also do away with the ambiguity which prevailed after the Vishaka guidelines. It will also provide an alternate forum to those women who file complaints against their bosses (or heads of a unit) where there is a constant fear that witnesses may be intimidated and prevented from giving evidence. While the definition, scope, and procedure laid out under the proposed legislation is elaborate, it is left to be seen how this new mechanism will be able to redress the atrocities suffered by women in the unorganised sector.

Women in the Sex Work Industry

The unorganised sector also includes women who work within the sex industry whose work does not even get recognition as 'work'. These women are not awarded either respect or dignity and violations of their rights are almost the norm. They are considered immoral, are stigmatised and subjected to constant human rights violations. Due to the stigma attached to their work, they are physically and sexually abused, exploited and harassed by the police, pimps and their clients, and are legally and socially marginalised by a society which criminalises prostitution, while at the same time availing of their services. In the discourse on sex work, the male client is conspicuously absent. This reflects an inherent acceptance of male sexual behaviour while stigmatising the women. Social stigma, taboo and prejudice are embedded in social structures, processes, law and the public imagination and serve to reduce and set limits to citizenship rights and social justice for women who sell sex.

An important factor which results in the violation of the rights of sex workers stems from the narrow perspective of sex work which views prostitution as violence. Within this framework, all women involved in sex work are deemed to be victims who have been coerced, bribed, blackmailed or forced into the trade. The view here is that no woman will 'choose' to be in sex work. Earning from sex work is therefore synonymous with sexual exploitation. This perspective views sex work as a dehumanizing business and, therefore, within this discourse there is no space for an assertion of human rights. The only approach to giving sex workers their rights is then to 'free' them from the trade and abolish prostitution altogether. This is termed as an 'abolitionist' perspective. Within this perspective, sex work is symbolised as oppression, victimisation and exploitation of women, and has been thought of as immoral and illegal. The women's movement also traditionally viewed sex work as the paramount symbol of patriarchy which objectifies women's bodies, and commoditises intimate sexual activity. Hence, terms such as 'female sexual slavery' and 'sexual victimhood' have been used to describe sex work. These perceptions about sex work are rooted in a reformist framework of 'protecting' women (Barry 1979). There is also a tendency to conflate issues of 'trafficking' with sex work and all cross-border migration of women with trafficking. Because of this conflation, any move to prevent trafficking by groups favouring abolition is framed within its own abolitionist perspective and does not sufficiently examine issues of trafficking and protection to trafficked women.

When all sex work is viewed as violence, issues of consensual and non-consensual sex get further problematised for sex workers, and rape and sexual abuse of sex workers gets submerged within the broader framework which perceives all sex work as violence. Hence, despite the fact that rape, sexual abuse and molestation have been key concerns of the women's movement, issues of sexual abuse of sex workers are seldom addressed. The conceptualisation of sex work as violence has served to constrain the feminist perspective which holds that sex work cannot be perceived as involving consent. But the reality is that in sex work, women give consent to sexual intercourse as a monetary transaction, but they also experience rape and sexual abuse. Hence, consensual sex and forcible sexual intercourse need to be viewed through separate lenses even for sex workers.

In contrast to the earlier framework which views all sex work as violence, an emerging perspective within feminism views prostitution as sex work and recognises the agency of women in sex work. This perspective does not subscribe to the image of sex workers as either 'victims', 'bad and evil' women or perpetrators of disease. This strategy helps sex workers to articulate the violation of their rights and helps them to claim their rights as workers and citizens. A rights-based approach, which acknowledges that women in sex work have rights and entitlements, would facilitate state and society to engage with this discourse and endow them with these rights.

In the context of Britain, Teela Sanders argues that relying on the rhetoric of a moral order and public nuisance that frames women either as nefarious outcasts who need containing or as innocent victims who need protection and relocation is a dated and unrealistic reflection of the majority of women who sell sex in Britain (2006: 11). In a similar vein, O'Neill argues that violence against women selling sex is endemic. Low levels of reporting and the marginal status of women who sell sex contribute to their vulnerability to sexual violence. Stigma, taboo, prejudice and moral regulation that deem sex workers to be in need of rehabilitation serve to remove agency, disempower women and lead to a process of othering. Thus women are marked as marginal, as liminal, as beyond citizenship and inclusion. If women selling sex were able to do so freely, with the attendant rights enjoyed by other workers and citizens, then violence against them will be drastically reduced and women would not be suffering such endemic levels of violence (O'Neill 2008 : 89).

In India, sex work is not prohibited nor legalised and it hovers in between the realm of the legal and the criminal. This is because while sex work is not prohibited, the law prohibits solicitation in public places. This provision tends to be invoked to harass, intimidate and arrest prostitutes and bring them to book under the provisions of Immoral Trafficking (Prevention) Act (ITPA) of 1956. This Act seeks to prevent trafficking of persons and prohibits most outward manifestations of sex work, including running brothels. While ITPA does not specifically prohibit prostitution, law enforcement officials have continuously used it with criminal intentions to harass sex workers while forming a nexus between themselves and the pimps and brothel keepers. The prohibition against 'public solicitation' is constantly used by the police not only to harass sex workers but also to demand bribes or sexual favours from them. If their demands are not met, the police implicate them in false cases. They have to incur huge expenses to disentangle themselves from this vicious web of the police and the law. When they are arrested, they are charged with hefty fines and are forced to borrow money to pay off these fines. Due to this, the sex workers find themselves constantly in debt and in order to pay off these debts they are forced to engage in more sex work which forms a vicious cycle. A survey reported 70 per cent of sex workers being beaten by the police and more than 80 per cent as arrested without evidence.[52]

The various collectives of sex workers advocate that legalisation will not help the women involved in sex work. On the contrary, it would only result in more state control over sex workers, hamper their mobility and increase their vulnerability to police violence and mandatory testing for HIV and STD. According to them what is needed is decriminalisation of sex work rather than licensing. This position is also endorsed by groups such as Sanlaap in Kolkata who run rescue homes and work within the perspective of rescue and rehabilitation of sex workers (Sleightholme and Sinha 1996).

The issue of decriminalisation seems to be on the government agenda. In 2005, the Department of Women and Child Development (WCD), Ministry of Human Resource Development proposed certain amendments to the IPA with a view to controlling trafficking and the spread of HIV/AIDS and also suggested decriminalisation of sex work. But the WCD failed to consult sex workers and AIDS service organisations and hence several provisions in the proposed Bill were opposed by groups working with sex workers, sex workers collectives and NGOs working with AIDS prevention. A revised Bill came up for Cabinet approval in September 2007 but due to lack of consensus among the Ministries of Health and Home Affairs, the Bill was referred to a Group of Ministers (GOM) for further deliberation. One of the main issues that the GOM was expected to examine was if and how the proposed amendments will affect HIV prevention among sex workers and clients under the National AIDS Control Programme.

The above discussion serves to highlight the fact that the Government of India has officially recognised the importance of involving sex workers in HIV prevention work, but it has not taken responsibility for the structural issues that make sex workers vulnerable to police violence and their lack of remedies under the criminal legal system. Hence, public health efforts, which have increased women's visibility, get undermined by the backlash of police abuse. While one branch of the government—the public health service—relies on the non-governmental sector and collectives of sex workers to spread the knowledge about condom use among high risk groups, another branch—the law enforcement establishment—continues to violate the rights of the very same persons who provide these services.

The violent backlash of sex worker visibility and the mismatch between different sectors of government threaten the work and successes of HIV prevention efforts by forcing people underground, halting work and discouraging people from accessing services. This backlash has been detrimental to the human rights of sex workers, denying them their rights to safety, access to health care and citizenship rights.

There has been some sustained effort to reduce violence and repression at the community level. This includes organising and mobilising sex workers to fight for their civil and human rights. The Sonagachi project in Kolkata which has organised sex workers into collectives and promoted sex worker solidarity as a way of fighting violence and injustice towards their community is one such example. The project aims not only to reduce sexually transmitted diseases and promote condom use, but is also involved in community mobilisation of sex workers as peer educators focusing on their overall health, social and economic well being and human rights. The organisation of sex workers, Durbar Mahila Samanwaya Committee (DMSC) began as a small collective of sex workers who were involved in STD/HIV Intervention Programme. The Veshya Anyay Mukti Parishad or VAMP, a collective of around 5,000 women in sex work, is based in Sangli–Nippani, the border districts of Maharashtra and Karnataka. This is yet another example of sex workers coming together to demand their rights as workers and citizens. The success of the contemporary sex workers' rights movement resists characterisation of women in these collectives as weak, abducted, sold into the industry and working against their will, violated and helpless (Shah 2004).

Concerns about the safety issues and the endemic nature of violence experienced by women selling sex should be at the centre of attempts to develop a transgressive feminist analysis of the relationship between sex work and violence using participatory methodologies. Feminists in this area working together across the binary thinking of 'sex as work' or 'sex as violence' need to develop knowledge that intervenes in policy and practice. This is crucial to the development of more women-centred policies and reform.

Issues Related to Trafficking and Children in Sex Work

Voluntary and consensual sex work by adult women needs to be distinguished clearly from issues of trafficking and the violence inflicted upon children and adults who are forced into sex work. Since the concerns of these two groups are separate, there is a need to formulate two different strategies to remedy the problems.

The increasing demand for, and supply of, children into prostitution is a direct result of the helplessness that is experienced by families from the mainstream and communities of women in sex work, who are lured and exploited by this criminal nexus. Through abduction, kidnapping, coercion or marriage, vulnerable young women and children become victims of traffickers. At times there is also collusion between families who are lured into selling their daughters to traffickers. Children are forced into sex work and become susceptible to physical, sexual and emotional abuse. Women in sex work express their helplessness and anger when their children are subjected to such torture. Women react not to 'making money from sex' per se but to the violence they experience within the institution of sex work, both as children and as adults.

Children of sex workers need special care and protection. Due to their mothers' profession, they are constantly stigmatised and are devoid of the opportunity of a normal childhood. Some efforts are being made to help these children to lead a life free of stigma and enjoy the same educational and other opportunities as any other child would. The Supreme Court has provided several guidelines for the safety of children forced into sex work.[53]

Issues of trafficking and migration also need different frames of analysis just as trafficking and sex work needs to be differentiated. Trafficking in women needs to be understood within a continuum of women's movement and migrations. The need is to critically examine the intersections of migration, trafficking, labour, exploitation, security and terrorism, women's rights, sexuality and human rights. Any analysis of the complexities of the transnational female migrant must extend beyond the confining parameters of the current conceptual and operational work on cross-border movements which views all such movement with the lens of trafficking. To this end, diverse conceptual frameworks that need to be applied to understand and redress the vulnerabilities of the migrant woman in the causes, process and end conditions of her migration in order to evolve alternative approaches to migration and trafficking.[54]

While both male and female migration is driven by economic reasons, female migration is impacted much more by value-driven policies, that is, those policies that contain gender-biased and other assumptions about the proper role of women. There is also a difference in the kind of work available to male and female migrants in destination countries. Males expect to work as labourers, whereas women find work in the entertainment industry or the domestic work sector.

We need to accept that migration does not take place only between the developed First World and the under-developed Third World and that there is greater cross-border migration within regions than from the Global South to the Global North. This is particularly true with respect to the Asian region. For example there is considerable migration from Bangladesh to India with numbers varying from 13 to 20 million.[55]

The cross-border movement of the transnational migrant female subject is inadequately addressed in law and policy. This inadequacy owes in part to two conflations: the tendency to address women's cross-border movements primarily within the framework of trafficking and the conflation of trafficking with prostitution. In order to make migration policies (both international and national) conducive to women's rights, we need to consider the nuances in the relationship between trafficking and migration and de-link trafficking from prostitution.

There is a need to develop a human rights approach to trafficking and, further, develop specific and contextualised strategies and arguments to extricate the genuine concerns related to trafficking of persons from the unstated or moralistic concerns with migration, prostitution or national security.

Violence by the Family and the Community

Violence within the family has been a concern for the Indian women's movement since the early eighties. The issue was articulated primarily within the realm of criminal law and was articulated as cruelty, dowry harassment and dowry death, and addressed the of extreme violence suffered by young brides in their matrimonial home. The campaign resulted in the introduction of some new provisions within the Indian Penal Code (IPC). Because of its private nature it was difficult to prove the offence under the existing parametres of the criminal justice system, certain procedural and evidentiary rules were also changed. The changes, which were effected, can broadly be summed up as follows:

Section	Description of Offence
S.304B	Dowry Murders
S.306	Abetment to Suicide*
S.498A	Cruelty to Wives

*Only the evidentiary rules of this pre-existing section were changed.

Murders, suicides and cruelty suffered by wives (whether dowry related or otherwise) could be made culpable under these provisions in addition to the pre-existing sections listed below which deal with violence in general:

Section	Description of Offence
S.302	Murder
S.304	Culpable Homicide
S.323-6	Simple/Grievous Assault

While these provisions addressed issues under the criminal law, it was felt that there is also a need for a civil law to protect women from violence both in their marital as well as their natal homes. After a decade-long campaign, finally a new Act titled The Protection of Women from Domestic Violence Act, 2005 (PWDVA) was enacted to provide speedy remedies to women who are subjected to domestic violence. The Act recognises a woman's right to reside in a violence-free environment, both in her parental home as well as in her matrimonial home and provides remedial measures in the event that the rights are violated. The three most important features of this enactment are:

- It provides a broad definition to violence which includes physical, emotional, sexual and economic perpetrated upon women and children.

- It provides a statutory right to every woman to shelter under the notion 'shared household'. Though this statute does not provide a woman title or interest in the dwelling house in which she is residing, it grants legal recognition to this right of residence and protects her against dispossession through injunctions and protection orders.

- It secures the rights of women whose marriages are not valid under the law or those women who have never been married but have been living in relationships in the nature of marriage.

Due to a sustained campaign which ranged over three decades, today there is a wide acceptance that Indian women are subjected to extreme violence in their homes. However, several other types of violence which a woman is subjected to with the sanction of the family and the community have not been sufficiently addressed. Some of these are known by certain specific names such as 'honour killing', 'acid throwing', 'sati', 'witch hunting', etc. Collectively these incidences bring to the fore the extreme violence to which women are subjected by their natal families, martial families, the local panchayats and from partners in intimate relationships. The violence which women are subjected to within the domestic sphere is reproduced in different ways like a kaleidoscope of images refracted through broken mirrors.

'Honour' Killings

Since women are deemed to be the depositories of the honour of the family and community, they are subjected to a very strict sexual and moral code and any transgression of this makes them susceptible to extreme violence at the hands of their own natal families.

Young couples who exercise their choice to get married often get trapped within family feuds or caste and community hostilities. The use (and abuse) of police power at the instance of parents with regard to marriages of choice is in direct contrast to women's autonomy, agency and free will. Most often, these marriages are opposed because the boy and girl belong to the same *gotra* or sub-caste and are within the ambit of the village *biradari* where every girl and boy is considered to be related by blood like a brother and sister and marriage within the biradari violates the incest taboos of the village. But if the girls strays too far away from her religious group or social class, that too can invoke the wrath of the natal family. For instance, if an upper caste girl elopes with a lower caste boy or when a Hindu girl falls in love with a Muslim boy, crossing boundaries of Hindu upper caste dictates of purity and pollution, she and her lover/husband can be killed with impunity as per the community and family code of 'honour'.

In a society ridden with prejudices against lower castes and communal strife, a young couple who dares to cross community dictates is severely punished. At times the price for choosing a partner would be a gruesome murder or public humiliation of the couple or their relatives. The notion of women as sexual property of their families and communities is deeply internalized, leading to violence not merely by the larger community but also the girl's own family (Chowdhry 2004).

This crime forms the other end of a continuum of another gruesome crime, that of wife murder which is popularly referred to as dowry death. In both these crimes it is the natal family that needs to be implicated. Dowry-related violence and murder takes place in arranged marriages with the traditional paraphernalia and fanfare including dowry and exorbitant gifts. But when the girl is harassed for more dowry, she seldom gets support from her natal family to break the marital bond. Every time she returns to her family seeking help, the family drives her back to her husband's home until finally, one day, unable to bear the torture, she commits suicide or is burnt to death by her in-laws.

'Honour' killings are the flip side of this, where the girl makes her own choice and gets married sans dowry and other paraphernalia and gets killed by her natal family only for making a choice about her marriage partner against their wishes. The community is also implicated in this crime because the family seeks the support of the local panchayats and the crime is committed with their sanction and collusion. The local police is also implicated in this as many a time the eloping girl and her lover are brought back to the village with the help of the local police who also endorse the norms of endogamy and exogamy (AALI 2004).

In order to criminalize the choice of marriage by young girls, at times the fathers file complaints of kidnap and rape against the boy or man by falsely projecting even major girls as minors who are devoid of the legal authority to give their consent to marriage or sexual intercourse. Despite being aware of the fact that it is a marriage of choice and voluntary elopement, the police collude with the fathers to protect patriarchal interests and 'community honour'. Only if the girl is able to provide clear and unequivocal proof of her majority is she allowed to accompany her husband and cohabit with him. Otherwise, the father's word regarding her age is accepted and she is sent back to his custody, and criminal charges are pressed against the boy (Chakravarti 2005).

In rare cases where the girls vehemently refuse to return to the custody of their fathers, they are sent to state protection homes until they are majors. Even thereafter the girls are often not automatically released and the husband would have to initiate legal proceedings in order to have them released. Judges have commented that many of the habeas corpus petitions filed by either the young husbands or fathers of the girls for production of the girl in court are in fact cases concerning elopement marriages. This is a serious concern for the courts as the following recent judgments indicate.

In *Ajit Ranjan v State*,[56] the Delhi High Court advised the state administration to view these types of cases more as a social problem than a criminal offence. In this case, the husband had filed a Writ Petition under habeas corpus seeking custody of his wife who had been confined by her parents and was not permitted to return to him. The court commented that the changing social scenario in the country was leading to a situation where there were more inter-caste and inter-religion marriages, which meet with societal and familial resistance. The court noted that what was required was not action under criminal law, but counselling of the parties in order to arrive at an amicable understanding. In *Ashok Kumar v State of Punjab*,[57] the Punjab and Haryana High Court commented that couples performing love marriage are chased by police and relatives, often accompanied by musclemen. Often, cases of rape and abduction are registered against the boy. At times the couple faces the threat of being killed and such killings are termed as 'honour killings'. Often the state is only a mute spectator. The court directed the state to speedily evolve a compassionate mechanism to redress grievances of young couples and their parents.

While determining whether the choices made by young girls are valid, courts have to counter allegations not just of minority but also of unsoundness of mind. To augment their claim, natal families base their arguments on phrases such as 'hormonal imbalances' and 'flush of youth', all of which are presumably indicators of her immaturity and inability to make a prudent choice regarding her life partner.

The violent manner in which families and the caste panchayats (also known as *khap* panchayats), exercise their power over a young girl and her lover/husband has been very well documented by the media in the recent past. There have been instances where the girl and her lover have been humiliated, ostracized or even killed for defying the community norms. It is widely perceived that these caste panchayats are taking the law into their own hands, demanding that couples who disobey their diktat must be severely dealt with.

In a first of its kind, a Sessions Court in Karnal, Haryana, awarded the death sentence to five persons and one person was awarded life imprisonment in a case of 'honour killing'. Manoj and Babli, who hailed from Karora village, were murdered by the orders of the *khap* panchayat because they both belonged to the same *gotra* and yet got married. The boy's family had moved the court after the killings and those convicted included the girl's brother, uncles, cousin and leader of the panchayat.[58]

Isolated and insecure after the judgment of the Sessions Court, some twenty *khap* panchayats from Haryana and other states held a *mahapanchayat* to protest against the court's decision and pledging their support to fight the case of those who were convicted. They further articulated their demand of an amendment in the Hindu Marriage Act to completely ban marriages from the same *gotra* and village.[59]

At the other end, due to public pressure from secular and women's rights groups, the government has set up a Group of Ministers (GoM) to consider amendments to the IPC 1860, to extend the definition of murder to include 'honour' killings. Appropriate amendments will also be introduced into the Indian Evidence Act, 1972. The government is eager to bring about these amendments keeping in mind the sudden rise in such 'honour killings' in the recent past.[60]

Though the question about whether there should be a separate law to deal with 'honour' killings or amendments should be introduced into the IPC and CrPC has yet to be addressed by the GoM, the government has to deal with other difficulties. These include the fact that 'honour' killings are not classified as a separate crime and therefore no separate data is collected by the NCRB. Further, FIRs are lodged only in rare instances as the entire episode is a closely guarded secret.[61]

There is a call to 'ban *khap* panchayats' from rights-based urban groups. But the question that needs to be answered is what power these panchayats wield in the villages and why their verdicts are obeyed. Here we must also examine the role *khap* other local panchayats play in village life. All issues concerning village welfare, including resolving family disputes, are decided by the panchayats because the formal justice delivery system is far too alien, distant and expensive for the village community to access in order to resolve issues concerning the village. The time taken to resolve disputes, the uncertainty of the verdicts and the costs involved in terms of legal fees drive most people in villages to the local panchayats which deliver quick justice according to the norms of the community. These panchayats will cease to have power only when the formal system becomes more easily accessible to poor people living in remote villages. It is the duty of the government to make justice more accessible to the marginalised communities in rural areas and also take the responsibility of eliminating delays through a system of mediation which is cheap and is not clogged by delays.

In spite of the media glare and public outrage at these horrific deaths, the point that seems to have escaped public scrutiny is the responsibility of the natal family. In most cases, the girl's family has colluded with the panchayat in order to salvage the 'family honour'. The family generally succumbs to societal norms and beliefs. In other cases, it has not been the panchayat but the family alone that has decided to take the law into their own hands. A case in point is that of a powerful industrialist in Kolkata who was presumed to have caused the murder of his Muslim son-in-law in 2007 because he was opposed to his Hindu daughter marrying a Muslim in what is known as Rizwanur-Priyanka case in Kolkata in 2007.[62] The police played an active role in separating the couple who were married legally and also in projecting the murder as suicide. This case highlights that such incidents are not restricted to rural areas but are also widely prevalent in urban India.

While extreme incidents of murder might be rare among urban households, the pressure on the young girls to toe the family line in respect of their choices in marriage takes place all the time. Confining the girl to the home against her wishes, filing police complaints against the boy, and the police taking extra legal actions against him are some of the common tactics adopted by many urban families to put pressure on the girl to terminate an unconventional relationship and agree to a marriage of the parent's choice. The pressure is all the more when the boy is from a lower caste or belongs to a minority religion. These issues need to be brought within the purview of the type of violence experienced by girls in respect of their marriages of choice.

The violence which is carried out under the nomenclature of 'honour killing' is carried out primarily by members of the natal family who believe that they have the sole right to control the sexuality of unmarried girls in their natal household. This type of sexual control over the girl and her sexuality is exercised by the natal family both in urban and rural areas although the form it takes may differ. Hence even if the government enacts a new law to keep a check on the khap panchayats, the situation is unlikely to change. This is because it is essentially a social problem, where the natal family also needs to be squarely implicated. What needs to be addressed is this familial control and lack of options for young girls both at the time of marriage and also at the time of divorce in the event of domestic violence within the martial home. Any special legislation to deal with the issue must also be based on a realistic understanding of the rural situation where the community plays an important role in resolving local issues.

Acid Throwing

While 'honour' killing is violence unleashed upon a woman by her natal family and the local panchayat, the crime of 'acid throwing' is committed by deserted husbands and jilted lovers. 'Acid throwing', which is prominent in cities and smaller towns, is a more recent form of violence. Acid is thrown on the face and body of a woman, seriously burning and disfiguring her while leaving a permanent scar of this ghastly act. The perpetrators of this crime include rejected lovers, would-be suitors and discarded husbands. Victims of such attacks not only have to deal with the physical, mental and emotional trauma, but also the stigma and fear attached to such crimes. The medical and rehabilitation costs are not only exorbitant but also continuous. Further, their loss of income and livelihood after an attack of this nature is completely ignored.

A perverse logic seems to be the underlying motive for this ghastly crime that a woman's face is her fortune and the crime of acid throwing will cause permanent damage to a woman's looks and mar her chances of leading a normal life in the future. Since acid throwing rarely results in death, the victim has to endure lifelong suffering. Another motive seems to be the easy access to harmful acids like hydrochloric acid and sulphuric acid which have the capacity of corroding the muscle tissue and burning the victim right up to the bone marrow and causing loss of sight and permanent disfigurement. The act of throwing the acid does not need much preparation and can be carried out in the home, on the street, at a bus stop or in any public place. For these reasons, it appears to be gaining popularity in South Asia with cases being reported from Bangladesh, Pakistan and India.[63]

In response to the growing incidents of acid throwing, in 2002, Bangladesh enacted a special law awarding death penalty to offenders and also passed strict laws to curb the sale of acid. Under the Islamic law of Pakistan, the perpetrator must endure the same fate as the victim. Despite growing incidents, the Indian government has turned down repeated pleas and recommendations by the Law Commission and the NCW to include acid attacks as a separate crime under the IPC or to enact a separate law to deal with this issue.[64] The Supreme Court, in a public interest litigation filed by a victim, has also directed the government to study the legislation enacted in Bangladesh and enact a similar law in India.[65]

Stories of acid attacks are reported far less in the media as compared to stories of honour killings, dowry deaths, etc. However, a few cases have managed to find their way into national dailies and news channels. In 1999, Haseena Hussain from Bangalore was a victim of a gruesome acid attack by her former boss who doused her entire body with two litres of hydrochloric acid when she turned down his job offer. She had burns all over her body and lost her nose and eyesight. The accused was sentenced to life imprisonment. Further, he had to pay Haseena a compensation of Rs 2,00,000 in addition to a fine of Rs 3,00,000. This judgment of the Karnataka High Court[66] is considered to be a landmark case because for the first time substantial compensation was awarded to a victim of such a crime. In addition, the accused had to incur the medical expenses including the cost of plastic surgery. Further, the learned judges urged the state government to start a health and rehabilitation programme for victims of such crimes.

In the case of *Awadhesh Roy v State of Jharkhand*[67] the victim was standing at a bus stop when the accused poured acid all over her. He had a photograph and was blackmailing her but she refused to give into his demands. She sustained grievous burn injuries all over her body. The Sessions Court judge sentenced the accused to three years rigorous imprisonment. The sentence was upheld by the High Court but no compensation was awarded to the victim.

Acid throwing is only one of the many forms of violence which women who refuse the overtures of their husbands and lovers go through. Another often used tactics is to slash the girl/woman's face with a knife or blade and disfigure her completely. There are several such cases of young and older married women who have been subjected to this type of disfigurement. Even when conviction does take place it is so meagre that three months later the convicted person is out after serving the sentence and continues to blackmail the woman concerned while the woman has to deal with the disfigurement for her entire life.

A catena of judgments on the issue highlight that even if the accused is convicted, the punishment awarded is not sufficient in the absence of specific law on the subject. Moreover, in most cases, compensation for physical and psychological treatment, loss of income, medical expenses is not awarded to the victim. A specific law on this issue needs to incorporate within it the provision of compensation for the victim in addition to stringent punishment. The government also needs to set up a fund for relief and rehabilitation of victims who need long-term medical and psychological treatment and trauma counselling to cope with the situation.

The Crime of Sati and its Prevention

Another crime that is well known and much publicised is the burning of a widow on her husband's funeral pyre. This is an older concern which has been in the public domain for over two centuries. While the incidents of sati have been reduced there are occasional incidents which come into the public domain. As against acid throwing, which is considered a 'modern' form of violence, sati is an older form violence and claims its roots in religion and Hindu culture and the commercial motive of inducing a woman to commit sati gets entangled within rituals and a hallowed place for the woman who has committed sati and raises her to the level of a local deity.

There were widespread protests following the public murder of an eighteen-year-old girl, Roop Kanwar in Deorala, Rajasthan, in September 1987. As an outcome, one of the demands was for a legislation to deal with the issue of sati. The government was prompt in its response. Even before the embers of Roop Kanwar's funeral pyre had cooled down, the law came into effect. The state law, the Rajasthan Sati (Prevention) Ordinance, was passed in October 1987 in response to the protests by women's organisations both in Jaipur and in Delhi. But the demand for a central legislation continued. Hence the state legislation was soon followed by a central legislation in January 1988. The Commission of Sati (Prevention) Act, 1988 was passed through both Houses of Parliament with a minimum of debate or amendment. When the IPC was enacted in 1860, a special provision to prevent the commission of sati was not incorporated as it was considered that the sections on murder, suicide and abetment to suicide could adequately deal with the problem.

At the beginning of the19th century, the campaign against sati became a major concern for social reforms and there was a sustained demand for its regulation. As a response to this campaign, the first legislation against sati was enacted in 1827, in Bengal, and was followed by similar legislations in Madras and Bombay. The Act was challenged in the Privy Council by pro-sati religious factions on the ground of freedom of religion. This was countered by the argument that freedom of religion could not go beyond what was compatible with the paramount claims of humanity and justice. The argument of a woman's choice, which was the main premise while defending the Roop Kanwar murder, was not put forward then. But in recent cases, the issue of a woman's choice to end her life and become sati has been advanced to defend these public murders.

BOX 4   The Commission of Sati (Prevention) Act, 1988

The Preamble of the Act states:

An Act to provide for the more effective prevention of the commission of sati and its glorification and for matters connected therewith or incidental thereto.

Whereas sati or the burning or burying alive of widows or women is revolting to the feelings of human nature and nowhere enjoined by any of the religions of India as an imperative duty;

And whereas it is necessary to take more effective measure to prevent the commission of sati and its glorification.

By passing a law, the government has bestowed a special status to the public murders of widows and a religious and cultural context to the issue. The Act concedes that sati constitutes a special offence, distinct from murder and suicide.

The law is stringent and shifts the burden of proving the offence on the accused. It was believed that such a move would ensure convictions and act as a deterrent. But the ground reality does not support this premise. For instance, after the Deorala incident, most people who were arrested were mere bystanders. Under the Act, the onus of proving their innocence was on them. This violates one of the basic premises of criminal jurisprudence that the accused is innocent till proved guilty. While conceding that it might be necessary in the interest of justice to depart from this principle in crimes of a private nature like rape and wife murder, it was totally unwarranted in the case of sati where the crime is committed in full public view. Another alarming aspect of the Act is that in its zeal to protect women's rights, the Act stipulates punishment to the victim. A woman who attempts sati is to be imprisoned for one to five years and fined Rs 5,000–20,000.

However, the irony of the Act lies in the fact that despite its stringency, there were no convictions of the accused in Roop Kanwar's case, the very case which resulted in a sustained campaign to enact the legislation. So while the incident and the legislation created much hype its effect in punishing the guilty was nil. This indicates the haphazard manner in which the state machinery conducted the investigation and followed up the legal case. In fact the state machinery was implicated as they had also colluded in the act at the village level. Such collusions makes it difficult for an effective implementation of the Act and takes away its deterrent value. Hence the provisions of such legislation remain at a merely ornamental level rather than having any concrete effect in curbing the violence (Kishwar and Vanita 1987).

Witch Hunting

Witch hunting is a phenomenon that is common in rural and tribal areas of the country. It is a severe form of gender-based violence that unequivocally targets women and girls. Single and widowed women are most likely to be victims of this crime. Some of the most common reasons for branding a woman as a witch include property disputes, personal rivalry, land-grabbing and resistance to sexual advances. In a number of cases, widowed women have been forced by their husbands' families to give up the land that they have inherited, and if the women refuse to do so the family approaches the village *ojha* (village doctor) and bribes him to brand her as a witch. This method of intimidation is also commonly used against lower caste women who spurn the sexual advances of men from the upper castes. In certain other cases, strong willed and assertive women have also been targeted because they are perceived as a threat. Witch hunting is common among the Santhal, Ho,

Munda, Oraon and Kharia Adivasis. Women who are branded as witches are mercilessly beaten, publicly paraded naked, forced to drink urine or eat excreta, and in many instances even ruthlessly killed. According to a report, nearly 150–200 women are killed every year as a result of witch hunting.[68]

Various research studies have been conducted which highlight the linkages between witch-hunting practices and land ownership by women. Their findings reiterate the fact that witch hunting has been used as a means of land grabbing and exploitation of women, as most women who are accused of being witches are single women who possess some land. Naming such a woman as a witch is a ruse for taking over possession of her land. Occasionally, some cases of extreme torture and violations of human rights of women hit the news headlines. For instance, in 2005, Pusanidevi Manjhi was accused of being a witch by a powerful landlord in her village in order to usurp her land.[69] She was dragged out of her home, mercilessly beaten and kept in captivity for four days before she was rescued. In October 2009, the story of five Muslim women who were branded as witches in Jharkhand caused outrage across the country.[70] The five women, all widows, were dragged out of their homes, beaten, forced to eat human excreta and paraded naked in the village playground, in the presence of the entire village. Their crime: it was believed that the women practised witchcraft.

In many tribal communities, in accordance with customary laws, succession of tenancy rights over land pass through the male line, with women having only usufructory right over the land during their lifetime. The Supreme Court, in *Madhu Kishwar* v *State of Bihar*,[71] failed to intervene and strike down customary laws such as the Chotanagpur Tenancy Act 1908 as unconstitutional despite its admission that such laws blatantly discriminated against women. While this judgment reiterated and spelt out in unequivocal terms a woman's usufructory right over land during her lifetime, to the exclusion of all male heirs, activists working with tribal communities are convinced that witch hunting is used as one of the means to force women to abandon this right to their land.

Bihar, Jharkhand and Chhattisgarh have enacted state laws to curb the practice of witchcraft. The Chhattisgarh law is more specific and mentions that it is an Act to prevent atrocities related to witchcraft in its title which implies that the focus of the Act is to protect atrocities committed upon women who are branded as witches and not just to prevent witchcraft.

Bihar: Prevention of Witch (Dayan) Practices Act of 1999
Jharkhand: Anti-Witchcraft Act, 2001
Chhattisgarh: Witchcraft Atrocities (Prevention) Act, 2005

By and large, the law has remained ineffective with less than 2 per cent of those accused of witch hunting being actually convicted, according to a report by the Free Legal Aid Committee, a group that works with victims in the state of Jharkhand.

Conclusion

A range of issues concerning violence against women in public places are discussed in this essay within the framework of constitutional assurances to women and the efficacy of statutes enacted to address this violence. It is evident that violence against women is rampant in our society and reflects the patriarchal control to which women are subjected within the domain of their homes. But when the control is exercised in the public domain and is perpetrated by different segments, such as state, employers, family, community and people in intimate relationships, it gets amplified and multiplied and results in gruesome crimes against women in public spaces. As women expand the boundaries of their domestic life, and challenge patriarchal power and authority, the violence unleashed upon them becomes more severe. The logic of maintaining patriarchal power and control provides the justification for the violence.

When women are demanding safety in public places, they are, in fact, claiming their rights of citizenship. The gendered notion of citizenship is a complex arena that is constantly mediated by the family, community and state. Sometimes women bear the brunt of their community identity and are subjected to violence from the 'outside' as markers of their own community. At other times, the community and family itself reproduces the control exercised by them within the private sphere of the domestic arena, and bring it into the public domain as an example for all women to toe the patriarchal dictates and obey the proverbial 'Laxman rekha', the boundaries of morality.

It is this duality of the violence to which women are subjected that makes the arena of public violence a complex one and any attempt to redress this must take into account the complexities of their situation.

In order to grasp the wide ranging manifestation of this control, it is essential to analyse each of the segments of violence in public spaces within their own contours. However, collectively they form a continuum of a range of violence suffered by women as a group. The redressal to this violation would have to be negotiated through women's claim for citizenship and the constitutional assurances of equality, freedom and liberty. Unless the public spaces are rendered safe for women, women will not be able to reap the benefits of other constitutional assurances, such as political participation and workplace participation, to the fullest extent as women's mobility and their choices get hampered by this shadow of public violence hovering over them. Hence the state needs to provide special protection to this segment in order to fulfil its promise of equality and equal protection.

As Mukhopadhyay and Singh (2007) have stated, gender justice implies full citizenship for women which includes protection of human rights, restoration of democracy and reworking of ideas of citizenship to embrace the ideas of active citizenship rather than the notion of citizenship as a purely legal relationship conferring rights on passive subjects. Active citizenship implies participation and agency. An understanding of citizenship as a process that entails overcoming social exclusions which is perceived as being multidimensional and eradicating social, economic and political forms of marginalisations is essential. Within this perspective, safety and security in public places becomes a precondition for changing the passive citizenship of women into an active one with the full potential of participating in all spheres of life, in order to overcome their marginalisation.

While we trace the history of legislative enactments, issues such as rape, though they find a prominent place within the IPC (Sections 375 and 376), are by and large ineffective to deal with the complex situation which has emerged in recent times. Women's groups across the country have come together to draft a new legislation and present it to the government. But despite these efforts the new statute has not (at the time of writing) been introduced in the Parliament.

Where issues of communal violence and state responsibility are concerned, at present there is no law to deal with this issue. Again there have been efforts and committees have been constituted to frame a new law but these efforts are yet to bear fruit in terms of a comprehensive legislation. The Bill, drafted by the government in 2005 and 2009, has been rejected as the secular and human rights groups felt that there is a need to define newer crimes and lay down adequate procedures outside the realm of the IPC and other relevant criminal statutes. It has been suggested that in view of state complicity, and given the delicate balance in centre and state relationships, there is a need to set up a separate national level civilian authority to take charge of the situation when there is a breakdown of constitutional machinery at the district and taluka levels. In situations such as these, sexual violence against women needs a new definition and also special procedures since the provisions under the existing laws have failed to bring justice to women victims of sexual violence.

Where the workplace situation is concerned, one of the primary concerns here is the effective implementation of the Supreme Court guidelines and extending the benefits of these guidelines to women in the unorganised sector who need such protective measures the most. A new Bill on this issue is ready for introduction in Parliament. It extends the benefits of the guidelines to women in the unorganised sector by setting up Local Complaints Committees. Though such a provision will bring some respite to women in the unorganised sector, unless special commissioners are entrusted to investigate offences under this Act, and a state functionary is nominated to assist women during these procedures, it is doubtful whether the benefits of the new legislation will reach women from this sector.

When we address issues within the family and community, we confront specific types of violence which family members, intimate partners as well as the broader community (as part of civil society) inflicts upon women. While each of these has a specific history and trajectory, together they form a complex weave of patriarchal control over women's lives which leaves very little space for women to manage their own lives and make their own sexual choices as citizens with a right to equality and equal protection.

Any new legislation to deal with this range of problems will have to take into account the power natal families and natal communities wield over women in order to protect women's right to citizenship. When we examine the provisions of the sati legislation, it appears that such efforts to render the family and community culpable have so far been ineffective. It also becomes evident that India has lagged behind in enacting legislation even in cases of gruesome violence against women such as acid throwing, while Bangladesh and Pakistan have introduced certain legal provisions to deal with this issue.

It is hoped that the detailed discussion on the legal situation currently prevalent will pave the way for a more comprehensive debate which will help in bringing about necessary enactments which could address the concerns raised in this essay.

Notes

1. It is not my intention here to flatten out the political debate on citizenship which has moved away from the 18th and 19th century European notion which perceives a universal citizenship based on a unitary and linear model, which is devoid of any contingencies of difference. This notion of a 'universal' citizenship has been critiqued by several postmodern and feminist political theorists, who have in turn, advanced an argument in favour of a citizenship which is embedded within respective histories and cultures (Benhabib 1995). My intention here is merely to re-examine the sphere of the public and private notions of citizenship within which women's claims of citizenship have been framed within diverse cultures and the manner in which the struggle to enter the public domain has, in its wake, brought to the surface several locations of violence against women in the public domain.

2. *Tukaram v State of Maharashtra* AIR 1979 SC 185.

3. NCRB has reported a conviction rate of around 26–27 per cent for the years 2006, 2007 and 2008. This is at the Sessions Court level. Most convictions lead to appeals to High Courts and result in acquittals. So, the actual conviction rate is much lower.

4. See 'The New Rape Bill–Legislating Rape 'Out of Existence'!', in *Manushi*, A Journal About Women and Society, Issue No. 7 (1981), pp. 38–45.

5.   The Indian Evidence Act: S. 154 (4) (text of the deleted section): when a man is prosecuted for rape or an attempt to ravish, it may be shown that the prosecutrix was of generally immoral character.

6.   See the recent report by Human Rights Watch (2010) titled *Dignity on Trial*.

7.   2006 (3) JCR 43 (Jhr).

8.   MANU/MP/0265/2007

9.   This is the legal term used for a rape victim-survivor in law journals and legal texts.

10. MANU/DE/3091/2009.

11. The glaring lacunae regarding the issue of rape in medical text books is also visible in another text book, which is popularly referred to as HWV Cox *Medical Jurisprudence and Toxicology*.

12. *Bhansingh v State of Haryana* 1984 Cri.LJ 786.

13. *Vinod Kumar v State of Madhya Pradesh* 1987 Cri.LJ 1541.

14. *Babu v State of Rajasthan* 1984 Cri.LJ 74.

15. *Prem Chand v State of Haryana* 1989 Cri.LJ 1247.

16. *State of Haryana v Premchand* 1990 Cri.LJ 454.

17. *State of Punjab v Gurmit Singh* 1996 CrLJ 1728.

18. *Mr. Werner Wulf Ingo v State of Goa (represented by C.B.I.), through Public Prosecutor for C.B.I.* MANU/MH/0207/2009. Also See a news report in *Tehelka*, 'The Original Sinner in Paradise', 15 October 2010, available at http://www.tehelka.com/story_main5.asp?filename=Ne080714The_original.asp

19. **Indian Penal Code (IPC) Section 377: Unnatural Offences**—Whoever voluntarily has carnal intercourse against the order of nature with any man, woman or animal, shall be punished with imprisonment for life, or with imprisonment of either description for a term which may extend to ten years and shall also be liable to fine.

20. *S.J. v K.C.J.* DLT Vol. LXII (1996) 563.

21. **IPC Section 354:** Assault or criminal force to woman with intent to outrage her modesty: Whoever assaults or uses criminal force to any woman, intending to outrage or knowing it to be likely that he will thereby outrage her modesty, shall be punished with imprisonment of either description for a term which may extend to two years, or with fine, or with both.

22. *Sakshi v Union of India* AIR 2004 SC 3566.

23. *Naz Foundation v Government of NCT* 2010 Cri.LJ 94 Del.

24. Special Feature in *India Today* dated 31 May 1989.

25. *Daryaram v State of Madhya Pradesh* 1992 Cr.LJ 493.

26. See the news report, 'After MP, Jharkhand women paraded naked', *Times of India*, Bhopal, 23 June 2006.

27. Report of NCRB, 2005.

28. 'A Strong Message', Editorial, *Times of India* Mumbai, 26 September 2008.

29. 'Understanding the Khairlanji Verdict', *The Hindu*, Chennai, 5 October 2008.

30. *Central Bureau of Investigation v Sakru Mahagu Binjewar* MANU/ MH/0893/2010.

31. See the Fact Finding report by a Women's Panel headed by Syeda Hameed, Muslim Women's Forum, Delhi (April 2002), *The Survivors Speak*, Ahmedabad: Citizen's Initiative and the report by International Initiative for Justice (December 2003). *Threatened Existence: A Feminist Analaysis of the Genocide in Gujarat*; available at *http://www.onlinevolunteers.org/gujarat/ reports/iijg/2003/*

32. 'Gujarat Rioters Get Life for Rape, Murder', *Reuters Insider*, Mumbai, 21 January 2008, available at http://in.reuters.com/article/idINIndia-31509620080121.

33. See fact finding report by Multiple Action Research Group (2010) Kandhamal titled *The Law Must Change its Course*.

34. http://timesofindia.indiatimes.com/india/8-get-three-year-jail-in-Kandhamal-riots-case/articleshow/6627082.cms

35. 'Five Girls Rescued From Being Trafficked in Berhampur, Orissa', *Hindustan Times*, 20 April 2010, available at http://www.hindustantimes.com/Five-girls-rescued-from-being-trafficked-in-Berhampur-Orissa/Article1-533716.aspx; Santosh Digal, 'Churches to curb women trafficking in Kandhamal', available at http://in.christiantoday.com/articles/churches-to-curb-women-trafficking-in-kandhamal/5521.htm; 'Trafficking From Riot-hit Area Worries Church', available at http://www.ucanews.com/2010/04/27/trafficking-from-violence-hit-area-worries-church/.

36. Mihir Srivastava, 'The Siege Within—Goes On', *Tehelka*, 2 September 2006.

37. 'Recall communal violence bill, demands MPLB', *The Times of India*. Available at: http://timesofindia.indiatimes.com/india/Recall-communal-violence-bill-demands-MPLB/articleshow/5710092.cms#ixzz12W7hBgpP

38. http://communalism.blogspot.com/2010/01/national-consultation-on-communal.html

39. http://www.indianexpress.com/news/to-write-communal-violence-bill-nac-turns-to-activists/674685/

40. *C.B. Muthamma* v *Union of India* AIR 1979 SC 1868.

41. *Air India* v *Nergesh Meerza* AIR 1981 SC 1829.

42. *Neera Mathur* v *Life Insurance Corporation of India* AIR 1992 SC 392.

43. See para 106 at page 1856.

44. *Neera Mathur* v *Life Insurance Corporation of India* AIR 1992 SC 392.

45. AIR 2008 SC 663: (2008) 3 SCC 1.

46. Freedom to practise any profession or to carry on any occupation, trade or business.

47. 1997 6 SCC 241.

48. AIR 1999 SC 625.

49. 1997(6) SCC 241.

50. *Rupan Deol Bajaj* v *Kanwar Pal Singh Gill* AIR 1996 SC 309.

51. 1997 6 SCC 241.

52. Sangram, Point of View and VAMP (2002), 'Turning a Blind Eye: Of Veshyas, Vamps, Whores and Women: Challenging Preconceived Notions of Prostitution and Sex Work'. Also see Sleightholme Carolyn and Indrani Sinha (1996), *Guilty Without Trial: Women in Sex Trade in Calcutta*, Calcutta: Stree

53. *Gaurav Jain* v *Union of India* AIR 1997 SC 3021.

54. See Report of the Centre for Feminist Legal Research (2004) on the International Seminar on Cross Border Movements and Human Rights, New Delhi.

55. Ibid.

56. II (2007) DMC 136.

57. I (2009) DMC 120 P&H.

58. http://timesofindia.indiatimes.com/india/Khap-Panchyat-Death-sentence-for-5-in-Haryana-honour-killing/articleshow/5743038.cms

59. http://www.hindustantimes.com/Khap-leaders-to-oppose-verdict-in-Haryana-honour-killing-case/Article1-530654.aspx

60. http://news.rediff.com/report/2010/jul/08/divided-upa-to-form-gom-on-khap-panchayat-issue.htm

61. http://www.thehindu.com/news/article553498.ece

62. http://www.merinews.com/article/cbi-books-ashok-todi-for-murder-in-rizwanur-case/127116.shtml

63. http://en.wikipedia.org/wiki/Acid_throwing

64. http://timesofindia.indiatimes.com/india/No-change-in-law-needed-to-make-acid-attack-a-heinous-offence-Centre/articleshow/5804710.cms

65. http://www.thaindian.com/newsportal/uncategorized/acid-attacks-on-women-india-to-learn-from-bangladesh_10042926.html

66. *Joseph Rodriguez S/o V.Z. Rodriguez v. State of Karnataka* MANU/ KA/8317/2006
67. MANU/JH/0558/2006.
68. http://www.thehindu.com/news/article533407.ece
69. http://www.washingtonpost.com/wp-dyn/content/article/2005/08/07/ AR2005080700947.html
70. http://news.bbc.co.uk/2/hi/8315980.stm
71. (1996) 5 SCC 125: AIR 1996 SC 1864.

References

Agnes, Flavia (2005). 'To Whom Do Experts Testify? Ideological Challenges of Feminist Jurisprudence', *Economic and Political Weekly*, vol XL, no. 18, 1859.
——— (1995), *State, Gender and the Rhetoric of Law Reform*, Bombay: SNDT Women's University.

Baxi, Upendra, Lotika Sarkar, Raghunath Kelkar and Vasudha Dhaganwar (1979). 'An Open Letter to the Chief Justice of India' 4 SCC (Jour) 17.

Baxi Upendra et al. (2008). 'An Open Letter to the Chief Justice of India', in Mary E. John (ed.), *Women's Studies In India*, New Delhi: Penguin Books India.

Barry, Kathleen (1979). *Female Sexual Slavery*, New Jersey: Prentice-Hall Inc.

Benhabib, Seyla, Judith Butler, Drucila Cornell and Nancy Fraser (1995). *Feminist Contentions: A Philosophical Exchange*, New York: Routledge.

Bhattacharjee, Swati (ed.) (2008). *A Unique Crime : Understanding Rape in India*, Kolkata: Gangchil.

Butalila, Urvashi (2000). *The Other Side of Silence Delhi: Stories from the Partition of India*, New Delhi: Sage Publications.

Chakravarti, Uma (2005). 'From Fathers to Husbands: Of Love, Death and Marriage in North India', in Welchman, Lynn and Sara Hossain (eds), *Honour Crimes, Paradigms, and Violence Against Women*, London : Zed Books , pp. 308–31.

Chowdhry, Prem (2004). 'Private Lives, State Intervention: Cases of Runaway Marriage in Rural North India', *Modern Asian Studies*, vol. 38, no. 55.

Das, Veena (1995). *Critical Events: An Anthropological Perspective on Contemporary India*, New Delhi: Oxford University Press.

Dikshit P.C. (ed.) (2002). *HWV Cox Medical Jurisprudence and Toxicology*, New Delhi: LexisNexis-Buitterworths (Seventh Edition).

Kannabiran, Kalpana (2008). 'Sexual Assault and the Law', in Kalpana Kannabiran and Ranbir Singh (eds), *Challenging the Rule(s) of Law: Colonialism, Criminology and Human Rights in India*, New Delhi: Sage Publications, pp. 78–118.

Kishwar, Madhu and Ruth Vanitha (1987). 'The Burning of Roop Kanwar', in *Manushi—A Journal About Women and Society*, no. 42–43 (September–December), pp. 15–25.

Menon, Ritu, and Kamla Bhasin (1998). *Borders and Boundaries: Women in India's Partition*, New Delhi: Kali for Women.

Mukhopadhyay, Maitrayee and Navsharan Singh (eds.) (2007). *Gender Justice, Citizenship and Development* New Delhi: Zubaan.

O'Neill, Maggie (2008). 'Sex, Violence and Work: Transgressing Binaries and the Vital Role of Services to Sex Workers in Public Policy Reform', in Letherby Gayle, Kate Williams, Philip Birch and Maureen Cain (eds), *Sex As Crime?* Devon (U.K): Willan Publishing.

Roy, Anupama (2005). *Gendered Citizenship: Historical and Conceptual Explorations*, New Delhi: Orient Longman.

Sanders, Teela (2006). 'Behind the Personal Ads: The Indoor Sex Markets in Britain', in R. Campbell and M. O'Neill (eds), *Sex Work Now*, Cullomptom: Willan Publishing.

Shah, Svati P. (2004). 'Prostitution, Sex Work and Violence: Discursive and Political Contexts for Five Texts on Paid Sex, 1987–2001', *Gender & History*, vol.16, no.3, pp. 794–812.

Sleightholme Carolyn and Indrani Sinha (1996). *Guilty Without Trial: Women in Sex Trade in Calcutta*, Calcutta: Stree.

Subrahmanyam, B.V. (2002). *Modi's Medical Jurisprudence & Toxicology* (22nd Edition), New Delhi: LexisNexis-Butterworths.

Fact Finding and Newspaper/Journal Reports

Association for Advocacy and Legal Rights (AALI), 'Choosing a Life…Crimes of Honor in India the Right to, If, When and Whom to Marry', Lucknow: AALI, 2004.

Fact Finding by a Women's Panel headed by Syeda Hameed, Muslim Women's Forum, Delhi (April, 2002) *The Survivors Speak*, Ahmedabad: Citizen's Initiative.

Fact Finding report by Multiple Action Research Group, Kandhamal: *The Law Must Change its Course* (New Delhi) (Informal Publication by MARG), 2010.

International Initiative for Justice (December 2003). *Threatened Existence: A Feminist Analaysis of the Genocide in Gujarat*. Available at *http://www. onlinevolunteers.org/gujarat/reports/iijg/2003/*

Kandhamal: *The Law Must Change its Course*, New Delhi: Multiple Action Research Group, 2010.

Newsreport in *Tehelka*, 'The Original Sinner in Paradise', 15 October, 2010. Available at http://www.tehelka.com/story_main5.asp?filename=Ne080714The_ original.asp

Report of the Centre for Feminist Legal Research on the International Seminar on Cross Border Movements and Human Rights, New Delhi, 2004.

'The New Rape Bill–Legislating Rape 'Out of Existence'!' in *MANUSHI*, A Journal About Women and Society, No.7 (1981) pp. 38–45.

Human Rights Watch (2010). *Dignity on Trial*, A report, New York: Human Rights Watch.

Table of Citations

Air India v Nergesh Meerza AIR 1981 SC 1829.

Ajit Ranjan v State II (2007) DMC 136.

Anuj Garg v Hotel Association of India AIR 2008 SC 663 : (2008) 3 SCC 1.

Apparel Export Promotion Council v A.K. Chopra AIR 1999 S.C 625.

Ashok Kumar v State I (2009) DMC 120 P&H.

Awadhesh Roy v State of Jharkhand MANU/JH/0558/2006.

Babu v State of Rajasthan 1984 Cri.LJ 74.

Bhansingh v State of Haryana 1984 Cri.L.J. 786.

C.B. Muthamma v Union of India AIR 1979 SC 1868.

Central Bureau of Investigation v Sakru Mahagu Binjewar MANU/ MH/0893/2010.

Daryaram v State of Madhya Pradesh 1992 Cr.LJ 493.

Gaurav Jain v Union of India AIR 1997 SC 3021.

Gokul and Atmaram v State of Madhya Pradesh MANU/MP/0265/2007.

Government of NCT Delhi v Sant Ram MANU/DE/3091/2009.

Hare Krishna Das v State of Bihar, 2006 (3) JCR 43 (Jhr).

Joseph Rodriguez S/o V.Z. Rodriguez v State of Karnataka MANU/ KA/8317/2006.

Madhu Kishwar v State of Bihar (1996) 5 SCC 125 : AIR 1996 SC 1864.

Mr. Werner Wulf Ingo v State of Goa (represented by C.B.I.), through Public Prosecutor for C.B.I. MANU/MH/0207/2009.

Naz Foundation v Government of NCT 2010 Cri.LJ 94 Del.

Neera Mathur v Life Insurance Corporation of India AIR 1992 SC 392.

Prem Chand v State of Haryana 1989 Cri.LJ 1247.

Rupan Deol Bajaj v Kanwar Pal Singh Gill AIR 1996 SC 309.

S.J. v K.C.J. DLT LXII (1996) 563.

Sakshi v Union of India AIR 2004 SC 3566.

Sidhartha Vashisht @ Manu Sharma v State (NCT of Delhi) 2010 (4) SCALE 1.

Sidhartha Vashisht @ Manu Sharma v State (NCT of Delhi) 2010 (4) SCALE 1.

State of Haryana v Premchand 1990 Cri.LJ 454.

State of Punjab v Gurmit Singh 1996 Cri.LJ 1728.

Tukaram v State of Maharashtra AIR 1979 SC 185.

Vinod Kumar v State of Madhya Pradesh 1987 Cri.LJ 1541.

Vishaka v State of Rajasthan 1997 6 SCC 241.

'Neutral' Laws or 'Moral' Codes
Controlling and Recreating Sexualities/Intimacies

RUKMINI SEN

Sexualities and intimacies have become a part of social science discussions in three ways—either in establishing the heterosexual familial relationships as the normative or identifying 'deviant' patterns of sexual behaviour or the need for laws to sanction 'correct' sexual codes. In recent years, various incidents across the country have also made codes of accepted or abhorred sexuality and intimacy a subject for the media, women's movement, sexuality rights movement, judiciary and academics. Sexuality is not a private matter and is linked to public privileges and persecutions; it intersects with gender, law, religion and nationality, directly affecting health and human rights. It is a contested terrain the world over—although constructed differently in different places and at different times, it remains a site where power is played out (Misra and Chandiramani 2005: 131). In a paper on the nature and content of the sexuality rights course organised by CREA[1] and TARSHI,[2] it was mentioned how one of the participants in the course described the meaning of body. For her, 'each body part has possibilities for pain and pleasure, shame and empowerment'. While breasts can be a source of pleasure, they can also be the site of sexual harassment, and while some cultures see a woman's breasts as objects of sexual desire, others see them as repositories of milk (ibid.: 139). It is keeping this in mind that sexuality as an issue remains contentious, there is a gap between the sexual practices and the legal provisions, it is so deeply 'morally' embedded in the 'neutral' law that this essay shall provide an overview on how recent incidents and the colonial law only reinforce that there are moral and legal codes controlling and recreating sexualities and intimacies in India. This essay attempts the following:

1. Briefly discusses the Indian women's movement's perspectives on sexuality;
2. Takes up certain contemporary issues relating to sexuality, and interprets how the public sphere has responded;
3. Analyses the presence, absence and silences in the Indian laws on issues pertaining to sexuality.

The Indian Women's Movement and Sexuality

Within the women's movement, sexuality in the urban, middle class Indian context has not really been discussed openly, and if at all, it is linked to women (that is what the law also does) and restricted to either reproductive health or sexual violence. Non-normative sexual expressions, sex work or sexual pleasure by a woman in a heterosexual relationship, are still largely invisible. While autonomous women's groups have protested violations against non-heterosexual people, there has not been a more positive, proactive articulation of a woman's right to her sexuality (Sharma and Nath 2005: 84). In this connection, it is relevant to mention what members of a sexuality rights group wrote during the time of lesbian suicides between October and November 2002 and the campaign strategies that were taken up as a response. Although the women's groups willingly supported the need to lodge a campaign protesting against the suicide of three lesbian women,[3] yet the responsibility of writing the leaflet fell on PRISM.[4] This is what they composed:

Was suicide the only choice for these women? Violence against women means rape, sexual harassment, and bride burning. Violence also happens every time a woman is married against her will. It happens every time a woman feels guilty for wanting to be happy and every time that a woman must die because she is unacceptable to society. Lesbian suicides are a result of society's attempt to restrict women's choices and control their lives. We protest these deaths as Violence against All Women. (ibid.: 92)

It is quite clear that the attempt was to situate lesbian suicide as violence against women, like dowry murder or rape. What is however more important is to understand that the language of choice became popular only after the choice to same-sex partnership became a debatable public issue. The Indian women's movement, therefore, to the extent that it specifically foregrounds sexuality, has usually concentrated on the question of enforcing laws that would act as a restraint on long sanctioned male privileges over the bodies and lives of women. It is the legal domain that has produced some of the most detailed discussions on sexuality. Legal activists and feminists have also discovered the extremely problematic nature of the 'sex talk' and overall ambience of the courtroom during rape trials. This has led to situations where rape victims have suffered secondary victimization at the hands of defence lawyers and judges during the process of interrogation.

Women bear the marks, sometimes violent marks, of caste, ethnic and national imaginations. The middle-class, upper-caste woman has in some ways been the ground on which questions of modernity and tradition are framed; she is the embodiment of the boundaries between licit and illicit forms of sexuality, as well as the guardian of the nation's morality. Discourses about control of sexuality, both by state and non-state patriarchies, have been dominant. Technologies of surveillance and laws of prohibition are central to the understanding of sexuality and determine what shall be termed as sexuality.

Fissures between Moral Symbols, Women's Experiences and Constitutional 'Rights'

There have been various incidents across the country in the last few years which have received media attention, reinforced gender- and sexuality-based stereotypes, generated campaigns and agitations among members of civil society and, on certain occasions, impacted the legal system. Since these have been very well reported incidents, only a brief overview of the incident will be provided; what shall be highlighted is the main issues that were raised, and the response from civil society. A 'good girl' ought to be soft-spoken, polite and obedient. She ought to marry. She ought to be a mother. If she dares to stray a little out of these prescriptions, it is seen as a momentous act of defiance. If she chooses to marry a man of her choice, it can create considerable tremors, and if she decides to marry a girl, it rattles the sexual 'foundations' of society. This image of a 'good woman' needs to be in our minds as we go through the following incidents and analyse how there has been a deviation/challenge from that stereotype. People in India have time and again taken up the morality markers in their own hands. The following examples give us an understanding of what behaviour is unacceptable in public spaces. Violence maybe inflicted if that norm is deviated. There is also an indication how little space there is for the individual here, this is evident in individual adults not being allowed to drink in public (because they are women), discouraged from choosing their partners (because of caste endogamy), disciplined to control sexual desires (because sex outside marriage is wrong) and punished for showing affection in public (because Indian culture does not allow a public display of intimacy). Thus, what is culture, morality and, subsequently, proper sexual conduct is at times decided by fundamentalist religious groups or community members or even the courts of law.

'Bad' Women Drink in Public: Mangalore Pub Incident, 2009

This was an attack where more than a dozen men barged into a local pub in Mangalore in the night and beat up the women present stating they were going against Indian culture and tradition. The attacks were carried out by extremist Hindutva political groups. Following are the issues that one can raise as a sociologist as a response to the incident:

- Age old patriarchal societal norms being imposed on young urban working women. It was a direct attack on independent working women of contemporary India. The attack has resulted in the violation of the women's right of freedom of speech and expression.
- Lack of faith in law enforcement agencies—not one woman who was attacked that night has felt safe enough to come out as a witness against the attackers.
- The National Commission for Women (NCW) itself published a report blaming the women for drinking at the pub and referring to them as

prostitutes. If a body set up for the progress and protection of women imposes morality standards on women, is it possible for women to have faith in the larger political and legal structures to support them?

- There is a two-way attack that women face: (*i*) from the self-appointed custodians of Indian culture who try to impose their standards of morality on them, and, (*ii*) from the law enforcement agencies who by taking no action perpetuated such violence against them.

- Finding no support from state agencies or from society at large, women took matters into their own hands. They began a very successful campaign called the Pink Chaddi (pink underwear) campaign against the attackers. This campaign mobilised women and men on the internet against the attackers and their assumptions that they had the right to decide how and when women can access the public sphere, and exhorted people to send in pink underwear to the leader of the attackers in order to publicly shame him. Women from all walks of life, especially those who have never been involved in such activist movements before, came out in support of this campaign, which succeeded in its objective of shaming the man.

The Mangalore pub incident brings out the crucial connection between feminist politics and the question of culture. According to Tejaswini Niranjana, there is a need to look at the relation between normative femininity and Indian-ness, especially in the context of a colonial society when women in the 19th century were seen as repositories of tradition, although now the women-and-culture pair has sedimented into common sense. The social surveillance in public spaces had become commonplace and the lack of protests reflected a consensual attitude among the people. Arvind Narain refers to this spate of events, including the Mangalore pub incident, as 'social apartheid', a form of social surveillance of public spaces where interaction between people was being surveyed. The right wing groups took active part in such acts of cultural policing. It was as if the saffron colour had become a walking structure of power. While no law could book offenders in such cases, yet vigilante action was being taken against 'offenders' of cultural norms. They were then being produced before the police, in complete violation of the constitutional tenet of fraternity, that is the right to have intimate interactions, social interactions, across caste, class, community, etc.

As a response to the Mangalore pub incident as an immediate issue—but broadening it out with a focus on the plurality of our social life, the constitutional protections guaranteed to us as citizens and women's diverse efforts to gain cultural freedoms—the Indian Association of Women's Studies organised a Southern Regional Workshop at Roshni Nilaya School of Social Work, Mangalore, where 145 participants, individuals and organisations unanimously took the following resolution:

- We affirm that the Indian Constitution is based on the ideals of equality, liberty and fraternity, which are being systematically subverted in various sites, undermining the fabric of social relations.
- We are disturbed by the series of attacks on people, especially the young, who choose to live out the meaning of fraternity by interacting across boundaries of caste and religion. We are disturbed that these forms of attack continue and that it is becoming increasingly difficult for women to move about and interact freely.
- We are further disturbed by the attempts to constrain the expressions of women within narrow cultural codes through intimidation and violence.
- We believe that young people by living out the ideals of the Indian Constitution represent the challenge to the boundaries of class, caste and religion. In the context of these attacks, which threaten the plurality that characterises the very idea of India, we reaffirm our commitment to the fundamental ideals of the Constitution, and to uphold justice and democracy.

Indecency in 'enjoying' Heterosexual Company in Public Spaces: Operation Majnu, 2005

Operation Majnu was the name given to the moral policing drive organised by the Meerut police targeting couples in parks. The couples were accused of indecent behaviour and were rounded up by the police. Some of them were slapped and beaten up. In fact, boys and girls sitting together were harassed irrespective of whether they were actually a couple or were just siblings or friends. The entire episode was shown on television, as the Meerut police wanted to broadcast the success of their drive to the entire nation. The Meerut incident raises questions that are larger than those of framing and interpreting laws: What are the spaces our society creates for any kind of intimacy? How do notions of morality and immorality get framed in a society that, on the one hand, is eagerly embracing all things 'free'—from economy to lifestyle—and, on the other, wants to keep its tradition safe under lock and key?

- Though the police are well known for harassing young couples in parks in Indian cities this was the first time police-imposed moral policing came out in public.
- The guardians and upholders of our security turned attackers in this case.
- Young couples were treated as ordinary criminals. They were attacked without provocation.
- Since the entire episode was shown on television may of the individuals had to face societal stigma and harassment for a long time after the event.
- Such incidents only seek to drive issues on sexuality underground. This is highly unhealthy for a society; when sexuality is repressed it leaves individuals more vulnerable to harassment and exploitation.
- If there are no spaces for young heterosexual couples in Indian society what hope is there for gay and lesbian couples to come out of the closet?
- Such incidents are a direct attack on the right to privacy and autonomy which has been read into the right to life and liberty by the Supreme Court (SC).

Pre-Marital Sex and 'Indian' Morality: The Khushboo Controversy, 2005–10

Khushboo, a famous Tamilian actress, had remarked in an interview that in her view there was nothing wrong with pre-marital sex, that necessary precautions against AIDS should be taken and that men ought not to insist on virgin brides. These comments created a nationwide furore. Conservative Tamil groups filed cases against her in numerous courts stating that her remarks were a threat to public peace and order. In addition, she was levelled with charges such as criminal defamation and indecent representation of women. She was also forced to publicly apologise for her remarks on national television. Protests were held against her on the streets and mobs attacked her car wherever she went. Even those who came out in support of her were not spared. What did Khusboo really say?

Women in Chennai were lagging behind Bangalore in expressing sexual desires. But Chennai women are now coming out of hibernation. I see a lot of women going out, in pubs and discos here. Women are able to talk about sex without inhibition. Given our conservative Indian backdrop, women are slowly coming out. But I do have questions about this women liberation when cases like Stefani's accident are happening [this girl was chased and killed by drunken youth after a night party in a Chennai hotel]. But at the same time, I think sex education is a must in our schools. When the schools fail to teach sex, parents should educate their children about sex. In my opinion, sex is not only related to body; it's got a lot to do with our minds. Our society should liberate itself from such ideas that the brides should all be virgins at the time of marriage. No educated man will expect his bride to be virgin at the time of marriage. But when indulging in pre-marital sex, the girl should guard herself against pregnancy and sexually transmitted diseases.... When women express their sexual desires they are looked down upon. This attitude should change. Sex is about two minds.

In 2010, five years after the controversy, the SC dismissed all cases against the actress.

- A direct attack on a woman's right to freedom of speech and expression. The remarks seemed to have caused a huge impact because they were made by a woman and because they were on pre-marital sex.
- The SC pointed out that when two adults want to stay together, what is the offence? Living together is not an offence. According to the SC, the appellant's statement, published in *India Today*, is a rather general endorsement of pre-marital sex and her remarks are not directed at any individual or event, at a 'company' or an association or collection

of persons, and therefore it did not invite any case for defamation as defined under Section 499 of the Indian Penal Code (IPC).

- The SC, while dismissing the case, pointed out that criminal law cannot be used to interfere with the domain of personal autonomy. While this observation was helpful in the present case, such a view could be quite problematic in other cases, such as cases of marital rape where this could be misused.

- At the time of the controversy all political parties, even the opposition, were united in their stand against Khushboo's remarks. The state, the upholder of fundamental rights, did not provide her with any protection against the protesters; instead, they furthered the protests against her.

Indian Heterosexual Adults Denied the Right to Choose Partner: *Khap* Panchayats and Marriage

Khap panchayats are traditional village bodies, mainly in northern India, comprising the elders of the village. They prohibit marriage between individuals of the same *gotra*, calling it incestuous. They have issued diktats against couples who have entered into such marriages and have, on some occasions, condemned them to death. They have also resorted to kidnapping of children and banishing the families of the couples from villages. They are demanding an amendment to the Hindu Marriage Act, 1955, to prohibit such marriages. However, the following must be noted:

- Imposition of standards of morality in marriages in the garb of protection of traditional value systems has resulted in the violation of the right to life and right to privacy of individuals, together with the right to chose one's partner.

- A debate has been started surrounding tradition vs. modernity, community decisions vs. individual choice, customary practices vs. constitutional freedoms, and honour vs. liberty.

- If an amendment is made to the Hindu Marriage Act on these grounds it will become a state sanctioned morality standard on the people. This will set a precedent for state-imposed morality sanctioned by law in other spheres of life, such as same-sex marriages, women going to pubs, etc.

On 5 August 2010, the home minister has said that the Group of Ministers (GoP) is working on either amending the IPC or proposing a separate law on 'honour' killings. He strongly condemned the instances of murder of young couples married into different castes or driving them to commit suicide. There had been a proposal to amend Section 300 of the IPC which is on murder by adding a fifth clause to the section. It is proposed to read as follows:

Except in the cases hereinafter excepted, culpable homicide is murder, if the act by which the death is caused is done with the intention of causing death, or if it is done by any person or persons acting in concert with, or at the behest of, a member of the family or a member of a body or group of the caste or clan or community or caste panchayat in the belief that the victim has brought dishonour or perceived to have brought dishonour upon the family or caste or clan or community or caste panchayat.

The word dishonour would include unacceptable dress codes, choosing to marry within or outside the *gotra* or caste or clan or community, and engaging in sexual relations which are unacceptable. It is yet to be seen how the government responds; however, just having an amendment or a separate law will not really resolve the more fundamental issues of young persons' right to have control over their own lives, a right to association, movement and choice of partners.

The next two examples deal with the denial of right to choice and privacy. Both are connected with, on the one hand, how an individual may choose to lead his/her personal life and, on the other, how an individual makes a livelihood. In the latter, the state did not have the moral responsibility to provide alternate livelihoods to women who were considered to pursue an 'immoral' occupation (bar dancing), but had the power to close down bars in Mumbai. Men who want to execute their choice in personal lives are also under surveillance and punishment. It is interesting that in both these examples there is a conflict between choice and profession. On one occasion, the choice in personal sphere impacts the professional, while on another occasion, the choice of the professional impacts the personal.

The Aligarh Muslim University Case 2010

A sting operation was carried out by a news channel in collaboration with Aligarh Muslim University (AMU) officials on Professor Siras, Reader and Chair of Modern Indian Language at AMU. He was caught on camera having sex with another man. This resulted in his suspension from the university, though he was later reinstated by an order from the Allahabad High Court. A few days later, Siras was found dead at his university accommodation and it was suspected that he had been killed.

- This is a case where university officials tried to impose their preconceived notions of morality on Professor Siras. This resulted in a violation of his right to life and right to privacy. It sends out a signal to the larger society that anyone who deviates from the narrow perceived standard norm of morality will pay with his/her life.

- As a result of the favourable judgment on Section 377 in the Naz foundation case, Professor Siras was at least able to approach the court and get a favourable order and he was able to file an FIR against the persons who had conducted the sting. Such a verdict would not have been possible in the pre Naz Foundation judgment days, in an atmosphere where homosexuality *per se* was illegal. However, though the law in books has changed, Professor Siras's murder shows that there is still a long way to go before the societal mindset changes. Such incidents make it more difficult for people to come out of the closet because even if the law on paper provides protection to homosexual persons, the enforcement agencies are not able to enforce the law effectively.

- Professor Siras's case is not a stray incident. The incident has brought to light a series of attacks against the Lesbian, Gay, Bisexual and Transgender (LGBT) community within academic spaces in recent times. For example, Professor Panikkar was suspended from the Maharaja Sayajirao University (MSU) in Baroda right after he came out of the closet. He has not been reinstated till date. Aniruddhan, a junior research fellow at Chennai University, was unable to find a guide to support his dissertation for the very same reason. If academic spaces still judge people according to their sexual orientation what hope is there for the larger society to change?

A concerned citizens' initiative had launched a campaign in Delhi, writing a strong letter to the Chancellor and Vice Chancellor of AMU after the death of Professor Siras under suspicious conditions. The letter reflects some significant issues of the inter-connectedness of legality and morality:

1. Morality cannot be legally used as a ground for restricting the fundamental right to dignity, privacy and autonomy of any individual. AMU should appoint a committee to look into instances of such moral policing and surveillance.

2. Action should be taken against the journalists for trespassing, violating privacy and intimidation of Dr Siras at his home. The police should also determine whether they were acting independently or on behalf of their employers or acting on behalf of AMU authorities.

Denial of Right to Choose a Livelihood: Mumbai Bar Dancers, 2005

In 2005, a ban was imposed by the Government of Maharashtra on all dance bars. This was done by amending Section 33 of the Bombay Police Act, 1951. The grounds for the ban were that the bars promote trafficking, sexual exploitation of women, and deprave, corrupt and injure the public morality. The bar dancer and owner associations approached the High Court which struck down the ban on two grounds: that it violated Article 14 (Right to Equality) and Article 19(1) (g) (Right to Work). Deputy Chief Minister R.R. Patil, who made the ban his crusade to 'protect law and order' and 'save families from ruin', continues his moral tirade despite its obvious fallout on the lives of thousands of poor women and their families. After prohibiting dance, his government has not even tried to provide alternative work to a single bar girl. Patil justified the closure by saying that the dancing was obscene and that dance bars were pick-up joints and meeting places for criminals. However, the legal amendment he had passed in the Assembly allows dancing in three-star plus hotels, gymkhanas and clubs. So, if it is in an upmarket place, dancing is not vulgar, and no vice exists in that rarefied atmosphere. It is this discriminatory tone of the amendment to the Bombay Police Act, unanimously passed by the Maharashtra Legislature, which the High Court struck down as 'unconstitutional'. If women could be waitresses or singers in bars, why could they not be dancers? If other forms of dance, such as *lavani* and *tamasha*, were allowed, why not others? 'That some may be exploited is no answer to preventing others from earning their livelihood by a vocation of their choice, maybe sometimes involuntarily', the Mumbai High Court judges said. This incident highlighted the following:

- State-imposed morality standard on appropriate behaviour for women. The bar dancers were seen as promoting vulgarity and obscenity in society. However, no observations were made on the people who visited such bars. During the ban period, a number of bar dancers were arrested but no one raised the issue of arresting the people who regularly visit the bars.

- No uniform standard of morality was imposed. The law enacted was itself discriminatory. It allowed dance performances in hotels which were rated three stars or above in order to promote tourist and cultural activities. It was a direct violation of right to equality under Article 14 since it imposed a different law for the same class of people.

- One of the reasons cited for the ban was to prevent trafficking of women. However, most of the studies conducted during the period showed that the bar dancers were mostly from Mumbai and had willingly chosen to work in this profession. No note was taken of the bar dancer's choice or views before imposition of the ban on them.

The ban pushed these activities underground and forced women into prostitution to support their families thus subverting the entire purpose of having enacted the ban in the first place. As many as twenty-five bar dancers have committed suicide since the ban was enforced, according to official statistics. Women's activists and groups came out in Mumbai in support of the bar dancers. Flavia Agnes had taken the issue to the Bombay High Court in 2004 when she found that after police raided some bars, they took the women to the police station late at night. This is prohibited under the law. No woman police was present when the dancers were taken there. And several women complained of molestation and harassment by the policemen. The police had claimed that they raided the bars on the ground of obscenity. Ms Agnes pointed out the girls dance to film music using the same dance movements as stars do in films in what are called 'item numbers'. Why, she asked, was one allowed and the other considered obscene? Varsha Kale of the Womanist Party of India, who has enrolled many of the 75,000 bar girls into a registered trade union, the Bharatiya Bar Girls Association, questioned the role of the government in the proliferation of dance bars. She pointed out that after 1996 their numbers had grown rapidly. 'Why were licences given out so freely?' she asked. Today, there are an estimated 1,250 dance bars in Maharashtra and most of them have been established post-1996. In fact, the Association took to the streets and expressed the fear that trafficking in women would increase if the bars were closed. It raised the issue of rehabilitation and said it was unconstitutional to close the bars. Amidst this legal high ground on dance bars, a survey on the working conditions and background of women working in dance bars refutes the claim that they were trafficked in from Bangladesh, as suggested by some politicians, or that they are forced into sex work. The survey was conducted by the Research Centre for Women's Studies, SNDT University, July 2005, along with non-governmental organisations (NGOs) such as Akshara, the Forum against Oppression of Women (FAOW), Majlis, Point of View and Awaaz-e-Niswan. The main findings of the survey were:

- 500 women in 50 dance bars were interviewed.
- 17.4 per cent are from Maharashtra, contrary to the belief that most were non-Maharashtrians and from Bangladesh.
- Most dancers are aged between 21 and 25.
- Their average monthly income was less than Rs. 10,000; this was contrary to the perception that a bar dancer made lakhs of rupees every night.

There was a statement that was released by some of the above-mentioned groups in Mumbai and other parts of India in support of the bar dancers.

On the issue of women working in bars, the State is resorting to contradictory stands, on the one hand of 'sexual exploitation' of women working in bars and on the other accusing these very women of 'morally corrupting' the youth and society at large. Morality cannot be determined by the dominant and privileged sections of society.... Instead of creating spaces and conditions that ensure that women are not sexually harassed and that their rights are respected, the State has targeted the livelihood of women which might have lent their lives independence and autonomy and thereby freedom. By rendering women jobless and without financial resources, the State is making them much more vulnerable to abuse and exploitation. (Quoted in Menon 2008: 296)

There is a challenge made to the state construction of morality, and also a usurpation of the movement's rhetoric of sexual exploitation without obviously sharing the concerns of the women's groups.

A Way Forward on Adult Intimate Relationships? Naz Foundation Judgment, 2009

This is a landmark judgment, which, after a decade of struggle by different groups, decriminalised homosexuality in India. By acknowledging the distinct status of persons, whose only common bond is sexual orientation, and addressing them as a collective (actually using the phrase 'LGBT'), the Naz Foundation recognises the emergence of new social identities, while carefully sidestepping lingering concerns about their elite roots and urban biases. The mass publicity and fanfare heralding the decision presents a rare opportunity for activists to reshape public opinion and influence a wider social debate about gay rights. The judgment says that the state has no presumptive right to regulate private acts between consenting adults. It protects privacy.

There is a lot of positive response on the judgment comprehending the spirit of the Constitution and not the formalism of the constitutional provisions. It is the Constitution which creates an image of the excluded citizen. The abstract figure of the citizen needs to have a specific character so as to be deserving of rights. In India, in spite of the scope of the 'citizen' being expanded to include marginal figures like child labourer, prisoner, or street dweller, one of the excluded categories have been that of queer sexualities. This judgment is the first occasion where the concept of citizenship is understood. This understanding of citizenship does not cover areas relating to marriage, divorce or adoption, where the queer person is still the absent figure. Marriage as an institution is based on exclusion and exclusivity both of which are antithetical to any proper concept of democracy. Marriage presumes exclusivity, which as a choice is not by itself problematic. But the problem is that marriage as an institution occupies the normative field, leaving no space for non-normative, non-exclusive relationships. Not discussing issues surrounding marriage or family, this judgment reiterates the need to creatively interpret the Constitution because that is what will conceptually extend the rhetoric of the Constitution to unspecified spaces. The mystification of the family as a sphere of love and harmony has been one of the primary foci of the feminist critique. The family has been identified as one of the sites of oppressing any kind of sexual orientation other than the heterosexual one. The law protects the family structure and also produces the body as a series of binary opposites—male/female, healthy/disabled, heterosexual/ homosexual. The judgment questions the idea of 'normal', and also indirectly addresses disadvantage and not just homosexuals. Although the archetypical 'normal' person may not be impacted by the judgment, but therein lies the importance of the decision—by bringing within and raising a voice about any kind of minority identity. According to the Delhi High Court, if there is a constitutional tenet that can be said to be the underlying theme of the Indian Constitution, it is that of 'inclusiveness'. This court believes that the Indian Constitution reflects this value deeply ingrained in Indian society, nurtured over generations. The inclusiveness that Indian society traditionally displayed, literally in every aspect of life, is manifest in recognising a role in society for everyone. Those perceived by the majority as 'deviants' or 'different' are not on that score excluded or ostracized.

There are lingering concerns about whether the SC would override the High Court decision; the judgment merely talks about decriminalising and not doing away with the archaic Section 377 of the IPC, which has been the standing demand of the movement. Moreover, it is quite clear through the first two issues that these judgments do not immediately impact in transforming moral codes on sexual practices.

Some general observations from the above incidents on issues relating to morality, sexuality campaign strategies and the legal responses to them are the following:

- Issues of sexuality are definitely not personal or private, as one expects, rather they acquire a public dimension, especially with societal sanctions and legal doctrines trying to control sexual spaces.

- Sexuality is connected with marriage, cohabitation, the sexual act, partnerships that a person chooses to be in, certain economic activities which provide livelihood to some.

- Heteronormative sexuality is nearly unquestioned as a given, except for campaigns and movements by women's rights groups, or groups struggling for the rights of the LGBT community.

- Sexuality as an issue remains buried from the everyday educational environment although the media, films and serials portray the above mentioned themes widely and uncritically.

- When it comes to issues of sex and morality surprisingly all the political parties despite their varied ideology seem united on the issue and hardly anyone is seen to come out in support of the victims.

- Some of the cases have got favourable judicial support but these have been pyrrhic victories for the victims. The decision in Khusboo's case came five years after the controversy began and the Mumbai bar dancers had already lost their livelihood by the time of the decision. In fact, despite a favourable judicial decision, Professor Siras was murdered and his killers have still not been apprehended.

- Lack of teeth of the law enforcement agencies. The message sent out by the cases has been that conservative groups have more power to curb one's fundamental rights than the state has to protect them.

- Imposition of morality standards cut across class barriers. Both urban and rural women have been targeted.

Indian law on sexuality/sexual diversions: its words, meanings and silences

The concluding part of the essay examines the manner in which the Indian legal system looks at the issue of sexuality. It is noteworthy that nowhere in the law is there any mention of the word sexuality. What follows is a brief theoretical engagement with law's engagement with sexuality, where the colonial legacy to our legal provisions shall be confirmed. Devlin, in a public lecture, had affirmed that the original law of England was based on moral law, although in many respects it lagged behind it, for there were many sins, which were not punishable as crimes, his insistence on the difference between offences which were *mala inse* and those created by law which were only *mala prohibita*, creating a quasi-criminal law, has resulted in a general view that morality is the opposite of sin, and concepts of morality tend to be confined to the sphere of sex, and particularly to what the law regards as sexual offences. The distinction between the real criminal law and the quasi-criminal law in their relationship to morals is that in the former a moral idea shapes the content of the law and in the latter it provides a base upon which a legal structure can be erected. Crime means for the ordinary man something that is sinful or immoral and an offence, at worst, a piece of misbehaviour. Acceptance of the 'right-wrong' view of morality clearly indicates the relation between it and law, especially in the light of the definition of law based on its function to preserve peace and good order in society. Morality plays a major role in divorce, suicide, use of contraceptives, abortion and homosexuality. Male homosexuality was considered more immoral and repulsive than lesbianism when the law was developed. Law is a reflection of the beliefs and needs of the community it is intended to serve. It is neither rigid nor sacrosanct and as those needs and beliefs change, so the law must change with them. It is difficult to be certain at any time whether the law indicates the current morality or whether the few who have secured an amendment of the law are responsible for the development and rising of moral standards. If law lags too far behind current trends in morality, the law will become obsolete and fall into disuse. If the legislators allow this to happen too frequently, they only have themselves to blame if the society they serve appears to have abandoned respect for the rule of law.

There is both a lack of theorising on sexuality as well as an under-research on sexuality and social policy. Sexuality is an area of significant social change. This can be seen in changing social attitudes to marriage, divorce, single motherhood and homosexuality; in the diversity of household and family forms which exist; and in the impact of HIV/AIDS epidemic on sexuality, intimate relations, risk and health. The most recent legalisation of gay marriages has happened in Argentina, the first Latin American country to do it (July 2010). In order to understand the importance of sexuality in social policy, three issues maybe identified:

- Contraception, abortion, sexually transmitted diseases, reproduction, sex education, teenage pregnancy, single motherhood, lesbianism and homosexuality. Focus may be on needs and provision of services.
- Examining power relations which surround sexuality issues. Analysis of the direct and indirect ways in which lesbian and gay men can experience discrimination on the basis of their sexuality. They may also address the ways in which appropriate and acceptable sexuality is the means for establishing access to and eligibility for welfare benefits and services; as a criterion for eligibility to benefits in the critiques of the cohabitation rule.
- Theorising and critiquing the influence of dominant sexual discourses on social policy. Heterosexuality taken as an unquestioned norm/given, in all social policies.

The model of family under consideration has been heterosexual, and laws preserve and restore families. Another peculiarity with sexuality is that it is perceived as an intimate, personal and private matter. So there is an inherent contradiction between a *private* relation and a *public* policy. The individualisation of the experience of sexuality is a reason why it is marginalised as an analytic category. It is different from income support or health, housing, education, social care because it is seen as exciting, pleasurable, dangerous, personal and intimate. Sometimes, people conflate sexuality with homosexuality and one may be seen as promoting homosexuality or 'pretended family' relations.

Sexuality and the Indian Penal Code

All the incidents on sexual 'immorality' that were discussed previously can find resonance in the legal system. Some of the incidents would come under outraging modesty, some under indecency, and another under the notorious Section 377, a section connoting denial of liberty, justice and privacy in South Asia. If we focus attention on the IPC then it is in the chapter on 'offences against the human body' that issues of sexuality get discussed, still in a Victorian, colonial framework. It is not to say that there are no laws in the IPC that may be evoked when a woman is sexually harassed. However, these related laws are framed as offences that either amount to *obscenity* in public or acts that are seen to violate the *modesty of women* under Sections 294, 354 and 509 of the IPC. While Section 294 IPC is a law applicable to both men and women, the latter two are specifically oriented towards women.

Section 294   Obscene acts and songs (under the chapter 'of offences affecting public health, safety, convenience and morals').

Whoever, to the annoyance of others—

(a)   Does any obscene act in any public place, or

(b)   sings, recites or utters any obscene song, ballad or words, in or near any public place, shall be punished with imprisonment of either description for a term which may extend to three months, or with fine, or with both.

Section 354   Assault or criminal force to woman with intent to outrage her modesty.

Whoever assaults or uses criminal force to any woman, intending to outrage or knowing it to be likely that he will thereby outrage her modesty, shall be punished with imprisonment of either description for a term which may extend to two years, or with fine, or with both.

What the above provision indicates is the following:

- Women are the bearers of modesty and it is a criminal offence to violate that.
- This is intrinsically connected with women being the representatives of tradition and moral values of Indian society and therefore their modesty needs protection by the law.
- It is left to the subjective interpretation of people in the legal system to decide which acts can be considered 'outrageous'.
- Patriarchal notions of women as chaste and the bearers of purity and

honour are prevalent in the colonial code and are similar to the notion that drives reactions against women drinking in pubs.

Section 509   Word, gesture or act intended to insult the modesty of a woman (under the chapter 'of criminal intimidation, insult and annoyance').

> Whoever, intending to insult the modesty of any woman, utters any word, makes any sound or gesture, or exhibits any object, intending that such word or sound shall be heard, of that such gesture or object shall be seen, by such woman, or intrudes upon the privacy of such woman, shall be punished with simple imprisonment for a term which may extend to one year, or with fine, or with both.

What is evident from the two provisions is that there is a hierarchy between outraging the modesty of a woman and insulting her modesty. That is clear in the varying degrees of punishment associated with the two offences. There is a mention of privacy here, but that is quite different from the right to privacy language that has become common today. The logic of the pure, good woman exists in this provision also. Often, for want of no other provision, cases of molestation and sexual harassment are booked under either of the two sections. It was much later in the *Vishaka* judgment of 1997 that the SC provided a definition of sexual harassment at the workplace, a term unheard of within the criminal law jurisprudence on sexuality in India. According to the SC, such behaviour 'includes such unwelcome sexually determined behaviour (whether directly or by implication) as:

(a) physical contact and advances
(b) a demand or request for sexual favours
(c) sexually-coloured remarks
(d) showing pornography
(e) any other unwelcome physical, verbal or non-verbal conduct of sexual nature'. Since 1997, this remains a guideline with no real legal binding and there has not, till the time of writing been a separate statute since then.

Subsequent to Vishaka, there was another Supreme Court judgement (*Apparel Export Promotion Council* v *Chopra*), where the definition of sexual harassment was expanded and it was held that: 'any action or gesture which, whether directly or by implication, aims or has the tendency to outrage the modesty of a female employee, must fall under the general concept of the definition of sexual harassment'. Conservative notions of modesty and decency have become entangled with the definition of sexual harassment. Shame, humiliation and embarrassment are emotions expected from a woman who has been sexually harassed. More seriously, all women are expected to feel the same sense of outrage with regard to sexually-coloured behaviour.

In July 2005, the Supreme Court upheld the conviction of former DGP of Punjab, K.P.S. Gill, for outraging the modesty of a woman IAS officer, Rupan Deol Bajaj. While the conviction is laudable, the observations made by the apex court, particularly with regard to a woman's modesty, are not. In this case, the complainant was verbally assaulted at a dinner party and when she tried to leave, she was slapped by Gill on her posterior in front of all the other guests. The matter reached the SC, where it was held that

…the ultimate test for ascertaining whether modesty has been outraged is if the action of the offender such as could be perceived as one which is capable of shocking the sense of decency of a woman…the alleged act of the respondent in slapping the appellant on her posterior amounted to 'outraging of her modesty' for it was not only an affront to the normal sense of feminine decency but also an affront to the dignity of the lady.

There is no denying that the conduct of K.P.S. Gill under the circumstances was outrageous—an unwelcome sexual demand was made, resulting in a hostile environment. But the problem with the judgement is that it imposes attributes of feminine decency on all women. For example, there are some women who may pat friends or colleagues on the posterior and not consider it sexual harassment—just a display of affection. A sexually-charged office/workplace is not detrimental to women's interests; it only becomes so if the sexual atmosphere discriminates. When sexual harassment gets disassociated from discrimination it becomes hostile to freedom of sexual expression and, in fact, detrimental to the feminist agenda.[5] Dress codes for women in universities, company guidelines where consensual relationships need to be reported to the manager or director or where consensual relationships between co-workers are simply not allowed, or restrictions at women's hostels on timings and male visitors simply control anything related to sex, and not sexual harassment. In private companies, the fear of becoming entangled in sexual harassment cases where vast sums of money are involved leads to stringent company codes. Employers are duty bound to provide a safe environment, and if they fail to do so may end up having to face a suit for criminal liability. Therefore, extreme steps are taken to keep the workplace sexually sanitised.

It is equally important to remember that both these sections fall short of the section that defines rape in the IPC as peno-vaginal penetration against the will and consent of the woman. Thus, according to the prevailing colonial notion of sexual violence, anything short of penis penetration into the woman's vagina is outraging her modesty. Issues of penetration, proving consent, the possibility of the woman becoming pregnant, violation of a woman's purity and chastity are the connotations that emerge from the definition. Moreover, this provision is very clear about the fact that there is no rape within marriage, or, to look at it differently, husbands have complete control over their wife's sexuality. A woman's pleasure and desire associated with sexuality is not a part of the discussion on sexuality. Currently, provisions relating to sexual crimes are scattered across the IPC in Sections 375, 376, 377, 354 and 509. In their present form, these different sections on sexual violence do not constitute a clear and coherent set of laws. In 2010, Indian women's groups submitted a recommendation to the Ministry for Home Affairs, Government of India, asking for a separate chapter on sexual violence against women, recognising that sexual crimes form a continuum. This chapter intends to reformulate and bring together in the place existing crimes such as rape, outraging the modesty of a woman and sexual harassment within the broader crime of sexual offences. Sexual violence includes but is not limited to sexual acts which involve penetration by the penis. They include acts which involve penetration by other parts of the body and objects, as well as the use of criminal force, including stripping, parading and mutilation which are intended to sexually assault, degrade or humiliate those who are so targeted. This proposed revised framework recognises the structural and graded nature of sexual violence. The offences need to be graded based on concepts of harm, injury, humiliation or degradation, using well established categories of sexual assault, aggravated sexual assault and sexual offences.

In the absence of any provision on child sexual abuse, either cases are not registered or can come under another very controversial section, Section called 377, defined as unnatural offences:

Whoever voluntarily has carnal intercourse against the order of nature with any man, woman or animal, shall be punished with [imprisonment for life], or with imprisonment of either description for term which may extend to ten years, and shall also be liable to fine.

Explanation: Penetration is sufficient to constitute the carnal intercourse necessary to the offence described in this section.

That heterosexuality is not normal is evident from the law's efforts to criminalise homosexuality, and terming the practice as *unnatural*. It is however interesting to note that sex between two men is what is considered as legally unnatural because the Queen could not even perceive the possibility of two women engaging in a sexual relation and therefore the omission in the law. However, the exclusion in the law did not indicate that there were social sanctions favouring female sexual intimacy. There is an ongoing effort to amend or repeal this section by sexuality rights groups, women's groups and also child rights groups in the country, but in vain. The only positive move has been the Delhi High Court judgment in the Naz Foundation case which is the first step towards decriminalising adult sexual relationships. India has a long way to go, however, with respect to legalising adult same-sex partnership, eliminating discriminations on grounds of inheritance, employment, residential requirements, etc.

In 1992 the semantic category of Crimes against Women was coined and a new set of classificatory practices operationalised to generate data to cope with the demands thrown up by challenges from the women's status discourses. This shift was significant in that it distinguished general criminality from crimes specifically against women that violate their rights. This new category was now to act as an index of the *status of women*. The report listed the following crimes against women as enunciated in the IPC. Rape (376 IPC); kidnapping or abduction for different purposes (363-373 IPC); homicide for dowry, dowry deaths or their attempts (302/304-B IPC); torture, both mental and physical (498A IPC); molestation (354 IPC); and eve teasing (509 IPC). The report classified Section 354 as molestation and Section 509 as eve teasing. Molestation then was read against those offences that use force or assault to outrage the modesty of women. Eve teasing was recognised as a popular form of harassment of women in public spaces, but the popular understanding that it falls short of molestation underlay the distinction between molestation and eve teasing. Eve teasing was then classified as those offences that outrage the modesty of women by word, gesture or act, thereby reifying popular and normative distinctions between physical and verbal (or non-physical form) of harassment. It affirmed the idea that eve teasing is not assault and causes lesser 'hurt' than molestation.

Law Relating to 'Immoral' Work

The law in India, just as it criminalises non-heterosexual intimate relationships, similarly criminalises any sexual engagement that a woman is involved in to earn her livelihood. The reason why the following law on prostitution shall be discussed briefly is because prostitution is a sexual activity considered immoral and therefore for prostitutes to solicit clients is criminalised in India. Second, the extension of the ban on bar dancers is the criminalisation of prostitution. What comes out unambiguously from the legal provisions maintaining sexual standards is that the institution of patriarchal, heteronormative family is the most important unit to be protected under all conditions. It is due to this that prostitution is legally criminalised in India. Disregarding the debates about prostitution vs. sex work, the Indian legal system continues with an old law Immoral Traffic Prevention Act (ITPA). The law in the title mentions 'traffic', yet defines prostitution within the body, understandably using the two words interchangeably which obviously is conceptually incorrect. According to ITPA, 1986:

(f) "prostitution" means the sexual exploitation or abuse of persons for commercial purposes or for consideration in money or in any other kind, and the expression "prostitute" shall be construed accordingly;

h) "public place" means any place intended for use by, or accessible to, the public and includes any public conveyance;

8. Seducing or soliciting for purpose of prostitution. Whoever, in any public place or within sight of, and in such manner as to be seen or heard from, any public place, whether from within any building or house or not – (a) by words, gestures, wilful exposure of her person (whether by sitting by a window or on the balcony of a building or house or in any other way), or otherwise tempts or endeavours to tempt, or attracts or endeavours to attract the attention of, any person for the purpose of prostitution; or

(b) solicits or molests any person, or loiters or acts in such manner as to cause obstruction or annoyance to persons residing nearby or passing by such public place or to offend against public decency, for the purpose of prostitution, shall be punishable on first conviction, with imprisonment for a term which may extend to six months, or with fine which may extend to five hundred rupees, or with both, and in the event of a second or subsequent conviction, with imprisonment for a term which may extend to five years, and also with fine which may extend to five hundred rupees.

If the above is the language of the law, it is clearly criminalising prostitution, not considering the reasons why women get into prostitution or even taking into account women's voices about their body, sexuality, choice, or freedom. Without taking any onus on social and economic compulsions or a choice with which women are a part of this work, the law merely looks at this sexual exchange as immoral, harmful for public morality and therefore finds offence in the act. This is the only law in India which defines public place and talks about 'immoral activities' that should not be part of that space. In contrast to this text, the following is a text written by Veshya Anyaya Mukti Parishad (VAMP) and SANGRAM (Sampada Grameen Mahila Sanshta).[6]

Prostitution is a way of life like any other. It is a survival strategy that is parallel to any other occupation. Women in prostitution make money out of sex and we are the breadwinners of our families....Brothel owners, goons, police and the self-appointed crusaders of morality in society harass us, try to curb our independence and are forever trying to douse our spirit. Control structures have vested interests in criminalizing prostitution. What we demand is decriminalization of prostitution such that we can live safely and continue to choose to make money from sex without stigmatization…We believe that making money from sex is but selling a part of our body which is in no way different from selling our brains or physical labour.…We do not believe that sex has a sacred space and women who have sex for reasons other than its reproductive importance are violating that space…We protest against a society that deems us immoral and illegal mainly because we do not accept its mores, rules and governance. (Quoted in Menon (2008: 327)

What one can reflect upon from the above text is that:

- Prostitution can be a method of earning a livelihood.
- All the male actors associated with this 'immoral' activity harass the prostitutes, and in fact make money also out of the 'livelihood'.
- There is a sense of sexual liberation that the prostitutes experience, and challenge the societal and legal hegemonic norm that directly links sexual activity with reproduction.

Are There Strategies to Negotiate with the Hetero-patriarchal Ideology of Sexuality and Morality?

Women are continuously cautioned to 'behave properly', 'dress appropriately', 'restrict movements' vis-à-vis public spaces. A conscious newspaper reader will realise the amount of controversy dress codes of women teachers cause in schools and colleges. This is nothing but a restriction of freedom of choice. Where there are laws relating to sexuality, they endorse these social and moral negative sanctions. It is therefore important to unpack the socio-legal issues that have been discussed above. Some recommendations with which sexuality, public space, women's freedom can become part of academic and training discourses are:

- To discuss sexuality—its images, its stereotypes, questioning them and remapping them—more openly in training sessions with different government officials, grassroot level workers, students and teachers.

• To develop sex education training manuals in high schools and colleges.

• Gender and sexuality trainings with different stakeholders.

• Campaigning with respective government departments on the need for minimum effective infrastructure to be in place that can prevent sexual violence against women—like well lit roads, functioning helplines, police patrolling. Taking cue from safety audits done by different NGOs and trying to device better preventive strategies in more vulnerable areas.

• Training manuals for police, lawyers, counsellors, NGO personnel.

• Using the media—street theatres, posters and film clippings to discuss myths and realities of sexuality.

• Campaign to reform both substantive and enforceable components of laws on sexual violence.

It is a lengthy campaign, requiring people from different fields to interact and generate innovative strategies—short term and long term.

Notes

1. A human rights organisation that empowers women to articulate, demand and access their rights in the fields of sexuality.

2. It runs a helpline that offers information, counselling and referrals on sexuality and reproductive health.

3. These happened in different parts of the country because their relationships to each other were not accepted by their families and communities.

4. Non-funded, non-registered feminist forum of individuals in Delhi, inclusive of all gender sexual expressions and identities.

5. Gayatri Sharma, 'No Sex Please' Available online at http://infochangeindia. org/200602085632/Agenda/Claiming-Sexual-Rights-In-India/No-sex-please.html

6. NGO working with sex workers in Maharashtra since 1992.

References and Additional Reading

CEQUIN and CMS Communication (2009), *Perceptions and Experience of Gendered Violations in Public Spaces of Delhi.*

Chandiramani, Radhika and Geetanjali Misra (2005). 'Unlearning and Learning: The Sexuality and Rights Institute in India', in Geetanjali Misra and Radhika Chandiramani (eds), *Sexuality, Gender and Rights: Exploring Theory and Practice in South and Southeast Asia*, New Delhi: Sage Publications, pp. 131–49.

Green, L.C. (1970). 'Law and Morality in a Changing Society', *The University of Toronto Law Journal*, vol. 20, no. 4 (Autumn), pp. 422–47. Available online at http://www.jstor.org/stable/824884

John, Mary and Nair, Janaki (eds) (1998). *A Question of Silence? The Sexual Economies of Modern India*, New Delhi: Kali for Women.

Menon, Nivedita (ed.) (2008). *Sexualities: Issues in Contemporary Indian Feminism*, New Delhi: Zed Books.

Vishwanath, Kalpana and Surabhi Tandon Mehrotra, (2007). 'Shall We Go Out? Women's Safety in Public Spaces in Delhi', *Economic and Political Weekly*, April 28, pp. 1542–48

S. Khushboo v. *Kanniammal* in Supreme Court of India, Criminal Appeal No. 913 of 2010. Available online at http://nyayabharat.blogspot.com/2010/04/full-sc-judgment-of-khushboo-case.html

Sharma, Jaya and Nath, Dipika (2005). 'Through the Prism of Intersetionality: Same Sex Sexualities in India', in Geetanjali Misra and Radhika Chandiramani, *Sexuality, Gender and Rights: Exploring Theory and Practice in South and Southeast Asia*, New Delhi: Sage Publications, pp. 82–97.

Website Sources

Baxi, Pratiksha, *Sexual Harassment*, available online at http://www.indiaseminar. com/2001/505/505%20pratiksha%20baxi.htm

In Mysterious Circumstances, April 7, 2010, available online at http://www. outlookindia.com/article.aspx?264986

The Great Divide, April 10-23, 2010, available online at http://www.frontlineonnet. com/fl2708/stories/20100423270811700.htm

A Taliban of our own, 15 August, 2009, available online at http://www.tehelka. com/story_main42.asp?filename=Ne150809a_taliban.asp

Khap Panchayats not above the Constitution: HC, December 12, 2009, available online at http://www.expressindia.com/latest-news/Khap-panchayats-not-above-Constitution-HC/553305/

Khap Panchayats: A sign of desperation? May 7, 2010, available online at http:// beta.thehindu.com/opinion/lead/article424506.ece?homepage=true

Culture Police, March 28-April 10, 2009, available online at http://www.
hinduonnet.com/fline/fl2607/stories/20090410260710600.htm

Shocking Assault on Women in Mangalore Pub, January 26, 2009, available online
at http://news.outlookindia.com/item.aspx?652649

Quilts of Love, 2009, available online at http://www.tehelka.com/story_main42.
asp?filename=hub040709quilts_of.asp

Is love really in the air? available online at http://www.hindu.com/mag/2006/02/19/
stories/2006021900250300.htm

Love and hate, available online at http://www.hinduonnet.com/fline/fl2623/
stories/20091120262302500.htm

Hot news or not news? available online at http://www.indiatogether.org/2010/apr/
rvw-morality.htm

62% of Mumbai's bar girls are sole breadwinners: SNDT survey, available online at
http://infochangeindia.org/200506224437/Livelihoods/News/62-of-Mumbai-s-
bar-girls-are-sole-breadwinners-SNDT-survey.html

Morality check in Mumbai, available online at http://www.hindu.com/fline/fl2209/
stories/20050506001104700.htm

Women's groups express support for bar girls, available online at http://www.hindu.
com/2005/04/17/stories/2005041700611100.htm

Right to dance, available online at http://www.indiatogether.org/2006/jul/soc-
dancebar.htm

A freedom at stake..., available online at http://www.hindu.com/mag/2005/11/27/
stories/2005112700360100.htm

Pre-Marital Sex Not a Statutory Offence: SC, available online at http://news.
outlookindia.com/item.aspx?680626

Kushboo didn't direct remark at any person or group: court, available online at
http://www.hindu.com/2010/04/30/stories/2010043063021500.htm

Gender-based Violence Faced by Hijras in Public Spaces in Urban India

PRITI PRABHUGHATE, ERNEST NORONHA,
ALKA NARANG

Introduction

Transgender individuals in India are variedly called hijras, kinnars, arvanis in different parts of the country. Discourses on gender-based violence seem to largely focus on discussing issues of either men or women or both. There is scant research on gender-based issues with respect to the violence experienced by transgendered individuals—individuals who can neither be classified as 'male' nor as 'female'. This essay is an attempt to understand the violence, both overt, in the form of acts of aggression, as well as structural, in the form of exclusion from public life, as well as to public institutions like education, healthcare, and the discrimination that transgender people face in public spaces in urban India. Our essay draws on available literature and case reviews of hijras, as well as media clippings and anecdotal information available, as very little published literature exists on the issue. Also, most reviews so far have focused on violence faced in urban spaces—it is our contention, however, that attention needs to be paid also to conditions in semi-urban and rural landscapes if we are to generate a more accurate and informed position on violence. Similarly the nature and extent of violence faced by hijras in more private spaces like the family, and within the community has not been explored. Having said that, we do not wish to generalise about hijras, but we would like to use this opportunity to draw attention to issues of transgender individuals in India. Our essay, however, has certain limitations, the discussion presented here is based on issues of female transgenders only (male to female) and does not include issues of male transgenders (female to male). Secondly, though there are multiple identities and gender constructs under the transgender rubric, here we focus only on hijras.

Before we go any further, it is worth explaining some terms used in this essay:

- **Transgender** is an umbrella term for people whose gender identity, expression or behaviour is different from that typically associated with their assigned sex at birth, including but not limited to transsexuals, cross-dressers, and gender non-conforming people. Transgender people may be heterosexual, lesbian, gay or bisexual. The term transgender as it is used in the United States has limited resonance in many other countries. It does not convey many diverse expressions of gender identity or intersecting expressions of sexual desire, intimacy and gender nonconformity—for example, *bisu* and *waria* in Indonesia, *hijra* in India, *katoey* in Thailand, *metis* in Nepal, *zenana* in Pakistan. In many cultures, the terms, "third gender" or "other gender" are frequently preferred to transgender.
- **Transphobia** refers to an irrational fear or hatred of transgender people. These phobias manifest themselves in harassment, prejudicial and negative treatment, violence and other forms of discrimination.
- **Stigma** refers to a state of anxiety with which the stigmatised individual approaches interactions in society. Such an individual "may perceive, usually quite correctly, that whatever others profess, they do not really 'accept' him/her and are not ready to make contact with him/her on 'equal grounds'" (Goffman, 1963, p. 73) Stigma is both a 'trait' and an 'outcome'. As a trait, stigma is an attribute or a characteristic that is viewed negatively by society or culture. As an outcome, stigma occurs when the negative social meanings attached to the discrediting attribute become linked to the individual. This definition applies well to hijras as culturally their gender non-conformity is viewed negatively by people and in turn they get labelled as deviant.
- **Discrimination** refers to behaviours that include some form of

exclusion or rejection of members based on their membership of a particular group, in this case being identified as a hijra.

- **Violence** refers to the intentional use of physical force or power, threatened or actual, against oneself, another person, or against a group or community, that either results in or has a high likelihood of resulting in injury, death, psychological harm, maldevelopment, or deprivation. (World Report on Violence and Health, 2011)
- **Public space** for the purposes of this essay, public spaces are understood as social spaces, venues that are open and accessible to all individuals and groups at any point in time.

Background

As mentioned above, transgender is a general term applied to a variety of individuals, behaviours, and groups who tend to diverge from the normative gender roles. The term "trans-gender" itself is the symbolic representation of crossing boundaries, and it has been derived from two different languages; the Latin word 'trans' and the English word 'gender'. It does not denote any particular form of sexual orientation—indeed transgender people can identify themselves as heterosexual, homosexual, asexual, bisexual and other such identities. In India they are often known as "hijra" and are sometimes also referred to as "kinnar" an ancient term for hijras, which is used by some hijra groups as a more respectable and formal term since the Mahabharata era. There is a preconceived notion that hijras are "neither male nor female," and that the men are usually castrated (a few originally, although rarely, had ambiguous or hermaphroditic sexual organs) by which they are transformed from being disempowered males to being potentially powerful new persons who are attributed with certain ritual powers of blessing others.

Although the Hijra identity and culture had a public acceptance and space in ancient Indian society, colonialism and colonial law changed that by criminalising hijras. The 1897 amendment to the Criminal Tribes Act of 1871, subtitled "An Act for the Registration of Criminal Tribes and Eunuchs" required that a register be kept with the names and residences of all eunuchs who were "reasonably suspected of kidnapping or castrating children or committing offences under Section 377 of the Indian Penal Code". The law also decreed eunuchs as incapable of acting as guardians, making a gift, drawing up a will or adopting a son. This section of the law also criminalises certain kinds of sexual acts as "unnatural", a broad category that included hijra sex (seeing it as 'against the order of nature'). Little has changed in this law since colonial times, and today, our civil law recognises only two genders, which gives the police the right to exercise violence against hijras.

Serena Nanda, Professor Emeritus of Anthropology at John Jay College of Criminal Justice says: "The hijra identity is a complex one, overlapping with the western idea of gender and sex—male and female.... The hijras are also man plus woman, or erotic and sacred female men... The hijra of India poses a challenge to western ideas of sex and gender." (Nanda: 1993) This quote captures the ambiguity and mystery surrounding the hijra identity and transgenderism. It nints at ordinary people's lack of a mental schema to assimilate transgenderism into their worldview and the psychological heuristics employed by them to come to terms with transgenderism. These mental shortcuts range from thinking of hijras as being dangerous, criminals, individuals to be scared of, or thinking of them as inscrutable beings who possess supernatural powers to curse or bless others.

Contrary to the popular notion that hijras are hermaphrodites or people who are born with male and female sex organs, hijras are mostly people who are born with male physiology; adopt feminine gender identity, women's clothing and other feminine gender roles. Hijras may use male, female or gender-neutral pronouns, they insist that hijras, as a group, prefer to be referred to as a female or neither gender. Most hijras dress and lead their lives as women. Hence a hijra essentially moves about as a woman, but is not 'biologically' a female. They seek legitimacy and acceptance as women, but society does not accept them as women, neither does it look at them as men, causing confusion and resentment against them. This enunciation of the hijra way of being may sound very simplistic and unnecessary, but is very fundamental in understanding the place of hijras in the public space. Before examining the intersection of hijras and public spaces, it would be useful to look at what is meant by 'public' space in relation to 'private' space. Phadke (2010) offers some useful insights. She points out that public spaces are a part of a larger construct of the 'public sphere'. According to her "...public sphere includes not only public spaces, but also public institutions, roles, positions which are produced over a period of time transforming the economy polity and in turn getting transformed in significant ways." The interface of hijras with the public sphere as active agents engaging in transforming the economy and polity needs to be examined in detail. One can imagine that such an interface would be difficult, as there is no evident sociopolitical or economic environment that would facilitate such an engagement and foster dialogue. At this level, the violence faced by hijras may not always occur in the form of overt 'physical' violence, but is usually structural violence in the form of exclusion from public institutions, lack of participation in public activities, denial of their rights and discrimination. The absence of the ability and space to engage, benefit and contribute to important institutions in the public sphere, works against establishing the existence of the transgender/hijra identity, like the inability to participate in the mainstream workforce or seek ration cards or other such forms of formal identity markers.

Hijras and Public Spaces

Public spaces that form a part of the public sphere are also understood as spaces that are essentially 'male' and 'female', and have certain privileges associated with them. As articulated by Srivastava (2010) the 'public' often represents 'male' space, while the private represents 'female' space. Similarly 'public space' is seen as a domain of action, rationality, a realm where important matters of social life can be discussed, conversely the private is perceived as 'feminine', the soft sphere where other kinds of sensibilities come into play. Such a positioning reinforces male control and women's restricted access to public spaces. Thus the privilege of being seen in the public and the freedom to move about, and to access resources is the domain of men and not of women.

Before getting into a discussion on public spaces and the challenges they pose to hijras, it is important to understand that even if hijras give up their 'male' privilege, being born into and having experienced a social male identity, (albeit mostly coloured with stigma for being a non-confirming male) one can imagine that hijras, as compared to individuals born into a female identity, would have already experienced the privilege of public spaces as men, and therefore are more likely to be less afraid or inhibited in their access to open public spaces, for example traveling alone at night. It is important to keep this in mind while discussing the interface of hijras with public space. A counterpoint along the same lines is reflected in the tension that exists between feminists and hijras. Many feminists do not agree with the hijra self definition as victims. Instead, they argue that hijras use their identity expediently, conveniently accessing the male identity when they want, (as when they threaten women aggressively in public trains to get money) and similarly deploying the female identity when it suits them. Moreover it is also argued that the space for free expression has been a very hard won one, especially for lesbian women, and yet they have to constantly compete with hijras, to claim their space.

With the above caveat, our essay examines the division of public spaces and the gendered meanings associated with such a division. In the sections that follow we draw attention to the challenges faced by hijras, individuals who often give up their male privilege of access to the public sphere and public spaces by giving up their 'maleness', often irreversible by emasculation, but do not get their rightful place even in the private space of family, something that is often enjoyed by other women. Furthermore their non-conformity to either of the sexes, makes them more vulnerable to violence in public spaces as well as private spaces. Thus they face violence in different kinds of public spaces such as educational and health care institutions, public transportation and so on.

Anecdotal evidence suggests that public institutions do not assimilate hijras within them. Many transgenders report that they face discrimination and harassment in the educational institutions and are often forced to discontinue their studies. Similarly office situations also are noted to be discriminatory towards hijras, so much so that hijras do not easily get employment, whether in the corporate sector or elsewhere, and those rare individuals who do manage to get employment are often forced to wear male attire, and feel isolated at work thus creating conditions for them to quit. Most educational institutions and workplaces do not have anti-discrimination policies. With the exception of a few hijras who are successful, most are often reduced to sex work and begging.

Another institution under the domain of public sphere where hijras have been known to face violence is in health care. The desire to transform into a woman and possess a female body, often makes hijras seek health services for undergoing sex reassignment surgery (SRS). Many hijras also opt for castration as it is a sure way of gaining acceptance in the community and living permanently in hijra gharanas, or havelis with their gurus,* and of getting closer to possessing a female body. For hijras, castration symbolises permanent and irreversible transformation into femaleness. The demand for SRS is one of the most important entry points for hijras into the health service sector although there is considerable ambiguity around the 'legal' status of castration. Typically, if done correctly, SRS is conducted following pre and post operative counselling, and hormonal therapy under medical supervision. However, most places do not offer this psychological support. In the few places where counselling is offered , the pre surgical advice provided is designed in such a way that it does not help hijras to explore the various options available to them, but instead counsels them against undergoing a sex change operation!

In most developed countries, if hijras are assessed and diagnosed to have Gender Identity Disorder (GID), then psychiatrists help them in getting the necessary surgical and endocrinological interventions from qualified medical practitioners. 'India-specific' and 'hijra-relevant' diagnostic and treatment guidelines for GID need to be developed for this purpose. A significant event in the life of a hijra—such as SRS—often goes unsupported by the medical settings like hospitals and doctors who yet do not have clear, universal guidelines for conducting an SRS. Furthermore India's legal stance on SRS is unclear.

Easy access to traditional means of castration by traditional doctors or older community members makes some transgenders undergo emasculation by traditional means. Such procedures have been known to result in grievous injuries. Some castrations are also carried out by qualified doctors illegally but even here hijras are treated badly. A newspaper report from Tamil Nadu described the plight of a hijra who was operated on by a doctor in unhygienic conditions and she bled for 20 days after the surgery, being forced eventually to seek help from her biological family in Bangalore. This hijra reported that she faced discrimination and ill treatment from both her family and doctors in Bangalore who refused to treat her.

Another significant point of entry into the formal health care system for hijras is seeking treatment for HIV and Sexually Transmitted Infections (STIs). Current estimates suggest that the prevalence of HIV among transgenders is high, essentially meaning that a sizeable number of transgender individuals are likely to be infected by HIV. Such high rates of infection reflect how vulnerable hijras are and the hazards they are faced with due to sex work and poor access to other survival alternatives. In addition, they are stigmatised as being carriers of HIV both in the 'outside' world and within their community. Thus HIV is a major health concern for them. So it is that when confronted with a health set up transgendered individuals encounter transphobia from doctors who avoid rectal examinations, even if a hijra complains of rectal pain, bleeding or warts. Moreover doctors are reported to be uncomfortable discussing their sexual histories with transgendered individuals, and therefore are unable to do complete justice to their treatment.

Hijras also face discrimination from health personnel because of their association with sex work. A study of aravanis or hijras in sex work noted that they face discrimination in the Indian health care system in various ways: for example in hospitals where they are admitted into male wards, are addressed by using the male pronoun and are made to wait in male queues. Indeed, within the medical set up there is considerable confusion about whether to admit hijra patients in the male ward or the female ward, and this sometimes results in humiliation and at other times delays in getting treatment. Some hijras have revealed that because hospital staff do not know where to place them, they have been made to sleep on the floor, often next to toilets. When admitted into male wards, they sometimes face harassment and humiliation at the hands of other male patients.

Health care is only one area. Perhaps the most 'visible' place for hijras is public transportation, which they use in multiple ways. For example, public transportation provides an avenue for hijras to cruise and solicit clients for sex work, as well as to beg, and trains and buses are also used for personal commutes. A PUCL(K) report entitled 'Human Rights Violations Against the Transgender Community' documents the kind of prejudice that hijras face in Bangalore. It shows that prejudice against transgender people often translates into violence, which can be brutal and can take place in in public spaces, police stations, prisons and even in their homes. The main factor behind the violence is that society is not able to come to terms with the fact that hijras do not conform to the accepted gender divisions. In addition to this, most hijras have a lower middle-class background, which makes them susceptible to harassment by the police. The discrimination based on their class and gender thus makes the hijra community one of the most disempowered groups in Indian society. Another glaring example of violence in public transportation was brought to light in the *Indian Express* story about the ordeal faced by two hijras for travelling without a ticket in the ladies compartment of a Mumbam train. The two were beaten, stripped naked and eventually thrown into a prison for their 'crime' of ticketless travel. The violence faced by the two transgenders continued even in prison where they were not given clothes and were molested and stripped by police constables who claimed they wanted to determine whether the two were indeed eunuchs. It is paradoxical that hijras face harassment by policemen for indulging in 'unnatural sex', but they are often subjected to the same so-called 'unnatural sex' by the police. The example also highlights how probably social class and gender put hijras in a more vulnerable position.

In *The Third Sex and Human Rights* Rajesh Talwar (1999) highlights human rights abuses and legal problems faced by the third sex in India. He details the legal position regarding emasculation, marriage, adoption, petitions challenging the criminalisation of homosexuality as well as international human rights law and treaties that have a bearing on their status. He also shows how the media mirror and perpetrate a different kind of violence on hijras, placing them right at the bottom of the social hierarchy, effectively turning them into citizens without rights. Hijras are not even recognised as being disadvantaged and therefore unlike certain other categories—such as lower caste people—who are recognised as socially disadvantaged, hijras do not have access to any social protection in the form of reservations in employment and education.

As the Indian law recognises only two sexes, the authors point out that although transgenders now have electoral rights, enjoying full civil and legal rights is still a far cry for them. This means transgender people do not have the right to marry, and do not have access to a ration card, passport, a driving license, objects that give one an official identity. If a hijra's rights are violated or he or she faces harassment, it is virtually impossible for them to fight for justice or to claim their rights. The case of Kokila—detailed below—and the events that followed in her life illustrate many of the points made above.

Box 1   Case Study: Kokila

Kokila, a 21 year old hijra has been living in Bangalore for the last five years. She survives by doing sex-work, the only option available to most hijras. On 18 June, 2004 (Friday), around 8 p.m., while Kokila was waiting for clients, she was raped by ten men who forcefully took her to the grounds next to Old Madras Road. They threatened to kill her if she refused sex with them. She was forced to have oral and anal sex with all of them. While she was being sexually assaulted, two policemen arrived. Most of the men ran away from the scene but two were caught by the policemen. Kokila told the policemen about the sexual assault. Instead of registering a case and sending Kokila for medical examination, the policemen abused her, using filthy language and took her along with the two captured men to the Byappanahalli Police station. They didn't even allow Kokila to pick up her trousers from the ground and she was forced to be naked for the next seven hours.

In the police station Kokila was subjected to brutal torture. She was taken to a room inside the police station, stripped naked, her hands cuffed to a window. There were six policemen in the room, every single one of them was under the influence of alcohol. Many of them hit her with lathis and their hands, and kicked her with their boots. They abused her, using sexually violent language. The verbal abuses include: *ninna ammane keyya* (we will fuck your mother), *ninna akkane keyya* (we will fuck your sister), *khoja* (derogatory word used against transgenders) and *gandu* (one who gets penetrated anally, a derogatory word). She was assaulted brutally by policemen and suffered severe injuries on her hands, palms, buttocks, shoulder and legs. They also tortured her sexually by burning her nipples and *chapdi* (vaginal portion of hijras) with a burning coir rope. One policeman of the rank of SI (Sub Inspector of Police) positioned his rifle on her chapdi and threatened to shoot her. He also tried push the rifle butt and lathi into the chapdi and saying, "Do you have a vagina, can this go inside?" while other policemen were laughing. This is to humiliate a transsexual woman by insisting that she is not a woman as she was not born with a vagina. At around 11 p.m. the PI (Inspector of Police, the highest ranking police official of that police station) came into the room. He directed the policemen to continue the torture and they did so till 1 a.m. in the night. Despite begging for water she was not given any. The police tied her up and the Inspector of Police threatened to leave her on the railway track unless she confessed to the knowledge of the robbery of a diamond ring and a bracelet. They paid no attention to her pleading that she had no knowledge of the robbery, or the person they were trying to implicate in the robbery.

At 1 a.m., four policemen (including the PI and SI) dragged Kokila into a police jeep and took her to a hamam (bathhouse) run by hijras in the Krishnarajapuram area. They physically abused her and forced her to knock on the hamam door and call the hijras living there to open the door. At around 2 a.m., they took her to another hamam in the Garudacharapalya area. They broke open the lock of that hamam. They forced her to wear male clothes (shirt and trousers). They tied a towel to her head and threatened to shave off her hair. Police also searched both the hamams illegally.

At around 3 a.m., while on the way, Kokila begged the police to take her to the house of Chandini (a hijra human rights activist) who lived nearby. The police entered Chandini's house forcefully and searched the entire house despite severe protests by Chandini. Chandini told the policemen that they could not enter her house at night and without any valid reason and her consent. When she protested, the police threatened her and her husband with dire consequences. Finally, on Chandani's demand that Kokila be left behind, and her assurance that she would bring Kokila to the Police Station in the morning if her presence was required, the police left her residence at 3.30 am.

Kokila's complaint was registered in Ulsoor police station on 19 June 2004. The complaint was registered only after legal intervention and after putting pressure on various high-ranking police officials of Bangalore city for three hours. The IPC (Indian Penal Code) Sections in the FIR (First Information Report) are 506 (criminal intimidation—threat to cause death or grievous hurt), 377 (unnatural sexual intercourse), 504 (intentional insult with intent to provoke breach of peace), 324 (voluntarily causing hurt by dangerous weapons or means) and 34 (acts done by several persons in furtherance of common intention). Kokila has already identified four policemen who tortured her. She has also identified five goondas, who sexually assaulted her. These are not stray incidents but are part of ongoing police violence against hijras. The level of violence has increased after hijras, other sexual minorities and sex-workers started protesting against police brutality.

Similarly, Human Rights Watch cites a number of newspaper reports that confirm how hijras are targeted for violence and hate crimes.

On November 10, 2008, after several national newspapers reported that the Bangalore police had captured a "gang" of hijras who kidnapped children, castrated them and forced them into sex work, the city police forced about 100 hijras from their homes, suggesting a spreading pattern of prejudice-driven violence and abuse in the city. Police used these stories to justify the mass evictions of hijras from their homes.

These reports about hijras kidnapping children = a common myth in many parts of India—came amidst an apparent campaign by Bangalore authorities against hijras in the city where Bangalore's Deputy Commissioner of Police called for a "drive against the city's eunuch menace." Five hijras were arrested and charged with "extortion," and were beaten and sexually abused in the process. Police also arrested 41 human rights defenders—including hijras, dalits, women's rights and sex worker activists, and trade union activists—who came to their defense. When challenged on their unconstitutional actions, the police told some of the activists that they had orders from higher ups to round up hijras in Bangalore. The chain of incidents that followed after this particular instance demonstrates the exchange between the hijra community, (see Box 2) the landlords and the police and details the violence that results from structural discrimination coupled with anti-hijra prejudice. The example speaks volumes about the disempowerment of the hijra community and their lack of voice to fight for their rights and protect themselves.

Box 2   Police Violence

On November 8 and 9, five major newspapers in India, including two national dailies, carried news items about Bangalore police breaking up a "gang" of hijras. The gang allegedly kidnapped children, performed "sex change" operations on them, and forced them to become sex workers. The reports also claimed that the accused hijras were associated with Sangama, a Bangalore-based organisation that works to defend the rights of sexual minorities.

Immediately after these reports appeared, on November 9, the police inspector of Amrutahalli police station in Bangalore issued a notice to about 40 homeowners in the Dasarahalli neighbourhood - known for having a substantial hijra population—requiring them to evict all hijras who rented apartments or rooms from them. More than 100 hijras rented rooms there, and most found themselves on the streets. Several lost their security deposits, and some lost all their belongings. One hijra told newspapers and local activists that she could not even find an autorickshaw driver who was wiling to give her a ride because hijras had been labelled kidnappers.

Police claimed the hijras conducted "immoral activities" in their houses, and the eviction notice was, according to newspaper reports, also accompanied by verbal threats to the homeowners. Some of the homeowners told newspapers that they had never had trouble with their hijra tenants, but they were afraid to disobey the arbitrary command.

Evicted hijras told newspapers and local sexual rights activists that the police accusations that they engaged in "immoral activities" were unfounded, and that the kidnapping case brought against two hijras was being used as a pretext for the mass evictions. Police deny responsibility for the evictions, claiming the homeowners evicted their hijra tenants because of the charges of kidnapping in the media. However, *The Hindu*, a leading national daily, reported that it had a copy of the notice the police personally served to the homeowners.

Another segment within the transgendered identities is the lesser known and documented community of laundas or dancing boys, who traditionally perform at marriages. This community faces violence/exploitation due to their unique circumstances and are pushed into sex work and often are subject to sexual violence (see box 3)

Box 3   The Case of Launda Dancers

In India adolescents and young gender variant boys, male with a feminine 'demeanour'—that is effeminate males/males with feminine gender construction—are victims of social stigma and gross human rights violations, and as a result face serious barriers to joining mainstream occupations. This has led to a situation where, in the absence of any other alternative, many join the "hijra" (eunuch) community and undergo illegal, secret and crude castration operations at great risk to their lives. Anecdotal evidence puts the number of deaths due to castration at 50 per cent of those operated upon by dais, quacks and "surgeons" with questionable credentials. As an alternative they join the troop as launda dancers—the traditional dancing boys—and migrate to Bihar and Uttar Pradesh and in the name of dancing at ritual ceremonies, are forced into prostitution and face brutal violence.

The laundas of Bihar and UP define and spice up the entertainment barometer at marriages in the Hindi heartland. But deep within they nurse broken hearts and bruised bodies. They are the young torch bearers of an age-old popular tradition—upholders of the launda naach, an integral part of weddings in northern India, especially Bihar and Uttar Pradesh, where weddings are elaborate affairs with a fair rustic dose of merrymaking, drinking, music and dance. Here young effeminate boys dance in marriage processions and ceremonies, dressed in women's clothing.

Laundas used to be hired by poor families that could not afford more expensive women dancers. Gradually launda naach became very popular and an intrinsic part of marriage ceremonies especially in feudal areas of Bihar and UP. The dancers mainly belong to the lower middle class and poor families from West Bengal, Bihar, Uttar Pradesh and Maharashtra and also from Nepal and Bangladesh via West Bengal. They come to

Bihar and Uttar Pradesh during the peak marriage season between April and June in summer and December to February in winter.

Orchestra companies hire launda dancers on a lump sum contract, in addition to free food and lodging. But they give the dancers only a fraction of the amount they mint through them. The other mode of payment is through cash given at the end of each session. A performer could earn Rs 6000 to 12000 on a three-month contract depending on the dancer's looks, grace and dancing abilities. But the dancers point out they often gets less than their contractual fee, and sometimes nothing at all.

The groom's family usually hires the dancers. They have to dance all the way to the girl's family along with the baraat (groom's entourage). In rural areas this journey could stretch across several miles and span numerous villages. After going to the bride's house, they get to rest briefly during dinner, after which begins the climax item through the 'lagan' (marriage) ceremony.

The ceremony may start late in the evening and continue non-stop until dawn. Even if the boys feel tired they cannot stop as they are physically prodded to carry on, with pinpricks on the body. At times drinking water is also refused. As the night progresses the songs become risqué, and are complemented by vulgar and obscene body movements. By this time drunken men at the wedding party hurl abuse at the dancers. The dancers now become vulnerable to physical and sexual assaults. Often their backs are slashed with blades as they dance, particularly because they wear backless cholis. They're also bitten and sometimes cigarette stubs are ground into their bodies.

A group of 10 to 15 men can also physically carry a dancer to a field and gang rape him, this is not uncommon. The dancers often have to face torture. Resistance only leads to greater torture and sometimes even death. Most of them are semi-literate and come from poor backgrounds, some are educated and prefer to dance rather than become the butt of ridicule at their workplace. Within South Asia, male sex workers operating at public sites are primarily koti-identified, but not exclusively so. Most are from low-income groups where poverty and support for their families drive much of their sex work. In other words, there are several frameworks of male sex work. But the common part of all of them is violence.

Men are attracted to launda dancing also because of the money and because it gives them the freedom to express their womanly instincts away from the jibes of relatives and neighbours. In spite of the risk involved, very few actually want to quit their seasonal profession because there are no alternatives.

Launda dancers are often treated as objects of lust. They generally live in deplorable conditions, being relegated to outhouses and thatched shacks which are shared with goats and cows. The food they eat is lacking in nutrition, sanitation in their living places is non existent.

Also awareness about Sexually Transmitted Diseases, HIV and AIDS and safe sex is virtually non-existent among the dancers and those who abuse them. Nobody uses condoms, No awareness, no availability and no negotiation. Many myths survive and people love to believe that having sex with virgin children will cure them of STD's and augment their sexual virility. In parts of rural Bihar and UP men satisfy their wild sexual urges with these effeminate young men because they are available, and sex with them is more or less socially sanctioned like prostitution, and proves the man's mardangi or maleness. It is a matter of great prestige in the feudal set up to keep laundas in the house and is treated as a sign of virility and power.

After the season these boys are divided into groups. New boys or less experienced boys are sent back home but others may stay back or travel to other part of the country and join local seasonal celebrations.

Often live-in laundas end up becoming unpaid slaves, doing menial household chores, including looking after their man's children. Thus he not only becomes his owner's sex slave but also has to entertain his friends. However after some years of providing constant physical gratification and sexual services when they fall prey to some sexually transmitted disease, they are cast away. The findings also show that many misconceptions about the migration of adolescents and young boys for sexual exploitation remain and are firmly rooted in the continuing view that it is an issue related solely to homosexuality and child sex tourism. On the other hand they also underscore the overall vulnerability of all children, boys and girls, who are targeted by adults who seek to exploit them as sexual objects and demonstrate that those committing such crimes are largely individuals from the local heterosexual population and not solely homosexual men or tourists. While it is difficult to quantify the magnitude of the problem due to the lack of reporting or misreporting of cases, the studies nevertheless suggest that it is much bigger problem than previously recognised and that exploiters are local men and in some cases local women.

Through the anecdotes and reports presented here, our essay attempts to showcase some of the many issues that confront hijras and the multi-layered violence and discrimination faced by them in public spaces and institutions such as educational institutions, health systems, and law enforcement agencies like the police. Our essay articulates the daunting task hijras face while negotiating and claiming their place in 'public' spaces.

While the political organisation of hijras has been exemplary in certain instances as in Tamil Nadu, and hijras now have some recognition inasmuch as they can now get a passport, in some instances also a ration card, these can be seen as small victories that need to be scaled up. The paradox of the hijra existence is, as we have shown above, that while hijras/transgender individuals are probably one of the most visible communities in the public space, yet they remain largely invisible in the discourse on gender and rights. This is evident in the absence of engagement and participation of transgendered individuals in law, human rights, education, health and socioeconomic policies.

Conclusion

When people are deprived of respect because of their sexual orientation, gender identity and expression, they are much more vulnerable to human rights violations and the possibility of redress and remedial action is also reduced. Being faced with stigma, discrimination and violence at multiple levels is detrimental to the well-being of any human being and impairs their quality of life. Hijras and transgenders are also less likely to report the violence they face because of fear of state reprisal and penalties, or because they are concerned about being rejected by their families and communities. In this kind of environment, reporting human rights violations becomes too dangerous, and complaint mechanisms either do not exist or do not apply.

Even if a complaint is filed, investigation may be unlikely and violators are not held accountable—in fact they have immunity. Consequently, the victim's experience of the initial violation is compounded by the state's failure to respond or care.

There is an urgent need to develop and promote strategies to reduce the multiple stigma faced by hijras. Policy changes must be enacted to facilitate the protection of hijra rights and facilitate the uptake of services (social, legal, health, economic etc). Below we give some recommendations that can help to put positive steps in place (some of these are adapted from the Transgender recommendations for the approach paper for the 12th five year plan, UNDP (2010)).

Legal and Social Justice Reforms

Demonstrate progressiveness: A progressive revision of laws is an important step to eradicate the social prejudices against transgender persons. The International Bill of Gender Rights adopted by the International Conference on Transgender Law and Employment Policy in Texas, United States, in 1995 provides an ideal course to follow while considering legal reforms. It lays down that all human beings have the right to define their own gender identity; express their gender identity; secure and retain employment and receive just compensation; control and change one's own body; enjoy competent medical and professional care; sexual expression; form committed, loving relationships and enter into marital contracts; and conceive, bear and adopt children and exercise parental capacity. The Yogyakarta Principles—a set of international legal principles on the application of international law to human rights violations on the basis of sexual orientation and gender identity—also bring greater clarity and coherence to the human rights obligations of states. The principles were drafted by a distinguished group of international human rights experts at a meeting held in Yogyakarta, Indonesia, in 2006. These principles recognise that sexual orientation and gender identity are integral to every person's dignity and humanity and must not be the basis for discrimination or abuse. They also view critically the policing of sexuality, which remains a potent force behind continuing gender-based violence and gender inequality.

Legal recognition: This implies legal recognition of being the other gender following a sex reassignment surgery. Transgenders undergo SRS to live their lives as women. Hence it is an identity that clearly matters to them. There needs to be a recognition of the change in the gender status that needs also to be reflected in the current procedures that issue identity documents to hijras/TGs—as they are connected to basic civil entitlements such as access to health and public services, right to vote, right to contest elections, right to education, inheritance rights, and marriage and child adoption. For example before they undergo SRS transgender people possess male passports and school certificates in their male names. They need to change these to their female names once an SRS is performed.

Enumerate TGs in the census: There has been no enumeration of the transgender population in India and this means there is a gap in data on their socio-economic status. The 2010 census could have provided an opportunity to enumerate this section of the population. It is recommended that a plan of action be prepared with community groups and national development partners to map the transgender/hijra population across India. This can be of great help in designing any kind of legal, social and economic interventions.

Extend social protection policies: There is a need to extend available social protection policies to hijras. For example the Adhaar scheme can be extended to include hijras. This will give hijras civic identity and will ensure that they are a part of future programmes and thus would strengthen equity. Apart from providing identity, the Aadhaar unique identification number will enable better delivery of services and effective governance.

Initiate action against human rights abuse of TGs: We have shown above how hijras and the transgender population are often particularly vulnerable to forms of violence perpetrated by law-enforcing agencies such as the police. There are also extensive reports of physical and psychological molestation of 'effeminate' males in academic institutions and workplaces. It is important that direct law enforcement and judicial authorities (including police) set up special cells to look into human rights abuses (also dealing with incarcerated transgenders and hijras) and through the Ministry of Law look at broadening the inclusion criteria of existing legal redressal mechanisms like that of free legal aid by NALSA and its decentralised units, and lok adalats and similar systems of non- formal systems of justice.

Training law enforcement agencies: There is an urgent need to work with law enforcement agencies like the police to ensure that they safeguard and not harm the interests of hijras. This can be achieved by training police personnel and ensuring that perpetrators of abuse and human rights violations are held accountable. Similarly, the police need to be educated about Section 377 and its application to the transgender community.

Health Systems and Health Care Reform

Clarify the legal status of SRS: As highlighted above, India does not have clarity on the legal status of SRS. Despite this many transgendered individuals who seek SRS services. In the absence of a legal status of SRS, there are no standards set for conducting surgeries, thus increasing the vulnerability of transgendered individuals and setting their lives at risk. It is therefore recommended that SRS needs to be legalised, so that transgendered individuals can access services in public hospitals.

Standards of care to perform SRS: There need to be standards of care for performing SRS in the country to ensure correct, informed and ethical medical practices. Such standards should also incorporate compulsory training of medical personnel involved in SRS and HIV care of transgendered individuals.

Improved sentinel surveillance to capture HIV prevalence: The national HIV/ AIDS programme NACO to date does not have data on the prevalence of HIV among transgenders. It is recommended that NACO increases the number of sentinel surveillance sites for transgenders, thus gaining better and robust data and a more accurate picture on prevalence of HIV.

Sensitise health care providers on issues of the transgender community and provide them with the current state of research and training to make them competent in areas of sexual history taking, physical examinations and overcoming prejudices about this community. Broaden the medical curricula to include syllabi on sex, sexuality and gender to train health care providers on these.

Education, Employment Reforms

Our research shows that transgenders are excluded from educational intuitions and mainstream employment. It is recommended that anti discriminatory policies should be made at educational institutions and employment agencies. We suggest that transgendered individuals have reservation in educational institutes and workplaces. It is also recommended that schools of social work, psychology, sociology and humanities broaden their syllabi to include discourses of sex, sexuality and gender.

Evaluate, Replicate and Reapply

The state of Tamil Nadu is the only state that over years of successful activism and advocacy with the government has achieved the establishment of the Aravani Welfare Board and has brought about policy changes which have enabled transgenders to access better health and human rights (see Box 4). It is recommended that the Tamil Nadu success story to be studied and if necessary modified and replicated in all states across India.

Box 4   Tamil Nadu Aravanigal (Transgender Women) Welfare Board

**Tamil Nadu Aravanigal (Transgender Women) Welfare Board:
A Landmark Initiative**

The Aravanigal (Transgender) Welfare Board is a state government agency set up for the welfare of aravanis in Tamil Nadu. One of its kind in India, the Board is a result of a unique blend of community and government action. A blend so fine, its components enmeshed so closely together, that enquiries with three different respondents revealed three different stories about the genesis of the Board. Each of these might well have been integral to the formation of the board, which is what makes it a blend.

Asha Bharathi, former director of ThAA (Thamil Nadu Aravanigal

Association), spearheaded a massive rally of aravanis in Chennai in 2006. Four organisations took the primary responsibility of organising this rally: THAA (Chennai), SWAM (Chennai), Sudar foundation (Kanchipuram) and Snegyitham (Tiruchy). A few delegates met the Minister of Social Welfare and submitted a memorandum. Asha Bharathi (ThAA) and Shekar (SWAM) say that the event and the memorandum had the effect of hastening the processes of implementation of welfare schemes. Though the Government Orders since 2003 had been discussing aravanis welfare, this public demonstration and the visibility it received had a huge effect in catalysing the decision to put such schemes in place. Kannadi Kalai Kuzhu (Mirror Cultural Troupe) of Sudar Foundation, the only all-aravanis theatre group in the country produced two plays, 'Manasin Azhaippu (The Call of the Heart)' and 'Uraiyada Ninaivugal (Frozen Memories)' which portray various aspects of the lives of aravanis. They were produced with support from Voicing Silence, a project of the M. S. Swaminathan Research Foundation. Through its performances, the theatre group is said to have raised public awareness about aravanis. Ms. Ramathal, Chairperson of State Women's Commission, organised a 'public hearing' in 2007. Leaders, bureaucrats and opinion makers were invited to hear aravanis speak of the violence and injustice they faced. This was believed to be the most immediate factor that led to the setting up of the Board in 2008.

As a first step, the board has conducted an enumeration of the transgender population in all 32 districts of Tamil Nadu and in some places identity cards—with the gender identity mentioned as "aravani"—are being issued. The government has also started issuing ration cards (for buying food and other items from government-run fair-price shops) for transgender people. In addition, the Tamil Nadu government issued a government order in May 2008 to enrol transgender people in government educational institutions and to explicitly include the 'other' or 'third gender' category in their admission forms. Furthermore, it is only in the state of Tamil Nadu that, in collaboration with the Tamil Nadu Aravanigal Welfare Board, free sex reassignment surgery can be performed for hijras/transgenders in select government hospitals

Limitations

In this essay we have been able to deal only with the violence faced by hijras in urban spaces. However, research needs to be conducted on the situation of hijras in semi-urban and rural areas in India. Secondly, a large amount of literature is silent on the question of Female to Male (F2M) transgender people. Given the extent of violence and discrimination M2F transgenders face, it is necessary to undertake a study on violence faced by F2M transgenders too.

Furthermore, though we have some data on violence in public spaces by way of media coverage, issues faced by hijras in private spaces, namely within their biological families as well as violence within their families of choice (hijra gharana/jamaat) needs to be documented. It is therefore recommended that a larger report be undertaken to document the gender-based violence experienced by transgenders and the hijra community, to look into the issues of feminised males and the less talked about issue of intra-community violence.

Similarly there is a need to build better empirical evidence on instances of gender-based violence, stigma and discrimination and its linkages with health and the quality of life. Such evidence is needed to further strengthen programmes and current advocacy efforts, as well as inform service delivery.

References

Goffman, E. (1963). *Stigma: Notes on the management of spoiled identity.* New York: Touchstone.

World Health Organization (WHO) (2011) *World health report on violence and health* http://www.who.int/violevceprevention/approach/definition/en/index.html on January 13,2011)

Nanda, S. (1993) 'Hijras an alternative sex and gender role in India ' in Herdt, G. (ed.) *Third Sex, Third Gender: Beyond Sexual Dimorphism in Culture and History*, pp. 373–419. Zone Books: New York.

Phadke, S. (2010) 'Gendered Usage of Public Spaces' , Paper presented at NCW-CEQUIN-UNDP conference on Gender-based Based Violence in Public Spaces: Challenges and Solutions, 26–27 October, New Delhi.

Srivastava, S. (2010) 'Masculinity -its Role in GBV in Public Spaces', Paper presented at NCW-CEQUIN-UNDP conference on Gender-based Violence in Public Spaces: Challenges and Solutions, 26–27 October, New Delhi.

UNDP (2010). *Transgender Recommendations for the Approach paper for the 12th Five Year Plan*, UNDP: New Delhi.

Redeeming 'Honour' through Violence
Unravelling the Concept and its Application

PREM CHOWDHRY

The regional and national dailies are currently full of reports of 'honour killings'.[1] In fact, this crime has emerged as an important media news item and although problematic in its coverage, it has helped to draw attention to the shocking violation of constitutional and human rights. The growing recent interest can be traced back to a May 2010 case: Manoj and Babli, a young couple from Haryana, were killed on the orders of a *khap* panchayat for marrying despite belonging to the same *gotra* or *got* (patrineal clan). In a historic judgment, the additional sessions judge in Karnal district awarded the death sentence to the five accused and a life term to the sixth. This legal setback and media coverage resulted in a united demand from the *khap*s of Haryana, Punjab and Rajasthan that their caste customs be legalised or the relevant law regarding marriages be amended to bar intra-*got* marriage by declaring them illegal. This sensational case has meant that virtually every day now there is a press release about the so-called 'honour killings' from different parts of India, cutting across regions, caste, class and rural-urban divides. In response to this, social activists from Haryana and elsewhere have greatly accelerated their efforts at raising public awareness about the issue through public interest litigations (PILs) and other means. The rise in the number of cases, as well as in the number of couples seeking protection, fearing for their lives once they decide to marry or have already married,[2] and the efforts and intervention of activists has led the Supreme Court to step in and send notice to the Union of India and the ministries of Home Affairs and

Women and Child Development to explain what steps they have taken to prevent violence committed in the name of 'honour'.[3]

Indeed, recent research has made it amply clear that crimes committed to uphold honour are fairly widely spread not only across India but also in the entire Asian subcontinent.[4] The Asian immigrant communities from India, Pakistan, Bangladesh and East Africa, located in the West (especially in the USA, UK and Canada), cutting across faith, age, caste, class and racial groups, similarly show crimes committed to maintain the 'honour and prestige' of the family and community. India may lack the statistical evidence and even publicly deny the existence of such crimes in international fora,[5] but their existence cannot be wished away. It is a hard reality.

The analysis that follows is based upon my extensive fieldwork research in Haryana during 1999–2002,[6] and lays special emphasis on the operation of the concept of honour, the role of the caste/*khap* panchayats in regulating 'honour' and in supporting/advocating violence to enforce it. Although this essay draws its major insights from Haryana, my conclusions have resonances for other regions as well and the broad conceptual arguments may be useful in understanding the gender related manifestations of the issue elsewhere and in other situations.

I propose to tackle this theme in five sections: In the first section I shall very briefly analyse one of the cases to illustrate the working of the concept of honour in relation to intra-caste marriages which are currently in the news, as also its dealing by the caste panchayats. The second section will deal with the inter-caste marriages or elopements which are equally inflammatory and violent and have a wider social and regional reach; they cut across the rural and urban divide and include some of the most prominent cases of all times. The third section will go into the ideology and cultural aspect of the concept of honour and how its ideological reach determines its wider application in other public crimes related to women; it also grounds the ideological and cultural aspect in the contemporary material realities. Indeed, the changing political economy of post-colonial India and legal rights granted to women have led to the strengthening of the concept of honour, generating newer anxieties emanating from reasons other than the upkeep of culture and tradition, though these are certainly played through the desire and need to uphold these aspects. The fourth section seeks to understand the reasons behind the increase in the breaches occurring in the customary marriage norms and consequent violence; it analyses the changing socio-political milieu and the shifting caste-clan configuration generating fresh apprehensions regarding marriage in a highly restricted marriage market. The last section deals with the caste/community collectives as the main regulatory authorities of caste and customary norms; the motivations behind their dictatorial and violent assertion and their inability to come to terms with the modern day requirements of law and human rights as well as a greatly changed society; it also makes a brief comment on the possible ways to salvage the situation specially in relation to the violence inflicted by this collective.

Cases relating to honour and honour killings are, not infrequently, runaway marriages and elopements that infringe cultural norms and customary practices. Briefly and simply stated, the customary rules regulating marriages in most parts of India, especially northern India, are based upon caste endogamy, on the one hand, and clan, village or territorial exogamy on the other; neither is a legally recognised category for marriage purposes. The introduction of the modern concept of adulthood and the sanctity given to individual rights gives legal recognition to the individual settlement of marriage between two consenting heterosexual adults. Under the Hindu Marriage Act, 1955, except for certain prohibited degrees of relationship, the legal restrictions on marriage are almost non-existent.[7] This implies that under the law, both *sagotra* (kin in the patrilineal line of descent whose members claim descent from the same *gotra* ancestor) and inter-caste marriages are permitted among 'Hindus' (broadly defined as Hindus, Jains, Sikhs or Buddhists, by birth, upbringing or conversion), notwithstanding any text, rule or interpretation of the Hindu law or any customary usage.

In other words, under the law, there is freedom to marry who you like but not under the customary law. Any breach of the customary law and practices leads to direct violence perpetrated by the male family members on the couple generally and on the woman especially. Perceived as common occurrences these have shown a tendency to escalate over the years.

Decisively regarded as matters of 'honour'—family or private—they remain highly hushed up and confidential affairs, till they spill over into the public domain to be dealt with at the level of the community or by the state.

SECTION I

Intra-caste Marriages

Customarily, there are a number of rules and practices and degrees of prohibited relationships observed in respect to marriage in different regions of India. This is specially marked in the north/south divide.[8] Customary marriage rules in most parts of north India uphold caste endogamy and adopt the rule of *gotra* or *got* exogamy. Most castes groups, upper or lower, follow three or four *got* exogamy. A person is not permitted to marry into his or her own *got*, nor with the mother's, nor with the father's mother, nor usually with the mother's mother. The last bar is, however, not universal and the restriction is apparently declining. In effect, the *got* rules prohibit marriage with the first cousins of either the parallel or the cross variety. In certain instances, the principle of *got* exogamy is enlarged by clustering several other *got*s represented in the same village into an exogamous bloc. Marriage between these *got*s is prohibited or restricted.

In extension of the principle of 'kinship exogamy', there is a rule of territorial exogamy. Most caste groups, such as the Jats, expressly forbid marriage within the same village, and every village which shares a border with the natal village, or in which other clans of one's village are well represented. The combined effects of these rules of exogamy is that, apart from the three or four *got* exogamy mentioned above, a large number of *got*s have to be kept outside the purview of marriage. The inhabitants of a particular village cannot inter-marry in a large number of villages, especially adjacent villages or those that fall in the *khap* area (the area held or controlled by a clan). In all these villages, the tradition and customs of the dominant *got* are followed by all *got*s. If the dominant *got* observes the tradition of avoiding certain *got* for purposes of marriage, all other *got* in these villages will also follow this avoidance pattern. The inclusion of village exogamy (with its notions of locality being equivalent to consanguinity) observed by virtually all caste groups, high or low, and the existence of a large exogamous *got* bloc, introduces considerable complexity to the marriage prohibitions.

Culturally translated, the principle of village exogamy means that all men and women of the same clan, the same localised clan and the same village are bound by the morality of brother-sister and therefore that both sex and marriage are prohibited between members of any of these units (Hershman 1981: 133–34). This extends to the *khap* area involving more than one village and more than one *got*. Significantly, terms like *bhai* (brother*)* and *behan* (sister) in villages are even used for persons who are not related to each other. Transcending ties of biological kinship, they embrace all males or females of the village of one's own generation, notwithstanding caste affiliations. One of the important connotations of the term *bhai* is that a *behan*'s care and protection are entrusted to him. He is to safeguard her honour and not defile it. These prohibitions create the *bhaichara* (brotherhood) which establishes equality between all and denies all hierarchy. This is the idealised *biradari* (community)—both that of the village and the caste which has full *aika* (unity). Clearly, the most hallowed cultural concepts like *aika*, *izzat*, *biradari* and *bhaichara* are contingent upon maintaining the traditional marriage prohibitions. It is a breach in these prohibitions that provokes the *biradari* to use the traditional tools available to them in the form of caste or village or khap panchayats to stem such attempts.

Customarily, the *biradari* uses the traditional panchayat[9] or rather, one of a series of traditional panchayats to settle a variety of disputes regarding caste and inter-caste matters, transgressions, and questions of property rights, inheritance and disputes which threaten the peace of the village or the immediate region.[10] Questions of marriage and sexual affairs form a significant proportion of such disputes, and it is in this sphere that the panchayat frequently intervenes to impose 'justice' according to its own definition. Although very little is known about the working of traditional panchayats in contemporary times, but they remain an active force in rural north India.[11] In cases of contentious marriage, it is the caste panchayat of the *biradari* concerned that is called upon to settle matters. Recent cases show the frequent use of the caste panchayat, which has no legitimacy in law, attempting to change relationships and impose one of their own liking, subsuming the individual/family will to that of the village/collective and prioritising the village and *biradari's izzat* over that of individuals. I shall very briefly mention some of the recent 2010 intra-caste 'honour killings' in rural India:

- January 2010: Kavita of village Kheri in Meham subdivision of Rohtak district was forced to leave her husband after her marriage with Satish was termed illegal by the Benewal *khap* panchayat. The panchayat declared them brother and sister because they belonged to the same *got*. The couple had a son. Kavita lodged a complaint against the panchayat following which she was allowed to live with her husband but had to leave the village.

- In March 2010 there were two prominent cases: In one, the Phogat *khap* panchayat directed Randhir Singh of Samastipur village in Charkhi Dadri of Bhiwani district to sell his land and property, and leave the village for marrying his son Sribhaghwan to Anita of Makrana village of the same district. He was declared to have brought 'dishonour' to the village and community for breaching the time honoured prohibition of *bhaichara* by bringing about a marriage alliance between the two *gots*. The second case was similarly that of the marriage of Ajay of Bedwa village near Meham with Poonam of Ludana village. The Meham *khap* panchayat ruled that they belonged to the same *got* and marriage between them should not have taken place.

- In April 2010, Usha Rani Kashyap of Bhaiswan village of Gohana, Sonepat district, was hanged to death by her brother for her relationship with her neighbour, Rakesh Kashyap. The man's body was found hanging from a tree in the same village the next day. They belonged to the same *got*.

- The most noteworthy case that shot into prominence in May 2010 was that of Manoj and Babli, mentioned above, who were killed on the orders of the *khap* panchayat for marrying despite belonging to the same *got*.

I shall now recount an in-depth study of an intra-caste case that occurred in village Jondhi of district Jhajjar. The account that follows, based on my fieldwork, will throw light on the working of the caste panchayat and accentuate some of its more important features, which are indeed common to all the above stated cases, with slight variations in detail.

Case Illustration: Village Jondhi

A July 2000 case in village Jondhi demonstrates the awesome power of the caste panchayat; the brutal extent to which the village culture and tradition can be extended, the continued hold of caste customs and traditions and the challenges that these traditions and customs are facing. This case raises various questions regarding marriage and highlights the social ambivalence regarding issues of control, of prohibitive degrees and of incest.

In February 1998, Ashish, a Jat boy of village Jondhi in Jhajjar district, 25 years of age, married Darshana, a 16-year-old girl from village Dabari. This village adjoins Haryana but falls within Delhi. When the case surfaced in July 2000, the couple had a one-and-a-half year old son. Ashish was a truck driver by profession. As is usual with the majority of people from rural Haryana who work outside their village and state, Ashish and his wife and child were living with his family in village Jondhi. His immediate family included his father, Satbir Singh, and his grandfather, Daryav Singh, who lived with them. His extended family in this village, consisting of his five uncles and their families, comprised some 40 members.

Trouble around Ashish and Darshana's marriage arose nearly three years after it had taken place when it became public knowledge that a Dagar *got* boy had married a girl from the Gehlot *got*. Under the rule of exogamy, these two *gots* in village Jondhi fall in the category of prohibited *got* and cannot inter-marry. According to a 'tradition', allegedly dating back 500 years, the founder of the village Jondhi, a Jat called Jondh, Gehlot by *got*, had gifted 2,000 acres of land to the Jats of the Dagar *got*, a destitute family then living in the jungle, and settled them in the village. This gesture was claimed to have established relations of brothers, older and younger (superior and inferior) between the two *gots* that prohibited intermarriage between them. This tradition was claimed to have been duly respected by members of both the *gots* till it was broken by this couple. It incensed the Gehlot Jats who summoned a caste panchayat of the village to thrash out the issue and avenge the alleged insult inflicted upon the *izzat* of the entire village by such a marriage. Although a caste panchayat, its attendance is open to all the villagers. However, as the concerned matter is internal to the caste, it is left to the villagers to attend it or not. This is important, as the decision taken at the caste panchayat is binding upon all the villagers. Indeed, the co-operation of the entire village is needed to implement the decision of the caste panchayat.

The caste panchayat, in a public pronouncement, held the concerned Gehlot and Dagar families guilty of wilfully breaking a time-honoured village tradition. The Gehlot family of village Dabari came under severe strictures for marrying their daughter to a Dagar boy. The family was expelled from the *biradari* of Gehlots. In future, no Gehlot was to have any contact with them. The Dagar family was also vehemently denounced. It was alleged that the Dagars brought about this marriage 'knowingly, stealthily, and calculatedly'.

Unequivocally condemning the marriage, the caste panchayat ordered it to be nullified. This decision was in keeping with the popular concept of woman as the 'honour' of the community. Such a concept turned Darshana into an object of 'honour' for the Gehlots—an honour that could not be allowed to be abused at any cost. If this honour had been compromised or defiled by an act of marriage, such an act must be reversed and her status of an unmarried girl must be restored. Consequently, the couple was ordered to revert to their brother-sister fictive relationship, in keeping with the *got* status that had existed prior to their marriage. This was the only relationship between Gehlot and Dagar *got* which the Jondhi caste panchayat was willing to recognise.

To effect this transformation, the panchayat prescribed a ritual to be observed. One, Darshana was to unveil herself in the full assembly of the village. This was a symbolic turning of the *bahu* of the village into a *beti* (daughter). (No daughter is required to veil herself in her natal village.) Furthermore, she was to tie a *rakhi* on Ashish, publicly accepting him as her brother. Two, as a daughter, Darshana was to be married again. Her father-in-law, now transformed into her father, was to perform the *kanyadaan* ceremony for Darshana and give her away as a bride. The Dagar family was to bear the entire cost of her marriage. The Dagars were made responsible for remarrying her. Three, the son of Ashish and Darshana was to remain with Ashish. Ashish's family was ordered to deposit Rs 5,000 in the account of his infant son as security. Four, all 40 members of this family were to be expelled from the village. They were given a week to make their departure. Five, the members of Ashish's family were ordered to sell off their land and other property in the village within a period of two weeks. Failure to comply with these injunctions would result in confiscation of their land and property by the panchayat and forcible eviction from the village. Six, in case the Dagar family allowed a week to lapse without complying with the panchayat's orders, they alone were to be responsible for any untoward happening in the village. The panchayat refused to accept any responsibility for their lives or property after a week.

The latter stricture was certainly a tacit approval of violence. Such cases are far more pervasive than acknowledged. They play an important role in maintaining structural and assumed hierarchies and are considered normal and legitimate. The Station Police Officer (SPO) maintained that the police intervene if and when the law and order breaks down or a complaint is lodged by one of the parties. This 'official' policy of wait-and-watch adopted by the state agency in such cases helps establish the might of the caste panchayat.

The caste panchayat's belligerent stand put the Dagars on the defensive. They reportedly requisitioned a larger body, that is, a *khap* panchayat (a multi-clan council drawn from wider clan areas, also known as *mahapanchayat*) to review the case. On 23 August 2000, a *khap* panchayat of both the *gots* assembled from different villages took place in village Jondhi.

The *khap* panchayat did not dissolve the marriage but refused to condone it. It also refused to review the decision taken by the Jondhi caste panchayat against the Gehlot family of village Dabari. Darshana's natal family was thrown out of their *got* for giving their daughter to a Dagar boy in marriage. They could no longer call themselves Gehlot. Socially boycotted for life, no member of the *got* was to associate with them in any way. All pleas for clemency were rejected by the *khap* panchayat. The *khap* panchayat further expelled the couple from Jondhi village for life. They were not even granted visiting rights. Their male child was exempt from this punishment, clearly on the grounds of patrilineage and sharing of blood. The other 40 members of this family in Jondhi were allowed to stay in the village but were expelled from the *biradari* for two years. After two years they could request the Jondhi caste panchayat for a review in order to seek re-admission to the *biradari*. Till then, there was to be complete social boycott of the family. Their *huqqa-pani* with other members of the village was banned. Neither could they participate in any of the village festivities nor could anyone else participate in theirs. Any infringement was to be severely punished.

The highhandedness of the *khap* panchayat forced the couple to go underground for a while. Darshana pointed out later that, had it not been for the child, the ending might well have been sordid and gruesome. Indeed, in several marriages that had transgressed the principle of territorial exogamy the couples concerned had been physically eliminated. The whole of north India is replete with such cases.[12]

The Gehlots isolated the concerned Dagar family and stopped their interaction with anyone, within or outside the village. They stationed their strongmen to shut out sympathisers. The Dagars, clearly on the defensive, accepted the 'fairness' of the panchayat's charges and criticised the marriage as well. Ashish's father and grandfather openly accepted their mistake and admitted their responsibility.

However, no voice was raised against the right of the caste panchayat to dictate marriage alliances. There was unanimity in the village about this matter being punishable. Opinion differed only on the nature of the punishment. When approached, villagers observed that 'if the culprits are not punished for breaking the moral and cultural code of the village there will be no difference between sisters, daughters and *bahus* of the village'. The hold of the caste panchayat on ruralites was complete in this respect. The village *sarpanch* of the gram panchayat, Pushpa Gehlot, summed up the popular sentiment by observing: 'Caste panchayats are empowered customarily to deliver judgments on various social issues. These must be honoured. In this alone lies the unity and prestige of the village generally and that of the *biradari* specially'.

Indeed, the role and attitude of the elected sarpanch is important to give legitimacy to matters such as these, which may not stand scrutiny under the law. The sarpanch, as the elected head of the gram panchayat, instituted by the government, has a lot of power and political leverage to intervene in matters which go against the law of the land and constitutional rights of individuals. But the sarpanches are not known to act against the dictates of the traditional panchayats. The traditional panchayats represent the *vox populi,* and to go against it would be electorally suicidal for them. It is a fact that panchayati raj is increasingly becoming a training ground for leadership at higher level and it is widely felt that the state leadership in Haryana may emerge from these institutions (Bathla 1994: 178). Therefore, instead of distancing themselves from the decisions of the traditional panchayats, the elected gram panchayat members and the sarpanch seek to emerge as supporters of the decisions of these panchayats. Indeed, in many cases the sarpanch leads from the front in favour of such cases. Such unqualified support from important personages associated with the state and government stands to stem any criticism and weaken any resistance that may arise.

This is not to say, however, that the sarpanch or the other members of the gram panchayat do not share the opinions of the traditional panchayats on social matters. They do. When approached, one of the gram panchayat members, endorsing the stand taken by the caste panchayat, maintained: 'We cannot allow the whims of individuals to divide our society'. Culturally, rural north India prioritises the collective interest over and above individual interests. The members of a family are expected, as a matter of course, to place the interests of the group above their personal desires. It is also clear that in matters such as these the caste panchayat enjoys even wider and higher political support than that of the gram panchayat. For example, the then Chief Minister O.P. Chautala, who visited Jondhi in the wake of this trouble, firmly maintained that 'whatever the panchayat (caste) decides is right'.

The Dagar community, despite offering initial support to Ashish, backed out after their own position in the village became secure. If Ashish's family had been more sound economically and more prestigious socially, his case probably would not have gone unrecognised and unsupported by his

otherwise powerful Dagar community, for there are instances where socially
and economically influential families have breached the *got* restrictions
successfully.

In arriving at its decision, the caste panchayat of village Jondhi had
treated the concept of *bhaichara* and the breach of the incest taboo by
the couple as the central issue. Incest is being given special attention in
view of the recent May 2010 demand by the khap panchayats of Haryana,
Uttar Pradesh and Rajasthan, that the Hindu Marriage Act of 1955 may
be amended to include 'incest' in its prohibitory categories, which in rural
areas, as pointed above, is a very wide category. It embraces all inhabitants
of a village; all *got* represented in the village who may be located anywhere,
as well as the inhabitants of those villages which share a boundary with it,
by creating fictive brother-sister relationships between them. Any breach
in this is considered a serious transgression and dealt with summarily.
Yet experience shows that the charge of incest is not applied uniformly
to all caste groups in the village. In case one of the parties is of a different
caste, the issue is altogether different. It becomes a caste issue and not
one of incest.

On the other hand, incest within the family is generally buried under
the carpet. The concept of incest is not extended to family relationships
involving unequal power relations between senior males and junior females
or any other prohibited category of people. This counterposes fictitious
incest *versus* real incest. Activists involved in the women's movement in
Rohtak, based upon their experiences in the villages of Haryana, informed
me that incest has assumed truly frightening proportions. The daughters
and sisters are however afraid to voice it, as it would reflect on the 'honour'
of their families, for which they feel responsible. Police officers similarly
vouch for the widespread incest in families. According to them these cases
come to light only when they result in suicides or murders.[13] In some
instances, the woman may approach the caste panchayat. The few cases
that are brought to the notice of the panchayat, however, are not dealt with
in any satisfactory way.

A recent example from village Hathanganna in Gurgaon district is a
case in point. The caste panchayat, summoned twice in a case where a

woman accused her father-in-law of attempting rape, did precious little. On the first occasion the panchayat summoned the father-in-law, gave him a strict warning and advised the couple to ignore the instance and settle it among themselves. The second time, when the father-in-law repeated his offence, the panchayat expressed its inability to do anything and advised the woman to take recourse to the law, but when the woman tried to register an FIR at the police station, the police refused to do so. In matters such as these, the bonds of community or ideology shared by the police and the traditional panchayat, and not the law of the land, determine the action or inaction of the law-enforcing agencies. The woman then moved the court at Firozpur Jhirka. It was here that the judge instructed for a criminal case to be instituted against her father-in-law.

The caste panchayats are clearly uncomfortable and unwilling to deal with the question of incest *within* the family, especially when it concerns their own caste members. This may not necessarily be the case while dealing with other caste groups, especially the lower castes. When it comes to other so-called inferior caste members, the upper caste members take a high moral stand and impose very stringent sanctions.[14]

SECTION II

Inter-caste Alliances

As stated above, under the law, inter-caste marriages are permitted, but not under the customary law. Historically, the accepted stand of the British colonial authorities, enforceable in the courts, was against a recognition of inter-caste marriages, in keeping with the strictures found in the classical Hindu law, enunciated by members of the highest caste—the Brahmins.[15] Inter-caste marriages were considered by the British administrators, ethnographers and commentators on law and society to have existed in the past, and to have become obsolete by the second half of the nineteenth century.

The judicial records of the colonial period are littered with a number of cases of runaway women with male guardians seeking to retrieve their daughters from the men the daughters chose to live with by charging the other man with kidnapping, abducting and inducing the daughters to compel them into marriage. Such cases (which were essentially inter-caste liaisons) were considered to be 'very frequent', next only to cases of 'rioting and hurt'. On the basis of the existing data at the High Court level, it is not unreasonable to assume that the available cases of runaway women were but a few compared to what might have existed in the judicial records. Several others would not even have reached either the police or the court stage. Those cases of elopement and marriage that reached the state level of intervention were not given the legal sanction of a valid marriage because the 'consent' of the guardian had not been forthcoming.

For an inter-caste marriage to be accepted in the colonial courts, the existence of a local and caste custom to this effect had to be established. Such a stand encouraged claims and counter-claims, contributing to the crystallisation of certain trends in the shifting cultural practices surrounding marriage. Clearly, the colonial intervention had introduced complexities and ambiguities in the legal processes and their interpretation. Such a situation spoke for fluctuating verdicts, especially as it was interpreted and implemented by culturally and socially embedded members of colonial society and created a great deal of confusion in judicial decision making. Each case set a precedent for all subsequent cases, even where they contradicted actual practice. Legally, therefore, independent India inherited a situation in which inter-caste marriages were highly contentious and lacked legal validity.

Some of the recent and well known inter-caste/community cases of 'honour' killings come from not only rural but also urban regions of India, extending from north to south, cutting across class lines. The media has come a long way. From disregarding the news of 'honour' killings and considering it as essentially belonging to the 'other' India—the rural hinterland—to sensationalising it as belonging to a 'feudal mindset', the media has been forced to accept its existence in educated, modern, urban metropolitan India. The cases, some very well known and many obscure or little known, have been multiplying. Some of the recent high profile cases are those of:

- Bibi Jagir Kaur, as the first woman President of the SGPC (Shiromani Gurdawara Prabhandak Committee), Punjab, was a high profile minister in the then ministry of Prakash Singh Badal. Early in 2000, her pregnant daughter Harpreet, who married Kamaljeet, a *mona* (shaven) Sikh from a different caste, secretly and against her mother's wishes, was killed after a forced abortion, allegedly at the instance of Jagir Kaur. Bibi Jagir Kaur is held as an example of one who 'justifiably subscribed to violence against daughters if they transgressed boundaries'.
- Nitish Katara was abducted and killed by Vikas Yadav, the son of D.P. Yadav, a Member of Parliament from western Uttar Pradesh in 2002, for being friendly with his sister Bharati. The couple had planned to get married. Katara, belonging to a different caste, was totally unacceptable to the Yadavs. The killing was to preserve their 'honour'.
- Rizwanur Rahman, a 30-year-old computer graphic trainer, secretly married Priyanka Todi, daughter of an affluent businessman, in August 2007 in Kolkata. The Todi family, under false promise, took their daughter home for a few days after the marriage. She never came back. Rahman, who tried to get her back, was severely harassed by the police and others. Within a month he was found dead near the railway track in Kolkata. 'Honour' had taken its toll.
- Nirupama Pathak's case, May 2010, is most recent and is still being investigated. From all accounts it looks like an 'honour killing', self or induced. Belonging to two different castes, Nirupama's Brahmin family would not accept her wanting to marry Priyabhanshu, a fellow scribe, who belonged to a lower caste than her own. Also pregnant, she was found dead in her parental house in Jharkhand.

For detailed analysis of factors operating behind inter-caste marriages, I shall take up the village Nayagaon case in Haryana which I investigated in detail to underline some of the finer points at stake in the operation of concept of honour.

Case Illustration: Village Nayagaon

In March 1994, in village Nayagaon in Haryana (less than 25 kilometres from the national capital), Asha was hacked to death with an axe and so was her lover Manoj, who was from Balaur, an adjacent village, by her six out of seven uncles. Asha belonged to the numerically and economically strong Saini caste in the village. The Sainis are locally considered a higher caste in relation to the Ahirs—a caste group to which Manoj belonged. The boy was declared to be an 'upstart' by the Sainis. According to local accounts, Asha openly asserted her right to choose her life partner. She reportedly told her family members not to interfere. Manoj and Asha had become intimately involved as high school students and carried on for two years before Asha's family discovered them. Asha was beaten and warned repeatedly but she continued to meet Manoj stealthily. Her defiance had brutal consequences.

The uncles who perpetrated this crime surrendered to the police through a lawyer. It is unclear why they did it. An important reason that emerged out of the discussions was a sense of pride and achievement that they experienced for having punished the 'guilty'. 'Why should they hide it? They have done nothing wrong' was the dominant sentiment. Their lawyer disclosed that the case was fought on the plea that it was not a premeditated murder and the deed was done in a fit of anger-cum-passion on discovering the two in a 'compromising position'. Although no witnesses came to testify, the culprits were given 20 years of imprisonment. This harsh punishment was totally unprecedented and was condemned outright by the villagers of Nayagaon, across caste and communities.

The case was under appeal in the High Court when I was doing my fieldwork in 2000–1. The defending lawyer, when interviewed, was very confident of getting a mitigated sentence on appeal because of the grounds on which the case had been contested. This seems entirely plausible. It has been argued by legal experts on the basis of certain case studies that the Indian Supreme Court often mitigates the sentences in homicide cases on considerations of 'justifiable grievance' provided by 'grave provocation' (Dhagamwar 1992). Thus 'loss of honour' constitutes in their eyes a sense of grievance, which implicitly provides a 'justified motive'. In other words, a man may kill with little or no reason if a woman's character can be said to be bad or loose. Such reasoning is contrary to the stand of the Indian Constitution that recognises the right to life and the right to equality of all without exception. It is certainly not limited to virtuous men and women. In practice this seems to be the case.

According to the residents of Nayagaon, Asha's uncle did what was necessary and what any one of them would have also done. The uncles, according to them, by eliminating the lovers restored not only their own *izzat* or honour but also that of the community and the village as a whole. This was declared to be the only time-honoured and traditional way of dealing with such cases. Several cases were cited in which members of these two caste groups took similar steps.

The rural opinion is heavily in favour of punishing those who 'violate social norms' of rural society so that 'others can learn a lesson'. The peer group (which includes *netas* and other social bigwigs) condones this attitude and action. They openly defend the right of the peasantry to punish anyone who breaks the caste rules and codes of honour. Regarding infliction of extreme violence in certain cases, caste members see the killings as 'executions' and 'just punishment' awarded for breaking caste norms and boundaries of honour. In all such cases, the villagers in general and leaders in particular prioritise the village or caste *izzat*. Two of Asha's uncles who were out on parole at the time when this fieldwork was done, were not treated as criminals but with due respect (*izzat*). A repeat of this can be noticed in the recent June 2010 case of a murder of an inter-caste married couple, where the killers have been hailed as 'heroes'.[16]

All that was emphasised, in both the villages, was that the girl was *badmash* (of loose and bad character). It was rumoured that she had had two abortions. The girl was said to be enjoying herself or '*maza loot rahi thi*', suggesting that the question of marriage was never raised or entertained by either of them. In Balaur village, Manoj was absolved of all the responsibility and only Asha was held responsible. The people's verdict reveals patriarchal attitudes towards women and acceptance of the notion of honour as residing in the body and behaviour of women. Such an ideology provided justification for eliminating her if she were to tarnish this 'honour'.

There was also a feeling among the Ahirs that Manoj should not have been killed when the fault lay entirely with the girl. Asha was spoken of as someone with insatiable lust who was constantly throwing herself at a reluctant Manoj. Manoj's father regretted that the Sainis did not take him into confidence in this matter. He was confident that he would have sorted it out with his son, something which, he taunted, 'the Sainis were not able to do with their girl'. According to most people in the two villages, the killing of the girl was certainly justified but they question the killing of the boy, although for different reasons.

In Nayagaon, it is openly maintained that had it not been for the killing of the Ahir boy, the uncles would not be in prison. According to them, the question of their confessing and surrendering to the police would not have arisen as *they were fully entitled to deal with their girl, as they liked and deemed fit.* After all, it was a matter of their 'honour'. No one would have come to testify against them. In such instances, violence and death are considered preferable to condoning/accepting such a marriage. The acceptance of inter-caste marriage as a possible solution to the growing incidents of violence was lost in the ideology of lust, morality and honour.

Indeed, it is a well known and openly stated fact that a large number of girls who are forcibly 'retrieved' in cases of elopement or marriage are either murdered or encouraged by family members and the community to commit suicide. A girl's death is seen as the only way in which the 'honour' of the family can be salvaged. To this may be added the financial burden of marrying off a girl who was said to have eloped. In the dowry economy of north India, such a girl is even more of a burden than is normally the case.

It may be underlined that cases of breaches show a gendered response. A number of instances show that women are more likely than men to become victims of violence. However, the Dalit men are an exception. They are invariably killed, making a mockery of the state-sponsored reward instituted and periodically increased for encouraging Dalit-non-Dalit marriages in Haryana.[17] This gendered response of the upper castes for 'honour' in a bitter struggle with lower caste groups for assertion of their power and domination leading to violence has its parallel in other parts of India as well.[18] Recently, in May 2010, a high caste Reddy girl and her Dalit husband, married for just three months, were 'stoned to death for honour' in Krishanjiwadi village in Nizamabad, Andhra Pradesh.[19]

SECTION III

The Ideology of Honour: Cultural and Material Underpinnings

What is this ideology of honour that sanctifies such violence? An analysis of the ideology highlights it as a gendered notion producing inequality and hierarchy. Both men and women embody notions of honour, but differently. The woman is the repository and the man is the regulator of this honour. Therefore, the greatest danger to the ideology of honour comes from the woman. One oft-repeated phrase is: *Ladki ke saath uske kutumb ki izzat judi huee hai* (the honour of every family is connected to its girl). Honour so posited in a woman is importantly located in her body. A woman dishonours her family by what is considered her shameful physical behaviour. This stretches from observing *sharm* and *lihaz* (modesty and deference) to her sexuality. Honour is the overarching concept, which regulates and puts into effect the practice of purdah and its attendant ideology of seclusion as a controlling device.[20]

Why does honour lie in the body of a woman? The answer lies partly in the specific construction of procreation, which is conceived in terms of the male seed germinating the female earth or field (Dube 1986). In this, the male semen is perceived to create while the woman is seen as the passive recipient. This social perception of the male creative ability acts as the foundation upon which the notion of honour is built. The ideology of the seed and the earth, going back to ancient times, forms a part of the literate tradition as well as a part of customary law and popular consciousness. According to this, the blood that flows in the child's veins comes from the father's seed and gives a child (particularly a male child) its identity as belonging to the father's lineage. Semen is commonly considered as concentrated blood and there is a clear notion of a common bloodline for agnatic kin continuing through male members who serve as links for the passing of the common blood to the next generation through their semen. The practice of caste endogamy, preserving caste boundaries and caste purity, ensures this patriliny and lineage. It implies the need for control of female sexuality to assure the paternity and lineage of the offspring.

Therefore, a man's honour is predicated largely on his ability to impose this control over his womenfolk. This means that a woman has no control over her own self. All decisions regarding her body must be made by the male members of her family—the upholders of her honour. The familial ties are extended through ties of blood to the clan and then the caste/community. The blood tie makes them co-sharers of this honour. They must all join to safeguard and preserve its purity. The imagery of blood kinship or *bhaichara* (brotherhood) virtually excludes women from this powerful and hierarchical *biradari*.

In patrilineal communities this cultural understanding provides the ideological basis for legitimisation of crucial principles of kinship and their operation in respect of inheritance of all resources, whether land or labour in an agrarian economy. By equating the woman's body with the field or the earth and the semen with the seed, the process of reproduction is equated with the process of production and rights over the children with rights over the produce. In other words, the seed/earth symbolism of reproduction sustains an ideology of honour in which strategic resources of both types—material as well as human—remains in the hands of men. Clearly, honour is not merely a cultural construct. It is grounded in material conditions and social worth. As such, both production and reproduction need to be controlled, as autonomous reproduction spells danger.

For reproduction to be a legitimate act, marriage must be within the group that seeks to reproduce itself in terms of status and control over property. It then becomes an alliance between two families and kin groups involving a series of material transactions and counter transactions, with emotions being subordinated to wider 'utilitarian' considerations. This makes reproduction or marriage a social rather than an individual act. Desire, choice and love are thus separated from the institution of marriage, which is about social reproduction and not about individual needs and their fulfilment. The dominant morality does not expect emotional and erotic satisfaction in marriage and regards love and sexuality with distrust and suspicion. In fact, it is not merely that a woman and a man get married; it is a woman's family that ties the marital knot with the man's family. Therefore, the emphasis is not necessarily on the individual, though s/he remains a vital consideration, but mostly on the family. It is the family/

caste/community nexus which produces the crucial test of a status marriage and upward mobility.

Consequently, the wider social, caste and customary considerations have meant that marriages in most parts of rural and urban India are arranged marriages—arranged by senior males and females of the family strictly within the caste. For a woman, hypergamy, that is, marriage with a man of higher social status is always desired. In arranging this family members or kin, both male and female, as well as friends, often act as go-betweens. The earlier use of a professional mediator, generally from the *Nai* (barber) caste, as a negotiator of marriage, has all but disappeared. Instead, professional negotiators in the form of a marriage bureau have become a visible presence. Use of technology has also meant placing advertisements in the newspapers and even on the internet, stating caste, clan and other vital statistics and even video clippings for the intended spouse. Indeed, the demand for 'suitable grooms and brides' specifying their caste groups has promoted a huge matrimonial business. There are also modern day caste associations which are in the forefront of arranging marriages within their caste groups.

Apart from the arranged marriages, there are also the so-called 'love arranged' marriages (essentially a middle-class term which seeks to accommodate 'modernity') in which the self-chosen partners get the approval of their families to get married. However, this emotional structuring of a relationship is contingent upon following the dominant caste and community, as well as appropriate class status and marriage norms. Breaches are not tolerated. Moreover, an overwhelming majority of those interviewed, both men and women, believed that the choice of spouse is best decided by parents, rather than by the individuals concerned.[21]

In matters of marriage, the overarching ideology of patriarchy, kinship and caste, which lie at the root of honour, is easily and most commonly translated into a comprehensible ideology of guardianship of a woman. This becomes the guiding force for all relationships between males and females. A female, minor or adult, is always under guardianship. While single she is under the guardianship of her father, or if he were dead, of other male relatives. With marriage she comes under the guardianship of her husband;

on his death until remarriage she is under the guardianship of his family, whether she is minor or major. In actuality, neither an unmarried girl nor a widow is allowed to exercise her choice in the marriage partnership. A widow, unlike an unmarried woman, may resist remarriage but she cannot marry without the consent of her conjugal or natal family males. Given the strong hold of patriarchy, this male control over a woman, minor or major, single or widowed, is never slackened throughout her life. It is a mere change of authority, from that of her father and brother to her husband and her son.

It is this ideology of honour and guardianship that acquires wider dimensions in its applicability. It no longer remains confined to the domain of the family/kinship and caste but spills over into the public realm where it gets manifested in the ideal of masculinity—in 'guarding' and 'policing' female behaviour, freedom of movement and sexuality. It is basically the desire to follow these ideals that is largely responsible for producing moral policing of women in different regional and social contexts. If women's public behaviour is not in accordance with what some males decree to be 'honourable' it leads to infliction of violence on them. In the opinion of such males, women, by their ' indecent western' behaviour, stand to 'shame' or 'dishonour' all: their families, friends, community and even the larger 'Indian society' and ultimately the nation itself. This has meant that not only in rural areas, with a highly segregated society, and the semi-urban and small townships like Meerut,[22] but even in the metropolitan cities like Bangalore and Pune and in the capital itself, there is heavy surveillance by the moral police cutting across political and social lines.[23]

The ideological and cultural patterns working behind the concept of honour, delineated above, are substantiated by material realties. Indeed, under the changed political economy of post-independent India, the material conditions have come to assume even more importance in the operation of 'honour'. With the females being given legal rights to inheritance and the right to marry whom they wish, the question of honour has surfaced in a big way. One of the major changes that strengthened the so-called concept of honour is the enactment of the Hindu Succession Act of 1956.[24] It amended and codified the law relating to intestate succession among Hindus and brought about fundamental and radical changes in the law of succession, breaking violently with the past. It abrogated all the rules of the law of succession hitherto applicable to Hindus, by virtue of Hindu law or any custom.

The Act enabled, for the first time, daughters, sisters, widows and mothers (along with the male members) to inherit land with full proprietary rights to its disposal.[25] This has aroused tremendous anxieties in rural society. In the event of its proper implementation, the patrilineal and patriarchal hold stands to weaken and even be demolished in time. This Act affected greatly the code of honour regulating marriage alliance, that is, village exogamy and caste endogamy. For instance, the land of the village is taken to belong to the male descendants of ancestors who originally settled and worked on it, the male agnatic descendants, as members of the localised clan, alone are considered to have reversionary rights in the estate. Land is ordinarily not to be alienated outside this group. The only ideal and '*izzatwala*' (honourable) pattern of inheritance is acknowledged to be by males from males. Basically, this means that daughters and sisters who are potential introducers of fresh blood and new descent lines through their husbands are to be kept from exercising their inheritance rights. The introduction of a rank outsider into the family who can and may claim the property on behalf of his wife needs to be effectively stopped. As an outsider he remains outside the influence of the family and caste/community rules and ethics which ensure a patrilineal inheritance.

Similarly, location of a married daughter within the natal village also spells danger to patrilineal inheritance as it facilitates and could lead to assumption of land inherited by her. It is small wonder then that the *khap* panchayats of Haryana, Uttar Pradesh and Rajasthan have demanded an amendment to the Hindu Marriage Act, which allows such marriages to take place. Consequently, one of the major effects of the Act of Succession has been to tighten the noose of control over females, unmarried or married, especially in relation to her marriage. Thus, the tightening of restrictions on marriage practice has had the effect of negating the progressive fallout of the inheritance enablement law on female population.

The significance of this practice can be easily visualised if it is juxtaposed to the custom prevalent among the lower castes. These castes allow flexibility in the rule of patrilocality. In other words, since the land and its ownership are not in question, the family of a married daughter might settle in her natal village. With the result that the *ghar jamai* (resident son-in-law) phenomenon among lower castes is not uncommon in rural Haryana-Punjab or across the border in western Uttar Pradesh (Kolenda 1982). Yet, at the time of marriage, the principle of village exogamy is as rigorously enforced as the prohibited degree of clan (*got*) and other taboos by the lower caste groups. A failure to observe these norms brings up the question of honour as much for the lower castes as the upper castes and any breach in it is violently dealt with. This is in keeping with the norms set by the dominant landowning caste groups. It is clear that the cultural codes of honour can and do function autonomously without necessarily having any social and material factors underpinning them.

As the Act of Succession evoked great tension in the rural society, the landowners of Haryana-Punjab were unanimous about the urgency of abolishing it in order to uphold their 'honour' and the 'honour' of their 'timeless traditions'. The other caste groups followed suit. On the one hand they tried to abolish it through the legislative procedures and on the other they accelerated their attempts through the caste panchayats to control its fallout effects. Consequently, three to four attempts were made in the Assembly of Haryana-Punjab (1967, 1977, 1979, and 1989). All these moves have failed but not the spirit behind them. The recent demand of the *khap* panchayats to amend the Hindu Marriage Act is yet another attempt in a similar direction. Attempts are also being made to seek a ban on same-*got* unions through the courts. All these are likely to meet the same fate as the attempts to abolish the Act of Succession.

Clearly, the legal acts have introduced anxieties stemming from different reasons and not necessarily out of concern for caste endogamy or village exogamy or even upkeep of honour, culture and tradition, even though these anxieties are played through these concerns and in fact reinforce them. Since the social, legal and political changes cannot be further resisted, cultural practices and notions of 'honour' have gained paramountcy. Consequently, the resultant violent opposition to breach of marriage norms or codes of honour overrides any education or modernising process that the rural families may have undergone. In fact, this opposition is almost always based upon the grounds of honour, tradition and culture vs. modernism and westernisation. Significantly, cultural ideas tend to benefit social groups that construct or promote them. The operation of concepts of honour and shame operate to restore the male, familial and community domination considered to have been compromised and endangered by the post-colonial legal enablement.

SECTION IV

Changing Social Milieu: Growing Marriage Anxieties

Although there is no statistical evidence, breaches of customary norms in marriages, whether inter-caste or intra-caste, are perceived to have escalated over the years. The roots of this lie in the rapidly changing social milieu. The process of political democratisation and the opening of economic opportunities have altered local power dynamics, complicating relationships between members of different caste groups as well as between members within a caste group. The traditional linkages of unequal status, hierarchy and prestige are challenged and replaced by new norms based upon notions of egalitarianism, citizenship and entitlement. Certain shifts are occurring simultaneously. On the one hand, caste solidarities are crystallising, and on the other, education, reservations, and opening out of the economy are eroding the system of caste by changing the material base for different caste groups. There is a certain amount of de-linking between caste, occupation and power in contemporary India. Other identities have taken over. A politically convenient self-classification is assumed or discarded according to the situation. Consequently, there is a conflict between traditional expectations and quest for status and power in caste terms and individualist aspirations, divorced from past or inherited identities. This contradiction has made the issue of marriage extremely complicated and conflict-ridden.

The social reality shows the growing resentment and assertiveness of the subordinate lower castes and classes, not infrequently resulting in inter-caste liaisons which infringe upon upper caste norms and sexual codes. For example, many Dalit youth, who can no longer be absorbed in agriculture or others who do not wish to, opt out of working as agricultural labourers and migrate to cities. It is a move by the Dalit youth to break away from the subordinate pattern of the past that is closely tied to agricultural work. Some of them, who have been able to take advantage of educational opportunities, have aspired and some even gained access to positions such as those of peons, clerks or drivers, or have been taken in the military service. Yet others have migrated to the cities and have become salaried workers. Consequently, many of them have been able to build brick houses in the village and also own cattle. Their standard of living not only equals that of the lower class, upper caste groups, but also sometimes has a distinct edge.

The educational aspirations of the Dalits and consequent disassociation from their traditional occupational roles are a considerable source of tension not only in the north but in other parts of India as well (Balagopal 1991, Kannabiran and Kannabiran 1991, Sanghtana 1991). The non-working by Dalits for the dominant caste group, for whatever reason, is taken as contesting upper caste dominance. The breakdown in the correspondence existing between caste and occupation is construed as an attempt to change caste itself; hence it is resisted by the dominant landowning caste groups. The latter greatly resent government scholarships for the lower caste children and reservations in government jobs which, according to them, have given the lower caste groups an edge over them. Education is considered to be at the root of all ills. Dalit-non-Dalit relationships/elopements/marriages are touted as the Dalits' ambition in life—to get assimilated among the higher caste groups (Chowdhry 2009). The Dalits, however, denounce any such aspirations and maintain that they were also zealous followers of rules of caste endogamy just like the higher castes.

In fact, there are a number of cases involving Dalits caught in the contradictions of caste endogamy, highlighting how most caste groups follow the dominant caste norms in this region. In October 2001, for example, a Chamar panchayat (of leather workers) expelled from the village the family of the girl who belonged to the Balmiki caste for breaking the norm of caste endogamy. The boy she was involved with belonged to the

Chamar caste, a higher caste than Balmiki. The girl herself is reported to have been killed.

My fieldwork reveals that the lower caste groups are as much 'honour bound' and status conscious as the upper caste groups. They also observe the norms of caste-endogamous marriage and deal with such cases individually or through panchayats in the same way as the higher castes do. Yet, given their weak socio-economic position they are unable to claim any such honour especially in relation to the higher castes. They may vaguely share in the honour of the village as a whole. This identification may mean going willingly or unwillingly along with the dictates of the upper caste leadership. Consequently, the only 'honour' which the lower caste groups may 'honourably' claim is in relation to members of their own caste and it lies in their ability to enforce it within their own caste group. Denied any claims of honour in relation to higher castes, the lower castes therefore become hypersensitive in defending it within their own caste. Such a concept of honour is not only claimed, but also defended and implemented.

Among the intra-caste cases, too, the post-colonial political economy suggests an increase. The most significant point to note and worth remembering is that intra-caste cases, which infringe the caste and customary codes, are not necessarily so-called runaway 'love matches', which may raise the ire of the caste and communities. Many times these are arranged matches, brought about by the respective individual and extended families and attended by members of their community. It is because of this factor that not only the individuals concerned come under grave pressure, but also their immediate as well as extended families.

For the eloping couples it can be maintained that they are defying the age old customs and revolting against the caste constrictions, which they may not believe in. In the given social milieu of education and higher mobility, and facing a globalised and consumerist society which has increased the intermingling of the sexes, it is not difficult to understand their defiance or 'revolt'. But why are the parents of young girls and boys breaching what are claimed to be the village and caste traditions?

In the answer lies the crux of understanding this problem. Over the years, the customary regulations governing marriages have had the effect of creating a very tight market for prospective brides and grooms. With the increase in population, the prohibited categories of people have tended to increase. For example, inter-village and regional migrations have resulted in a severe drop in the number of very small villages and corresponding increase in that of large and very large villages. This has had the effect of multiplying the number of *gots* represented in different villages. From two to three *gots*, villages may well have as many as 20 to 25 *gots*. An extension of the principle of village exogamy means that apart from three to four parental *gots* which have to be avoided, all the other *got* represented in a village cannot be entertained for marriage. This leaves the marriage market highly restricted. The extension of the concept of *bhaichara* (brotherhood) also means that all the neighbouring villages have to be similarly excluded.

These prohibitions imposed on marriages are greatly compounded by the fact that a girl has to be given in a hypergamous alliance, that is, she has to marry upwards to a man of higher clan and not a lower one. This is becoming increasingly difficult in an extremely fluid social situation where different groups are either claiming a higher or equal status or attempting to maintain their status against challenges and erosions effected by other clan groups within the caste fold. The changes occurring in ideas about rank and equality, along with the increasing differentiation of status, power and wealth developing within each caste are contributing to a re-evaluation of the relative status of different clans. The resultant collapse of the earlier relatively coherent, traditional hierarchy has led to breaches in the customary marriage norms. As marriage alliances are a significant means to establish one's status in society they assume great importance and demand sharper vigilance. The contemporary multi-directional pulls within a caste account for confrontation and violence in relation to contested marriage alliances.

Moreover, the whole of north India, especially Haryana, is also labouring under other problems. Briefly speaking, these relate to the extremely unfavourable sex-ratio, the presence of a large number of unmarried men, and the dowry economy. All these are interconnected. The widespread foeticide practised in this region in combination with suspected female infanticide through neglect and other causes has led to an adverse ratio of only 819 females to 1,000 males. In the estimate of the activists these census figures of 2001 are on the higher side. According to them, the female ratio in many villages is as low as 500–550. With the declining number of women, the anxiety to control them and use of violence to effect this control has steadily grown. Indeed, this uneven sex ratio is creating havoc in matters of marriage in more ways than one

In a situation where, as stated above, status hypergamous marriage is also the customary norm for a girl's marriage, there is a surplus of brides at the top but a pronounced deficit at the bottom. This situation is compounded by the very large number of unemployed men in Haryana. The unemployment figures have more than doubled in less than 20 years from 3,59,255 in 1980–81 to 8,11,359 in the year 1999—a staggering rise of 125 per cent. Whereas between 1981 and 1991 the population increase in Haryana was 27.40 per cent. The limited number of employed males who alone are considered 'suitable boys' means competition to net them in marriage. The existence of surplus girls in this stratum feeds into the dowry economy, successfully defeating the economics of demand and supply.

Such concerns leave the unemployed males to either settle for lesser matches or not get married at all. Consequently, a substantial number of the unemployed is to be found among those who are unmarried. In the 1991 Census, 36.24 per cent of men in the category of 15–44 years of age (the so-called reproductive or marriageable age) are shown to be unmarried.[26] In districts like Rohtak, the percentage of unmarried males between the ages of 15–44 is as high as 44 per cent.[27] Existence of a vast number of such males has a decisive effect on the problem under discussion. The enforced bachelorhood has meant a growing law and order problem, sex-related crimes, violence, increase in drug and alcoholic intake and its related troubles. Unable to get married themselves, or reduced to purchasing brides from any caste group and region (Andhra Pradesh, Kerala, Orissa, Bengal, Mizoram, Assam, Bihar and Nepal), this male segment shows great resentment of any breach in customary marriage norms. They are in the forefront of initiating all action against the culprits and are major implementers of the diktats of the caste panchayats.

SECTION V

The Caste Panchayat: Salvaging a Situation

In the present milieu the marriage restrictions are extremely hard on both the sides—for the boys as well as for the girls. Importantly, these breaches are attempts to open out the marriage market. However, such attempts by the 'erring' individuals and families provide an occasion to the caste panchayat to assert itself. This intervention is also an assertion of the united power and domination of upper caste, senior male members over younger men and women. It represents a direct attempt at retention of power by the caste leadership which is fast being eroded and challenged by aspirants from different socio-economic strata as well as by the younger generation. In the colonial period, these caste panchayats held an important position. In post-colonial India, the traditional power base stands considerably eroded with the introduction of different state structures such as the elected statutory panchayat (since 1950) and an election mechanism based upon equal citizenship and adult franchise. The statutory panchayat, which has become the focus of political life of the village, has thrown up new, socially mixed groups, in many cases drawing substantial representation from the lower social strata. In the changing scenario, the traditional leadership of village bigwigs, derived from the ranks of those born to power and prestige, is being pushed to the margins of the power structure.

This diminishing power is sought to be resurrected through the traditional panchayat who use social problems, like cases relating to questions of marriage, for legitimating its authority. In this a large collection of people come together temporarily and rather promiscuously for a certain specific purpose. What follows is claimed to be an open, fair and democratic decision. A close observation of the proceedings suggests the contrary. For one, it is a wholly male body; two, on many occasions, one of the concerned parties is not even present or is too thinly represented; three, women are not even allowed to enter the panchayat premises (not even the one who is a party in the dispute), although, more often than not, the decision involves them in an important way. The woman is represented by her male family members. The male head of her family is held responsible for her conduct.

Moreover, the youth, usually the affected party, is not allowed to voice its opinion, especially when any other older male member of the family is present. They are reprimanded, 'Why do you speak when your father/elders are present?' In rural north India, age and experience are still respected, though change, howsoever slow, now favours the youth. The decision of such a body, with the older generation monopolising and directing its course, is projected and implemented as a unanimous decision democratically arrived at and dissenters are dismissed as of 'no importance'.

For arriving at a decision, the traditional panchayat mobilises a large number of people on the basis of family, kin, *got*, caste, community and village, including persons from outside the local area. By bringing in a wider *biradari* from outside the village, links are activated which make the panchayat look more powerful. Issues such as the breaking of social taboos, customs, rituals and hierarchy are used as mobilising strategies. Being highly emotive issues, these succeed in uniting people and closing ranks and cleavages in rural society. In this the concept of village honour based upon idealised norms and village *unity* produces a powerful plank.

The dominant caste groups, though severely divided into factions and interest groups, throw their might behind the traditional panchayat. In cases such as these, they cannot afford to split their own ranks or caste. A show of solidarity serves them in a twofold way: (*a*) it helps them to present a united caste-*biradari* front despite their political and party differences. Such a front comes in handy in demanding political and economic concessions from the state; (*b*) it helps them in establishing their might in the village against other caste groups, specially the lower castes, reaffirming the existing hierarchy and caste/community domination.[28]

The illegal verdicts of the panchayats, however, can be legally challenged. There is always the potential danger that dissenters may move the court. Not many people exercise the option of going to court, but some do. However, recourse to the court over 'personal' issues internal to the caste is not generally approved and remains a last resort. Any attempt to reverse the panchayat's decision may well lead to permanent antagonism, revenge and violent retribution. For the ruralites, the financially draining courts, based upon different principles, are hardly equipped to resolve questions of marriage. In case recourse to law is taken, it is done only against grave social pressure and incurs a great deal of community displeasure. Moreover, in cases regarding contentious marriages or elopements state agencies like the police and the local administration are known to throw in their lot on the side of traditional authority. In northern India, the police are heavily drawn from the dominant upper caste groups, and are acknowledgedly casteist. In law-keeping, the socio-political role of such a force has proved to be highly dubious.

The court can and, at times, has declared a marriage legal. But the difficulties remain. A recent July 2009 case from district Jind in Haryana underlines the utter futility of even getting a positive verdict from the High Court. The young husband, Ved Pal, succeeded in getting a court order against the verdict of the caste panchayat. He had been forcibly separated from his wife on the ground that their marriage was incestuous as they belonged to the same *got*. When Ved Pal went to legally retrieve his wife, he was savagely murdered. The warrant officer and the police party of 15 who had accompanied him in this mission fled from the scene. Such cases can be multiplied. Moreover, a court can hardly stop the social boycott or ostracism inflicted upon the couple or the family. Taking recourse to the law is not considered an effective solution in such cases as the caste panchayats make a mockery of the law of the land.

However, it is also true that any recourse to the court of law leads to a dramatic loss of the caste panchayat's prestige as well as its delegitimation. It is a public demonstration of the refusal to obey its dictates. Also, going to court means a further transgression of the norms of community, compounding the earlier transgression. It is construed as an even greater challenge to the panchayat's decision, leading to a further hardening of its posture. The traditional leadership considers the judiciary, run by people who have no knowledge of rural culture and customary practices, to be working against caste and community norms. Anyone taking recourse to it is similarly condemned and stereotyped as 'westernised', 'urbanised' and 'modernised', and out of touch with rural realities. The state and its laws are blamed for all those marriages, which go against traditional norms and customary practices.

In such a situation what can be done to salvage the state of affairs? How can a much needed campaign for choice in marriage address and counter the violence of the family and the sanction, support and participation in killings by a large section of community to which the victims belong? The answers are not easy. A lot of them lie in the sphere of the law itself. The law must protect the right to choose a partner. As of now, some of the required legal changes are reportedly on the anvil.[29] Here are a few suggestions in relation to the state, the civil society and the khap panchayats in order to safeguard the citizens' fundamental rights in asserting choice in marriage:

1. **State accountability**: In questions of marriage the role of the state remains highly ambiguous.[30] It emerges as providing a space for social change as well as space for intervention to stem the process of social change. However, it must be recognised that the state's responsibility in combating such crimes is undisputed. The state agencies, whether political, legal or administrative, must be made accountable for safeguarding the citizens' fundamental rights in asserting choice in marriage; implementing existing laws; for failing to take and follow up appropriate measures, or adopting measures to prevent the commission of these crimes, as well as effective investigation and prosecution of perpetrators of these crimes. Provision should be made for exemplary punishment of the state functionaries, at all levels, in case of dereliction of duty.

For enforcing this, the onus is on the top-most level of our society—the politicians. Politicians who are even afraid to condemn the criminal activities of these unconstitutional bodies are hardly going to encourage any harsh measures against the traditional panchayats or rather against their caste constituencies and vote banks. In Haryana, for example, former Chief Minister O.P. Chautala had firmly maintained in an earlier case (cited above), that in social matters the *khap* panchayat has the right to decide. In the Manoj-Babli murder case he has openly supported the call of the *khap* panchayat to amend the Hindu Marriage Act. This has also been supported by, what the media describes as 'young, educated and modern',

Congress MP Navin Jindal, as also some other Congress MLAs like Shadi Lal Batra and Jagbir Malik. According to the media reports, the current Chief Minister Hooda, after prevaricating, has finally thrown his lot with the *khap* panchayats by declaring himself against same-*got* marriages.[31] The lead given by the politicians is only going to encourage the other state functionaries, like the police and the administration, to follow suit. In order to guard against the politicians' shenanigans, the state responsibility has to be underlined. The state or its functionaries must not be allowed to invoke custom, tradition or religious considerations to justify violence, or they must be prepared to be penalised. There is a need to develop penal sanctions against state functionaries who promote violence, directly or indirectly.

The state should also devise ways to adopt appropriate educational measures to modify social and cultural behaviour that sanctions such crimes. Awareness raising programmes should be followed to educate the state functionaries and the people of their rights, including all freedoms sanctioned under the Constitution including that of exercising choice in marriage.

State protection must be made available to couples who choose to defy tradition. High powered special cells could be constituted in every district to enable couples to approach them for purposes of marriage and safety. Women must be compulsorily placed by the state in 'protective custody' pending judicial decision rather than be forced to go back to their parents, as is done in most of the cases, to be victims of violence, inflicted or self-induced.

2. **Civil Society**: There is an urgent need to involve different segments of society in an attempt to evolve a solution to this problem and build a consensus against such crimes. For this, all forms of protests, ineffective or suppressed now, need to be encouraged. If needed, protestors should be given state protection. One major target for this attempt should be the youth who are the foremost segment of society who stand to be directly affected by customary and caste-related traditions. Women need to be encouraged to mobilise and work against violence of all kinds, public or private. It may be noted here that the major opposition to all such moves has come from

women themselves. This is amply demonstrated in all the cases which I investigated, including the one given above. While men take a back seat or in some cases even succumb to the illegal and draconian decisions of the caste panchayats, it is the women concerned who refuse to relinquish their rights. In the recent Manoj and Babli case, it is Chandrapati, the mother of Manoj, who initiated and carried to fruition a determined fight against the murderers, leading to their conviction. In this fight, very valuable help, moral and material, was rendered by women's organisations, but it essentially remained Chandrapati's fight and her refusal to crumble against heavy odds, which won her the day. The need is to strengthen the hands of both private and public institutions, NGOs and women's organisations and acknowledge the work that they are doing. Although difficult, in these efforts party labels and affiliations should be forgotten to accommodate all against a common concern.

3. **The traditional panchayats:** These need to be made representative of different segments of society. Women, among others, for example, must be allowed full participation in the community life and in decision making—be it family, village, caste or *khap* panchayat, where they are totally absent now.

Further, steps must be taken to make the traditional panchayats responsive to social needs. Historically, there is evidence to suggest that from time to time the *khap* panchayats themselves had initiated certain alleviating measures to correct the situation by relaxing the prohibitions on marriage between certain *gots*. For example, the Gulia and Kadyan *gots* were deemed to have originated from two brothers and marriage relations between them were prohibited. This was relaxed under British rule. Similarly, marriages between Kadyan and Jakhad *gots* were also prohibited. In 1946–47, this restriction was thrown open. More recently, in April 1995, a *sarv-khap* panchayat of the Chhahal and Mor *got* declared that members of these two *gots* could inter-marry. The prohibition on inter-marriage between these two *gots* was apparently instituted so long back that no one even remembered its origin. The decision of the *sarv-khap* panchayat was a ratification and formalisation of the already changing, and indeed changed, position.

The question is why this cannot be done now. The panchayats must be made to move towards this end. The need is for the state to encourage the reformist agenda of the traditional panchayats, which would remove the imposed restrictions on marriage. In fact, the reformist agenda of the caste panchayats must be made obligatory to their survival. They must be made to take up issues such as female foeticide, dowry, ostentatious weddings, erasing marriage restriction in both inter-caste and intra-caste marriages among other socially relevant issues. Why cannot the traditional panchayats adopt this reform agenda now when there is clearly a greater need of it today than ever before?

Notes

1.   There is a need to challenge the use of the word 'honour' in relation to crime. This usage rationalises and legitimises the crime by creating a notion that the crime is committed to 'save' one's 'honour'—a highly elusive and indefinable notion—and the society is bound by tradition to protect this.

2.   According to the Chandigarh lawyers, the Punjab and Haryana High Court receives as many as fifty applications per day from couples seeking protection. This is a staggering tenfold rise from about five to six applications a day, five years ago.

3.   The notice was sent on a petition moved by an NGO Shakti Vahini, on 21 June 2010, by Justices R.M. Lodha, and A.K. Patnaik to the centre and states of Punjab, Haryana, Rajasthan, Himachal Pradesh, Madhya Pradesh, Uttar Paradesh, Jharkhand and Bihar, seeking their response to the 'honour killings in their states.

4.   For the most comprehensive research, highlighting activist and practice-oriented academic perspectives from different countries of Europe, the Middle East, Latin America and South Asia, involving different religious communities see Welchman and Hossain (2005). Also see, Jafri (2008), Jasam (2001), Shah (1997), and Hussain (1997).

5.   S.S. Ahluwalia, the Indian representative at the United Nations Social, Humanitarian and Cultural Committee firmly rejected charges of honour killings of women saying the report of the United Nations special rapporteur in this regard was based on 'hearsay' and lacked credibility. See *The Indian Express,* 12 October 2002.

6. This paper draws upon and extends the discussion presented in Chowdhry (2007a).

7. Certain persons however could not marry under this Act: those related as *sapinda* (shared body relationship), unless the custom or usage governing them permitted marriage, those with a living spouse or those of unsound mind, suffering from mental disorder and incapable of giving consent, and those subject to recurrent attacks of insanity and epilepsy. See Section 5 of the Hindu Marriage Act, in Desai (1966: 599–751). The age limit of 15 years for the girl and 18 years for the boy sanctioned under this Act was raised to 18 and 21 respectively by the Child Restraint (Amendment) Act 2 of 1978.

8. For these regional diversities and their accommodation and articulation in the politico-legal regime of post-independent India, see Uberoi (2002).

9. I am using the term 'traditional' panchayat to distinguish it from the statutory panchayat established in post-independence India. This usage in no way means that this pre-colonial and colonial body was in any way a non-changing, static institution. Like caste, traditional panchayat has also undergone changes over time.

10. Retzlaff distinguishes four different kinds of traditional panchayats in northern India: one, caste panchayat; two, general meeting panchayat or the village multi-caste panchayat; three, the farmer-retainer panchayat; four, the single purpose panchayat. See, Retzlaff (1962: 18).

11. According to Hershman, the clan and caste panchayats in Punjab have lost the authority they had exercised in the past, when they acted as courts and arbitrators in disputes affecting their members. According to him, cases are seldom submitted, as they once were, to the elders of the *biradari* or caste panchayats to decide. The situation in Haryana and Uttar Pradesh would appear to be different in this regard from that of Punjab. See Hershman (1981: 35–36).

12. For details of these cases see, Chowdhry (1997).

13. In January 1998, for example, in village Ichhapuri, district Gurgaon, a woman killed her *jeth* for his incestuous designs on her. See *Dainik Jagran*, 7 January 1998, p. 4.

14. In a 1994 case from village Bhiwadi, the all-caste panchayat, dominated by the dominant Ahirs of the village, blackened the faces of a woman and her father-in-law and paraded them naked in the village for allegedly indulging in incest. Reportedly, the lower caste members of the victims' community

sided with the Ahirs in inflicting this punishment. A few villagers who protested were hounded out. The police did not even turn up. The matter was later hushed up under directions from the politicians. Case reported in *Dainik Jagran*, 19 April 1994, pp. 1, 11.

15. For details see Chowdhry (2007b).

16. An inter-caste married couple, Kuldeep (Rajput) and Monika (Gujjar) from Wazirpur, near Ashok Vihar in Delhi, after four years of their marriage, along with another girl, Shubha, were killed in June 2010 allegedly by the brother and male cousins of the girls. The uncle of one of the accused openly took pride in the act, and informed the newspaper journalists and television channels that '*samaj ke liye yeh murder zaroori tha…is kaam se in larkon ne sahi kiya hai* (For the good of the society, this murder was necessary. These youngsters have set a good example). See *Times of India*, 24 and 25 June 2010, p. 1.

17. In such marriages, each girl or boy from the scheduled caste receives Rs 25,000. This amount includes Rs 10,000 in cash and Rs 15,000 in fixed deposit for six years in the joint account of the couple. This amount has been raised recently. However, there were hardly any takers. According to figures available Rs 2 lakh were distributed under this scheme in the year 1999 and Rs 3 lakhs in 2000. See *Dainik Bhaskar*, 10 August 2000, p. 7.

18. For this, see a most incisive report by Sanghtana (1991); also see, Balagopal (1991) and Kannabiran and Kannabiran (1991: 2130–33).

19. See *Times of India*, 28 May 2010, p. 1.

20. G.D. Mandelbaum (1988) argues how the concept of honour and the practice of purdah operate to control female sexuality.

21. A series of surveys conducted among the youth of major cities of India showed an overwhelming majority (84 per cent) opting for arranged marriage. This is when they have ample opportunity to interact with the opposite sex. For details of the survey see *Hindustan Times*, 16 February 2003, Sunday magazine, p. 1.

22. In December 2005, a police assault in Meerut mounted under the code name of 'Operation Majnu' (operation lovers) on young couples in a public park has seen its repeat in most cities, in one form or the other. In a bizarre display of police brutality the Meerut (UP) police physically assaulted couples, slapping, punching and dragging the 'offenders' under Section 294 of the Indian Penal Code (IPC) in a drive against 'obscenity'. It specially targeted women, forcing them to face television camera crews.

Such instances of violence in pursuance of the ideology of 'honour' and guardianship can be multiplied manifold across India, even in the capital Delhi. It is a similar behavioural pattern at work when the rejected suitors throw acid on women or even kill those who assert themselves and rebuff their 'romantic' overtures. The ideology working behind these is the same: women are not free to exercise their choice in these matters.

23. For instance, in February 2009, women outside a pub in Bangalore were abused and beaten up by goons who did not like their 'behaviour'. Since then moral police has been regularly on the prowl in the city attacking various entertainment places. On Valentines Day in 2010, the Pune police turned moral police by instructing the youngsters not to indulge in any 'love celebrations'.

24. For details of the Act and its comparison with the earlier situation existing in British India, see the Hindu Succession Act, No. XXX of 1956, in Desai (1966). Also see, Gupte (1981).

25. This equal share of intestate succession however did not extend to the concept of joint family property where a son's share in the property is calculated to be five times that of the daughter's share. For details see Carroll (1991).

26. A total of 1,438,997 males in the age group of 15–44 years out of a population of 3,970,390 males are unmarried. See *Census of Haryana,* 1991, Socio-cultural Tables, Series 8, Part IV-A, Chandigarh, 1994, p. 22.

27. In Rohtak, out of a total male population of 977,075 between the age group of 15–44, 547,922 were unmarried. See *Census of Haryana,* 1991, Socio-cultural Tables, Series 8, Part IV-A, Chandigarh, 1994, pp. 22–23.

28. This has been repeatedly witnessed in cases like that of lynching of Dalits in Dulina in 2005 and in Gohana in 2007, and now most recent one of April 2010 in village Mirchpur of Hissar district, where a section of Jats torched a dozen Dalit houses, leading to the burning alive of a polio-stricken girl and her grandfather. In cases where violence is resorted to, to implement the panchayat's decision an even more effective weapon is placed in their hands. Significantly, the desire to enforce their domination and prove their strength is an interest that is amply shared by other members of dominant caste groups.

29. Changes on the anvil are: amendments to The Indian Penal Act, The Indian Evidence Act and The Special Marriages Act. A host of other measures to deter violence associated with marriages inflicted by the family members

or the caste/community collective are also being discussed. For example, the existing criminal law requires the prosecution to establish guilt of the accused, the new law will reverse the onus of proof; the accused will have to prove their innocence. The law enforcement agencies would also have the power to arrest and act against community leaders who may be spurring or condoning violence. The proposed law also proposes to factor in punishment for the intangibles of social humiliation—social boycotts, hurting, ostracizing, denying water and rations or exiling those who defy the community's diktats. Even the High Court of Haryana and Punjab as in its latest directive (June 2010) to all the District and Session judges of Haryana, Punjab and the Union Territory of Delhi, has instructed that trial of runaway couples must be concluded within three months of the filling of the charge sheet.

30.   For details see Chowdhry (2004).

31.   See *Times of India*, 4 June 2010, pp. 1, 16.

References

Balagopal, K. (1991) 'Post Chunduru and other Chundurus', *Economic and Political Weekly*, vol. XXVI, no. 42, pp. 2399–2405.

Bathla, Har Bhagwan (1994) *Panchayati Raj and Political Parties: an Empirical Study at Grass-root Level in Haryana,* Kurukshetra: Nirmal Book Agency.

Carroll, Lucy (1991) 'Daughter's Right of Inheritance', *Modern Asian Studies,* vol. 25, no. 4, pp. 791–809.

Chowdhry, Prem (1997) 'Enforcing Cultural Codes: Gender and Violence in Northern India', *Economic and Political Weekly,* vol. 32, no. 19, pp. 1919–28.

_____ (2004) 'Private Lives, State Intervention: Cases of Run-away Marriage in Rural North India', *Modern Asian Studies*, vol. 38, Pt I, pp. 55–84.

_____ (2007a) *Contentious Marriages, Eloping Couples: Gender, Caste and Patriarchy in Northern India,* Delhi: Oxford University Press.

_____ (2007b) 'Fluctuating Fortunes of Wives: Creeping Rigidity in Inter-caste Marriages in the Colonial Period', *The Indian Historical Review*, vol. XXXIV, no. I, p. 210–43.

_____ (2009) "First Our Jobs then Our Girls': The Dominant Caste Perceptions on the 'Rising' Dalits', *Modern Asian Studies*, vol. 43, prt 2, pp. 437–79.

Desai, Sunderlal T. (1966) *Mulla Principles of Hindu Law,* Bombay: N.M. Tripathi Pvt. Ltd.

Dhagamwar, Vasudha (1992) *Law, Power and Justice: The Protection of Personal Rights in the Indian Penal Code,* New Delhi: Sage Publications, pp. 303–10.

Dube, Leela (1986) 'Seed and Earth: The Symbolism of Biological Reproduction and Sexual Relations of Production', in Leela Dube, Eleanor Leacock and Shirley Ardener (eds), *Visibility and Power: Essays on Women in Society and Development*, Delhi: Oxford University Press, pp. 22–53.

Gupte, S.V. (1981) *Hindu Law*, vol. I, Bombay: All India Reporter.

Hershman, Paul (1981) *Punjabi Kinship and Marriage*, Delhi: Hindustan Publishing Corporation.

Hussain, Neelam(1997) 'Narrative Appropriation of Saima: Coersion and Consent in Muslim Pakistan', in Neelam Hussain, Samiya Mumtaz and Rubina Saigol (eds), *Engendering the Nation State*, vol. I, Lahore: Simorgh Publications, pp. 199–259.

Jafri, Amir H. (2008) *Honour Killing: Dilemma, Ritual, Understanding*, Karachi: Oxford University Press, Pakistan.

Jasam, Saima (2001) *Honour, Shame and Resistence*, Lahore: ASR Publications.

Kannabiran, Vasanth and Kalpana Kannabiran (1991) 'Caste and Gender: Understanding Dynamics of Power and Violence', *Economic and Political Weekly*, vol. XXVI, no. 37.

Kolenda, Pauline (1982) 'Widowhood among 'Untouchable' Chuhras', in Akos Oster, Lina Fruzetti, Steve Barnett (eds), *Concepts of Persons: Kinship, Caste and Marriage in India*, London: Harvard University Press, pp. 172–220.

Mandelbaum, G.D. (1988) *Women's Seclusion and Men's Honour: Sex Roles in North India, Bangladesh and Pakistan*, Tuscon: The University of Arizona Press.

Retzlaff, Ralph H. (1962) *Village Government in India: A Case Study*, Bombay: Asia Publishing House.

Sanghtana, Samata (1991) 'Upper Caste Violence: Study of Chunduru Carnage', *Economic and Political Weekly*, vol. XXVI, no. 36.

Shah, Nafisa (1997) 'Role of the Community in Honour Killings in Sindh', in Neelam Hussain, Samiya Mumtaz and Rubina Saigol (eds), *Engendering the Nation State*, vol. I, Lahore: Simorgh Publications.

Uberoi, Patricia (2002) 'Kinship Varieties and Political Expediency: Legislating the Family in Post-independence India', *International Research Centre for Japanese Studies*, International Symposium, vol. 19, Koyoto, Japan, pp. 147–76.

Welchman, Lynn and Sara Hossain (eds) (2005) *'Honour': Crime, Paradigms, and Violence against Women*, London and New York: Spinifex Press, Victoria and Zed Books.

Gender-based Violence in Public Spaces
Consequences and Cost

NANDITA BHATLA

+·+

Background

Gender-based violence (GBV) is a pervasive phenomenon that impacts the daily lives of women and girls across the world, and yet is the most ignored and normalised form of abuse. It is estimated that 'around the world at least one woman in every three has been beaten, coerced into sex, or otherwise abused in her lifetime. Most often the abuser is a member of her own family' (Heise et al. 1999).

Within South Asia, GBV takes on particularly violent characteristics. The spectrum of GBV ranges from the universally prevalent problem of domestic violence to region-specific forms such as 'honour' killings and acid throwing. Evidence demonstrates that all violence against women is a consequence of gender inequity and discriminatory hierarchies of power between men and women. Misguided gender norms continue to fuel various forms of violence, whether in public or private spheres, and it cannot be reduced without redefining what a woman means in society.

The last decade has seen increased discourse around the issue of domestic violence, specifically Intimate Partner Violence (IPV), a form that has the magnitude of a silent epidemic raging within the four walls of homes, oft considered as a 'safe haven'. This discourse is being propelled by evidence and efforts to develop interventions to break norms around violence as a 'personal or private' issue; and that of the inevitability and normalcy of violence within marital relationships. Domestic violence frequently happens behind closed doors, making it difficult to prosecute offenders and uphold law prohibiting this violence. Further, without social and economic empowerment, many women are hesitant to confront abusive family members because of the potential consequences. Given these challenges, policy around domestic violence and violence against women can be difficult to justify through empirical evidence alone. One method of overcoming this obstacle is to estimate the 'cost' that violence incurs on society—in economic and social terms; on individuals' lives as well as on society as a whole. 'Costs' are described in terms of the social, health and economic consequences to a more specific estimation of the 'monetary or economic cost'. The monetary cost is constructed by measuring and quantifying the various consequences (as a whole or specific measurable elements) that households and national economies experience due to violence. It is also recognised that though monetary cost can never fully capture the toll that devastating experiences of violence can have, such an exercise can be crucial to demonstrate impact and act as an advocacy tool for justifying policy decisions for allocation of resources and necessary political action. IPV and sexual assault are two forms for which economic estimates exist, especially in the developed nations. The need for undertaking such exercises stems from similar concerns, across forms of GBV. The inevitability and normalcy of violence targeted towards women, whether in private or public spheres, minimises response and creates apathy that de-prioritizes this concern. Highlighting the consequences or 'costs' of specific forms of violence is a necessary and powerful tool to draw attention and urge political action.

To start discussing the costs of any form of GBV, one must answer the question: What is needed to estimate costs? Looking to the rich body of literature on calculating costs of IPV studies[1] in the early 1990s one finds various costing definitions and methodologies for cost estimation. Basic elements of these include having clear and precise operational definitions, mapping the help-seeking behaviour of women experiencing violence (as defined) and services available, determining the various types of costs to be estimated, and gathering relevant data to undertake the costing exercise. These various elements indicate that a minimal amount of clarity and data on the extent and nature of violence need to be established to undertake econometric exercises of cost estimation.

This essay presents a preliminary discussion of the 'costs' of specific public forms of gender-based violence. It undertakes a conceptual exercise on the framework of defining GBV in public spaces, including operational definitions of cost and GBV in public spaces. It also reviews existing methods for estimating and quantifying the cost of IPV and discusses their relevance for estimating the cost of forms of public violence, particularly within the South Asia context.

Concepts and Definitions

Defining Violence in Public Spaces: Who and Where

While GBV and domestic violence (DV) now have widely accepted definitions, violence in public spaces is not a well conceived holistic category. This essay will examine violence in accordance with existing definitions which define GBV by the setting and the identity of the perpetrator in relation to the victim.

Through its General Recommendation 19, the Committee on the Elimination of Discrimination against Women (CEDAW), at its eleventh session in 1992, took the important step of formally including GBV as a form of gender-based discrimination. To quote:

CEDAW General Recommendation 19 on VAW views gender-based violence as a form of discrimination that constitutes a serious obstacle in the enjoyment of human rights and fundamental freedoms by women, and addresses intersections of gender-based violence with the different substantive areas covered by the articles of CEDAW. It defines gender-based violence as "violence directed against a woman because she is a woman or which affects a woman disproportionately. It includes physical, mental or sexual harm or suffering, threats of such acts, coercion and other deprivations of liberty".[2]

States parties were, therefore, requested to take appropriate and effective measures to overcome all forms of GBV, whether by public or private act.[3]

It is important to examine the reports of the UN Special Rapporteurs on Violence on the causes and consequences of violence in order to examine the way 'public' forms of violence are described and defined, as these also determine the data collection, reporting and accountability mechanisms for the state.

A comprehensive document presents a review of the 15-years of existence of the UN Rapporteurs of Violence, and provides a foundation for examining violence in public spaces. The section on the Definition and Scope discusses the specific public and private forms of violence with reference to the Declaration on the Elimination of Violence against Women (DE VAW). It states: The Declaration on the Elimination of Violence against Women (DE VAW) provides a more comprehensive framework on VAW in terms of definition, scope, obligations of the state, and the role of the United Nations. Specifically, it defines VAW to mean 'any act of gender-based violence that results in, or is likely to result in, physical, sexual or psychological harm or suffering to women, including threats of such acts, coercion or arbitrary deprivation of liberty, whether occurring in public or private life'. DE VAW further outlines the scope of private and public to include violence in the family, violence in the community, and violence perpetrated or condoned by the state, wherever it occurs.[4] Typically, the forms of violence have been categorised into the following three categories:

1. *Violence in the family*: such as DV; battering; marital rape; incest; forced prostitution by the family; violence against domestic workers and the girl child (non-spousal violence, violence related to exploitation); sex-selective abortion and infanticide; traditional practices such as female genital mutilation; dowry-related violence; and religious/customary laws.

2. *Violence in the community*: such as rape/sexual assault; sexual harassment; violence within institutions; trafficking and forced prostitution; violence against women migrant workers; and pornography.

3. *Violence perpetrated or condoned by the state*: such as GBV during armed conflict; custodial violence; violence against refugees and internally displaced persons.

These definitions do leave considerable gaps, as all forms of violence cannot be placed within mutually exclusive categories. These categories distinguish (*i*) the space or site where violence occurs, (*ii*) and/or the perpetrator, keeping the family as the pivotal point. The public-private dichotomy is emphasised in such a categorisation, to focus attention on the non-public—that which is often hidden, and can fall outside the ambit of law enforcement. All spaces that are outside the domestic and all perpetrators that are non-family (with the exception of the state) appear to be classified under violence in the community. Thus, violence against domestic workers is categorised within violence in the family, as it occurs within the household or the domestic space, even though it is not perpetrated by members in one's own 'family'. The definition of 'family' becomes an important consideration for classification of similar forms across the categories. A distinction is made between prostitution 'by family' and 'forced prostitution', presumably by members other than family. The complexities of sexual violence also provide another example of these gaps. Rape or assault committed by *non-family* (and non-state actors), and in spaces *outside* the home would be classified within the category of violence by the community. It is noted that marital rape and incest fall under the first category, though rape by 'other family members' is not specified. For this essay, a simplified method of categorisation will be used to exemplify the utility of cost estimation methodology for public violence.

The distinction laid out above, between public and private spaces, will define the scope of discussion here. In this essay, 'Public spaces' will be used synonymously with social community spaces, the space outside the boundaries of the home, but *not* within other institutions, and these will include streets, marketplaces, bus stops, and community forums such as panchayats. These are places that are directly impacted and governed by

FIGURE 1   **Categorising Violence**

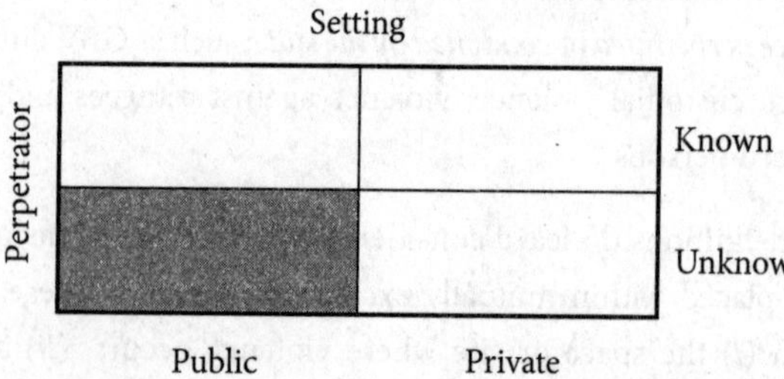

law and policy and that enable interaction with community/'non-family' members. If these social spaces render women vulnerable, it has the potential to add another layer of controls that will impact the everyday life experiences of women. Safety of these social spaces is emphasised from the view of advocacy to define specific interventions. The issue of safety in public spaces is not only a citizenship right that needs to be provided by the state, it is also a critical prerequisite for women to feel secure about entering and then moving in them and accessing opportunities for growth. For this, conceptual gender shifts of acceptance of women within these spaces must accompany strict enforcement regimes that respond efficiently to curb violence perpetrated on women.

Sexual harassment within institutions or brothels as sites of exploitation of trafficked women will not be included for detailed discussion here. This is for the purpose of delimiting the scope. While both of these are public sites (outside of the home), violence here is governed through additional mechanisms and dynamics. Commercial interests govern trafficking, that has established methods and routes with source and destination sites. On the other hand, 'institutions' is a generic term that can be further sub-categorised into several types, and have their specific laws, policies and regulations that govern them. Accountability and advocacy for violence-free environments within these institutions will have to take into consideration these additional guidelines and structures. For example, formal work institutions will be influenced by specific workplace policies, and the more recent guidelines for sexual harassment. This would require further deliberation, and hence is not included within here.

Violence inflicted during times of conflict and war will be excluded from the discussion as well. Times of war and conflict exacerbate all violence against women and girls. Escalated GBV has become an inevitable component of all conflict and a feature of conflict zones. Apart from the general social upheaval, social and economic crisis and increased vulnerability of women in public spaces during these times, violence perpetrated on womenfolk is also used as a deliberate strategy of revenge, humiliation and violation. Public space becomes even more unsafe for women, including increased risks of forced migration, trafficking and sexual violence. The role of the state law and order enforcement machinery becomes significant and perhaps this has prompted a separate categorisation, as discussed above. The dynamics underlying GBV during war and conflict are complex, with added determinants that differentiate its impact and incurred costs from that which occurs during times of peace. The specific forms of violence that will be focused on are discussed in the next section

Public Spaces as Sites of Violence

Before discussing any estimates of the costs of GBV in public spaces, it is important to consider the social theory and norms that govern public spaces and appropriate roles for men and women within those spaces. If law governs public spaces, why is violence tolerated and pervasive there? Gender norms define and describe public space and the behaviours that are perceived as acceptable or unacceptable. While the law for behaviour in public space may be presented as gender neutral, the reality is that there are implicit social rules and 'laws' that make violence acceptable. Notions of patriarchy dominate public space and contemporary moral sense. Public spaces, particularly within South Asia, are considered as primarily masculine spaces. Men leave their homes to engage in productive work and jobs, and also to spend time with peers in public spaces. While this may include playing games and healthy interactions, it may also be the site for collective behaviours that are potentially harmful. These include drinking, gambling and indulging in sexual harassment. While men are generally permitted in any and all spaces within the public sphere, private spaces are considered women's habitat. Women belong at home and a woman who goes out into 'male' spaces may face the consequences of this decision; from sexual harassment to more extreme forms of assault. Masculinisation of these spaces also places the responsibility of male sexual behaviour and boundaries on women themselves.

The conceptual explanation underlying the use of violence against women in public spaces to regulate and maintain these gender norms is a patriarchal paradigm of protection and punishment. Women are to be 'protected' and relegated to confines and controls dictated by patriarchy, and overstepping or violation of these justifies punishment. This overstepping or violation may be in terms of actual boundaries of physical space (say outside the home, of certain community spaces, etc.) as well as non-physical boundaries set by norms (such as taking certain decisions, or exhibiting certain behaviours and actions). Depending on the society, these rules are more or less relaxed, with loopholes that may permit women in certain spaces at certain times, and for reasons considered permissible and acceptable by that society. However, the penalty for breaking these rules is frequently a form of violence.

Forms of Public Violence in South Asian Spaces: Blurring the Lines and Social Conscience

This is the case in South Asia, where it is seen as natural to harass women in any public space (streets, markets, public transport), with more gruesome forms such as sexual assault. Rape is perceived as justified or expected if they are unmarried, unaccompanied, out at night, or seen in traditional 'male' spaces such as bars. A particularly disturbing and shockingly acceptable trend in certain communities is the violence perpetrated on women when they violate social norms, such as taking the decision to choose a life partner, compounded by breaking the hierarchy of the social order (caste, class, religion) resulting in acts ranging from public humiliation to murder in the form of 'honour' killings. These are forms where the lines of the public and the private become blurred in terms of both the site and the perpetrators (see Figure 1 above). The woman's actions are inextricably linked to family honour, and when she, by her acts, violates the norms of maintaining this honour, she is punished.

However, the punishment does not remain restricted to the family, and the boundaries of categorisation (as seen in Figure 1) become blurred. The community intervenes here in two distinct ways. First, family honour embodies within it a notional community, whether it is the actual physical community that the family resides in or it is the notion of larger community prescribed by birth and ancestral linkages. Thus, the girl[5] violates the honour of the entire clan, or caste. Second, because of this the community is involved as both the site and sometimes as co-perpetrators of this violence. Humiliation and killings happen in public spaces, often with the knowledge and participation (at least as bystanders) of the community members. A latent intent is also to set an example that will potentially prohibit others from repeating the violation. Interestingly, honour-related violence (HRV) finds mention in the description in the forms of violence on the rise in Europe (IPPF EN 2009). The same article quotes a UN estimate that 'every year 5000 women die in 'honor' killings.'[6]

Other forms of violence in South Asia that are enacted in public spaces, but with blurred boundaries of the private, are acid throwing and witch hunting. Witch hunting has attracted several studies and analysis, wherein it is analysed that labelling of certain women as 'witches' and then meting out gruesome violence against them including death is a 'convenient' way of doing away with these women, including for underlying gains such as familial property. In instances of acid throwing, the intent lies in a personal relationship and revenge, though both the relationship and the perpetrator may not involve the 'family' per se.

In India, such extreme events may be relatively less common[7] than other forms of GBV in public spaces such as sexual harassment or 'eve teasing', but they impact the public conscious increasingly with increased access to media through web-based media and general media coverage. All these forms are included within gender-based public violence, as they occur within the 'public space' and are perpetrated, in part, because of socially pre-described social roles.

A second related underlying concept, thus, is the need to distinguish actual acts of public violence and the threat of violence. The fear of violating norms and boundaries means that GBV will manifest itself in prohibitory forms as well, and these have a different set of impact and consequences that need to be considered. The threat of violence is necessary to highlight as this emotional manipulation perpetuates gendered notions of acceptable behaviour in public spaces as well as creates fear of the punitive consequences of challenging these notions. Thus, women shy away from being in the public, have restricted mobility and face numerous consequences such as denial to education and employment opportunities and services, denial of the right to participate in social, political and community processes, and denial of the freedom to exercise other civil and cultural rights. These are the costs women pay in terms of 'missed opportunities' or 'unrealized potential'. Many of these have been referred to as socio-economic violence, broadly understood as the cause and effect of the dominant power relations in society that result in denial for the weaker section. The specific acts of violence in public spaces can be classified in the categories of verbal and emotional violence (including name calling, eve teasing, threats, sexual advances and harassment, exhibitionism), and physical/sexual violence (includes groping, molestation, rape and beatings).

Consequences and Costs

Evidence: Existing and Needed

The first step in beginning to measure the cost of GBV in public spaces is to estimate its prevalence. Measurements for these forms of violence are sparse. The prevalence and extent of most of these forms of violence is difficult to estimate at a population level since there have been no large-scale household-based studies in India on these. What is available are routine data collected for those forms of violence that are seen as legally defined 'criminal' categories by the National Crime Records Bureau (NCRB). These include rape and sexual harassment.[8] In India, certain sections of the Indian Penal Code (IPC) establish the offence of insulting the modesty of a woman, whether by word, gesture or act: IPC, Section 509 (Sexual Harassment); Sections 354 and 354A (Molestation).[9] In Delhi, the Delhi Metropolitan Council has criminalised 'eve teasing', which is defined as words, spoken or written, or signs, or visible representations or gestures, or acts or reciting or singing indecent words in a public place by a man to the annoyance of a woman.[10] Sexual harassment is a preferred terminology over 'eve teasing', as the latter is seen to connote a 'lighter' or more casual intent and action. In 2007, NCRB reported 38,734 molestation incidents in the country, which was a 5.8 per cent increase from the previous year. Of incidents of sexual harassment, 10,950 were recorded, an increase of 9.9 per cent over the previous year.

Though admittedly under-reported and subsequently under-estimated in prevalence, the same report notes an increasing trend in cases of rape over the years from 2003–7. Rape cases are further categorised as incest rape and other rape cases by NCRB. The report also provides an age-wise distribution of the victims. It notes:

9.5% (1,972) of the total victims of Rape were girls under 15 years of age, while 15.2% (3,152) were teenaged girls (15-18 years). Nearly two-third (11,984) (57.7%) were women in the age-group 18-30 years. 3,530 victims (17.0%) were in the age-group of 30-50 years while 0.6% (133) were over 50 years of age. *Offenders were known to the victims in as many as 19,188 (92.5%) cases.* Parents/close family members were involved in 2.1% (405 out of 19,188) of these cases, neighbours were involved in 36.0% cases (6,902 out of 19,188) and relatives were involved in 7.5% (1,448 out of 19,188) cases.[11]

Studies that can be sourced for examining the 'missed opportunities' for women are few.

A recent document by the World Health Organization (WHO) that examines the role of gender in the achievement of the Millennium Development Goals (MDGs) describes that 'for some girls, lack of safety in or around schools is the chief obstacle to getting an education. In some countries, there are high levels of sexual violence and harassment from teachers and male students including rape, assault, and physical and verbal harassment'. It further recommends that 'Educational authorities must ensure that schools are safe places for all students, with special attention to the security of girls'. The PROBE report notes sexual harassment and unsafe environment in and around schools as a reason for fewer women opting to be teachers in the state of Uttar Pradesh. Similar effects of rigid patriarchal norms defined the experience of many women who entered the political scenario under the Panchayati Raj Act. Violence was often escalated, though no reliable data is available on the number of women who chose *not to* contest due to fear or other prohibitory factors.

A recent study undertaken in Delhi under the 'Safe Cities' initiative[12] in March 2010 aimed to identify factors that create greater safety and inclusion for women in public spaces in and around the city. It gathered information on the nature and forms of GBV faced by women in public spaces, and the role of governing agencies and police in safeguarding women's rights. In its key findings, the study states: 'Women and girls face violence and the fear of it on a continuous basis in the city. Due to fear and harassment, many women do not have the autonomy to freely move in a variety of public spaces such as markets, parks, bus stops'. Verbal and visual harassment were the most common forms reported by over 70 per cent women, while 31 per cent reported physical harassment.[13]

These data all suggest that recognised and reported violence prevalence is significant but presents only a margin of the reality. This partial empirical picture of violence in public spaces will require supplemental data collection using innovative data collection tools and survey designs to create a more complete picture of cost and consequence.

The Consequences of Violence

The consequences of violence are typically described in two ways: first, in terms of the impact of violence on key outcomes such as reproductive health, mental health, productivity etc.; and, second, by estimating monetary costs. While describing the impact, most documents use VAW as a broad category in their descriptions, while others have highlighted consequences of specific forms of violence, such as 'consequences of physical assault', thus making it difficult to use the public-private concept for further delineation. Several studies have been carried out in the industrialised countries, such as USA, Canada, Australia, and UK, wherein a well organised service provision system and strong routine data collection systems contribute to the feasibility of undertaking such exercises, as will be described in detail in this section. For instance, the World Bank in 1993 estimated that in industrialised countries, health costs for DV and rape account for one in five disability-adjusted life years (DALYs), lost to women aged 15-44 yrs. Every year lost due to premature death is counted as one DALY, and every year spent sick or incapacitated as a fraction of the DALY, with value depending on the severity of the disability (World Bank 1993).

The consequences of GBV have been positioned within different frameworks. Apart from a denial of fundamental human rights and freedoms, violence has oft been referred to as public health issue, and more recently as a developmental concern. It is argued that violence impacts the development processes and erodes its gains. Violence costs development, obstructs participation in developmental processes, and contradicts the goals of development.[14] This discussion can be used to frame the cost of 'missed opportunities' as a cost incurred due to GBV in public spaces, as described in the preceding section. Recent literature links violence to the achievement of the MDGs, wherein the achievement of specific goals is seen as being compromised due to lack of attention to underlying gender constructs, including violence (WHO 2005).

The specific health related physical and psychological consequences have been laid out by WHO, as presented below. Studies have also linked the experience of DV (in homes) to child survival. Overall use of health services is another parameter on which impact has been studied. For example, a VAW fact sheet[15] cites studies from Nicaragua, US and Zimbabwe that indicate that women who are physically or sexually assaulted use health services more than women with no history of violence.

Apart from direct consequences on the individual, the impact of violence is also captured through the burden that violence places on the economy; this is referred to as the economic cost of violence, and is calculated in monetary terms. The most rudimentary conceptualisation of costs is in terms of direct and indirect costs.

Direct costs include costs directly linked to responding to violence, which are largely the costs of service provision of different sectors (medical/health, law enforcement, judicial and social services).

Indirect costs represent the losses incurred as a result of violence, and these typically fall within aspects of social and economic well-being of an individual, covering aspects such as productivity, participation of labour force, suffering, and intergenerational effects as well. Duvvury et al. (2004) detail the types of costs calculated in indirect costs to include: (1) the value of goods and services lost in the forms of income loss through job loss or increased absenteeism, decreased productivity in the workplace, and decreased labour force participation; (2) costs of increased mortality and morbidity; (3) pain, suffering, and loss in quality of life; (4) costs of increased drug and alcohol use; (5) inter-generational transmission of violence; (6) behavioural problems of children; and, (7) reduced educational performance of children, to name a few.

TABLE 1   **Health Consequences of Violence Against Women**

NON-FATAL OUTCOMES *Mental health outcomes*	NON-FATAL OUTCOMES *Physical health outcomes*	FATAL OUTCOMES
• Fear • Anxiety • Depression • Low self-esteem • Sexual dysfunction • Eating problems • Obsessive-compulsive disorder • Post-traumatic stress disorder	• Injury • Unwanted pregnancy • Gynaecological problems • STDs including HIV/AIDS • Miscarriage • Pelvic inflammatory disease • Chronic pelvic pain • Headaches • Permanent disabilities • Asthma • Irritable bowel syndrome • Self-injurious behaviours(smoking, unprotected sex)	Suicide • Homicide • Maternal mortality • HIV/AIDS

Source: 'Violence against Women', WHO Consultation, 1996.

Discussions on classification of costs note the need to have a more nuanced framework for understanding indirect costs. The classification suggested by Buvinic et al. (1999) is widely accepted and quoted, as this provides a typology distinguishing different types of impacts and corresponding costs. These are:

1. **Direct costs:** refer to the value of goods and services used in treating or preventing violence. The costs include service-related costs as well as costs of programmes for prevention and advocacy. These compute expenditure on the following services: medical (hospitalisation, care in clinics and psychological counselling service), police, criminal justice system, housing (shelters and short stay homes) and social

    services aimed at prevention and advocacy such as trainings, advocacy
programmes, etc.

2. **Non-monetary costs:** capture human costs, including increased
   suffering, morbidity and mortality; abuse of alcohol and drugs; and
   depression.

3. **Economic multiplier effects:** This includes the broader economic
   effects of violence against women, that include aspects as increased
   absenteeism; decreased labour market participation; reduced
   productivity; lower earnings, investment and savings; and lower intergenerational productivity.

4. **Social multiplier effects:** are described as the impact of violence on
   interpersonal relations and quality of life. These include the effect on
   children witnessing the violence, reduced quality of life, and reduced
   participation in democratic processes.

It is obvious from this categorisation that different categories of costs
would require different methodologies, and corresponding data sets that
enable the essential parameters to be defined and quantified. For estimation
of costs for any form of violence, the following are critical: (1) defining
the form of violence; (2) measurement of the form of violence; (3) the
conceptualisation of the help-seeking behaviour of those experiencing
violence; (4) delineating the types of costs to be measured; (5) deciding the
appropriate methodology and analysis framework; and (6) deciding on data
collection methods to fill existing data gaps.

Most studies have focused on estimating the costs using either
direct costs of service provision, or estimating the economic multiplier
effects—both costs that are more easily quantifiable than other social or
intergenerational impacts; and these have been primarily around two forms
of violence: inter-personal violence and sexual assault/rape.

Computation of Direct Costs

The most common approach to estimating direct costs is the accounting
methodology (Morrison and Orlando 2004). In this, costs are calculated
for specific categories and total cost computed as the simple sum of all

distinct categories of costs. Thus, direct costs of a specific form of GBV will mean the sum of actual expenditures related to seeking health care services, judicial services and social services; assuming that a woman impacted by violence has chosen to seek all three.

The direct cost is typically calculated by establishing

1. the unit cost of each specific service
2. then multiplying the unit cost by the number of times the service was utilised.

This requires that there is reliable data on prevalence rates, service utilisation of specific services and calculation of unit costs. Population-based surveys that collect information on prevalence, response patterns and use of services as a result of violence are used to source information on women's use of medical and mental health services. Health care costs are usually gathered by a survey of medical service providers. (See Box 1 below that details steps followed, as set out by the Center for Disease Control [CDC 2003] for the estimation of direct costs.)

Estimation of the unit cost of service provision becomes critical in these methodologies. Duvvury et al. (2004) note that most studies rely on data from other studies that have estimated the cost of an average hospital visit, doctor visit, police action, etc., even if the utilisation of the service is not due to DV. Walby, for example, uses unit costs for medical services developed in the costing exercises for road traffic accidents. While using proxy data may be relatively unproblematic for medical services on the assumption that an injury is an injury regardless of the cause, it may not be suitable in the case of a police response, which varies considerably with both the level of the crime and the underlying situation that led to the crime. A similar situation is evident in the study by Yodanis and Godenzi (1999) in which an average cost of court cases is applied to all legal petitions filed by women, such as divorce, protection order, or separation order. This example is also relevant to the third issue of whether it is appropriate to apply the full cost of the service or only that proportion which reflects the cost of the service due to domestic violence.

BOX 1

Adapting from the method laid out for estimating the direct costs of intimate partner violence (IPV), by the Centers for Disease Control, USA, the steps for estimating (only) medical cost of any form of violence would involve:

Step 1. Determine usage of medical services by women who were injured as a result of violence experienced: need data on percentage of women who report using services as a result of the violence experienced.

Step 2. Determine usage of mental health services by women victimised as a result of violence experienced (irrespective of whether or not physical injuries present.) According to NVAWS data, 33 per cent of all IPV rapes result in usage of mental health services.

Step 3. Establish the unit cost of services used for medical and mental services separately.

Determine what services are likely to be used (such as ambulance transport, paramedic care, emergency room care, physician visit, physical therapy, inpatient hospitalizations, outpatient clinic visits).

Establish unit cost (based on specific Medical Expenditure Panel Survey and the Medicare 5 per cent Sample Beneficiary Standard Analytic Files)

Step 4. Calculate total direct costs as the product of unit costs times the number of times a service was used.

Similar cost estimate would need to be undertaken for direct costs associated with the police and judicial system.

Source: CDC (2003).

Though relatively easy to compute econometrically, direct cost estimates provide only a specific type of cost incurred on account of violence experienced, and do not account for the social or other economic impacts of GBV. There are also serious limitations of using this approach in the context of developing countries, where there are significant gaps in the required data to undertake this estimation accurately. For example, even if prevalence is known, accurate information on services utilisation rates may not be available. Further, in developing countries the actual availability of services is a critical argument, as under provision and lack of access are issues for political advocacy. This, coupled with strong social norms that enhance acceptability and tolerance of violence, while limiting women's mobility and discouraging use of 'external' services, may actually lead to decreased service usage even if services are available. In the absence of household surveys that may ask women the potential and actual use of services, records of service providers themselves are often a source for estimating utilisation and these are under-reported in any case. Thus, actual expenditures on services may be a particularly poor indicator in these contexts. Only two studies have been cited in literature that undertake direct cost estimates of IPV in developing countries, one in Jamaica and another in Chile.[16]

For public forms of violence discussed in this paper, similar limitations would apply. In India, as noted in the previous section, routine data on prevalence is available only for two forms of public violence—rape and sexual harassment. Since these are administrative data sets, the figures are prone to under reporting. Though estimates for most public forms of violence are not available on the proportion of women experiencing a particular form of violence, who actually report to any authority/service provider, the recent data from the National Family Health Survey or NFHS 2006 (IIPS and Macro International 2007) on IPV provides a trend. Of the women who reported experiencing violence, only 4 per cent reported that they had ever approached any external agency for help. The recent survey on public safety in Delhi is not a population-based estimate as the sample is drawn from women in public spaces as defined by the study; however, its findings highlight the problems of utilisation of formal services. Only 0.8 per cent respondents actually reported incidents of harassment to the police, and 58 per cent said that they didn't even consider approaching the police, given its attitude. Thus, even if a per unit cost of service in its most fundamental form is estimated, the utilisation rate can only be an approximation, generated by assuming the cost 'if all women were to avail the service' and presuming prevalence data is available. It is also important to include the victimisation rate (i.e., the number of times the incident occurs) because each incident of violence disrupts households, regardless of whether it leads to service utilisation

Estimation of indirect costs includes social, economic and intergenerational costs. The economic multiplier effects have looked at loss of jobs as a result of violence and/or increased absenteeism, framing it in terms of lost productivity. In the United States, it has been reported that 14 per cent of rape and sexual assault victims lost time from work as a result of their victimisation, 28 per cent of them lost 6-10 days.[17] A study in Santiago, Chile (Morrison and Orlando 1999) looks at reduced earnings as a way to measure loss in productivity, and estimates that women who do not suffer physical violence (domestic) earn an average of US$385 per month while women who face severe physical violence at home earn only US$150, in other words, less than half the earnings of other women.[18]

Indirect cost estimates that highlight the impact of GBV in terms of days of work lost have used the accounting approach. This would involve the following:

1. Estimating total number of days of paid work or household chores lost due to GBV: has to be collected through a specific question posed in survey.

2. Multiplying this by the mean daily earnings to yield a monetary estimate of lost earnings, whether this incapacitation is temporary (due to injury) or permanent (due to death or incapacitating injury) (Morrison and Orlando 1999).

In the case of recent estimates produced by CDC (2003), mean daily earnings are calculated for the mean age of women affected by the various types of intimate partner violence (rape, physical assault or stalking). In the case of non-paid household chores, an imputed wage is used.

Indirect cost estimates of the impact of GBV have also used estimated losses on women's labour force participation and earnings. This approach, employed by Lloyd (1999) and Farmer and Tiefenthaler (1999) for the US and Morrison and Orlando (1999) for Chile and Nicaragua, requires micro data sets that contain standard labour force information on women's participation, hours worked and earnings, as well as detailed information on women's experience with GBV.

Social costs associated with GBV have been the most difficult to estimate. Only a few studies have attempted to estimate the cost of the impact on children, and these include those that track grade repetition and parent notification of academic and disciplinary problems (Morrison and Orlando 1999) but did not attempt to capture the monetary implications of performance (Duvvury et al. 2004). The most nebulous category, and yet so relevant for costs of public forms of GBV that may not result in direct injury, is that of pain and suffering. Opinions differ on whether to impute a monetary value on pain and suffering. Kerr and McLean, Stanko, and others argue 'in no way can we 'cost' the horrifying physical and psychological damage of this violence to the women and children' (Kerr and McLean 1996: p. 3). In contrast, Miller, Cohen, and Wiersama (1996) argue 'intangible pain, suffering, and lost quality of life exceed all other tangible categories combined'. They urge the critical need to emphasise prevention in society. They further propose two approaches to the estimation of the cost of pain, suffering and loss of quality of life. The 'willingness to pay' estimates the willingness of individuals (and by extension society) to pay for lives free of GBV (can more specifically be a violence prevention service) using a specific contingent valuation methodology. Though this has not been used extensively, this could be considered for evaluation of the costs of public violence. The second approach is the 'willingness to accept' (or compensation). This is computed based on actual jury awards for identified individuals who were injured. This has been used in estimation of costs of sexual violence in Minnesota.[19]

Though powerful and relevant, these methods need to be examined and adapted for application to the developing countries. The willingness-to-pay method has been used in the environmental literature, but there is little application to injuries in most developing countries. Perhaps there is also need to call for jurisprudence on jury awards for pain and suffering, to more fully develop the compensation approach.

Moving Forward :

A review of existing data and methodology for estimating the cost of violence reveals that in order to estimate the cost of violence in public spaces, several gaps must first be addressed. First, complete understanding of violence in public spaces and the context around them is necessary. This would include:

1. Mapping public violence. Collecting data to understand how women perceive public violence and their perceived indirect costs.
2. Routine data collection of incidence of violence in public spaces.
3. Routine data collection at services accessed (identified through mapping of services such as health, legal, etc.) in response to violence in public spaces.

As described above, there are several methodologies that exist for estimation of cost of any form of violence. In addition, different forms would require adoption of different methodologies. With the exception of rape, literature on economic costs of other forms of public violence is limited. Not enough information exists to quantify and qualify the nature of GBV in public spaces to determine the best entry point for identifying and estimating costs. Basic to any estimation is a well developed data collection system that provides an operational definition, collects population-based survey data on specific measures to estimate aspects such as prevalence (the number of women experiencing violence) and the frequency/the number of incidents (victimisation rate). Econometric analysis then needs to be undertaken based on decisions on type of methodology and costs to be computed.

The second step is to collate secondary data on GBV, and identify gaps for which primary data collection is needed on a specific form of violence. The current data has limitations though, as it will inform only on crimes that are reported and those that are more serious; creating underestimations and under values. This data, in addition to mapping and review of service delivery (access, patterns of use, etc.) will help produce an estimation of violence. Because the perception of violence in public spaces impacts the lives of women and their mobility, discussion and debate can inform the designing of population surveys to be conducted to collect information on aspects such as the perceived limitations of women and girls in terms of mobility, perceptions of safety, experiences with GBV, perceptions of fear, and reactions to GBV. This essay initiates this discourse by laying out the issues that would require much greater deliberations.

Public safety is an issue of critical concern that must be addressed if societies ascribe to notions of inclusiveness and equity. Real acts of violence and the threat of violence, both impact women's lives as they move through public spaces. Notion of gender governing use of public spaces and the need for better response systems must be addressed to influence and deter the use of violence against women. Services and regulatory systems that are user-friendly, reliable and honest are needed for general public use. Scepticism and distrust of public systems will deter women from reporting acts of GBV and undermine efforts to address it. Policy must include consideration of creating safe and community friendly spaces; over and above better prosecution and punitive perspectives.

Notes

1. A comprehensive review is presented in Duvvury et al. (2004).
2. Fifteen Years of the United Nations Special Rapporteur on Violence against Women (1994-2009)—A Critical Review.
3. General recommendation 19, entitled 'Violence against women', 1992.
4. Ibid.
5. In many cases, depending on the caste composition, the boy may also be punished or killed. This is often when he is of a lower caste. We recognise that an analysis of patriarchy places both men and women as potential recipients of violence, apart from other social categorisations as class, caste and so on. However, this essay frames and considers GBV committed against women exclusively. Men and boys, however, may be considered victims of the social norms that may promote harmful behaviours, power dynamics and hierarchy of the sexes that may eventually lead to manifestations of violence against women.
6. See www.unfpa.org/swp/2000/english/ch03.html. in same report as IPPF EN (2009). The source of this data is difficult to trace.
7. It is difficult to distinguish between the actual prevalence and reported cases of these forms of violence. Most of them are not part of the legally defined criminal categories for which routine information is collected by the National Crime Records Bureau (NCRB).
8. The crimes against women reported by NCRB include kidnapping and abduction for specified purposes; homicide for dowry, dowry deaths or their attempts; torture, both mental and physical (Sec. 498-A IPC); molestation; sexual harassment and importation of girls (up to 21 years of age). However, the discussion here focuses on rape and sexual harassment and molestation, as laid out in the scope.

9. *Section 354 IPC:* Whoever assaults or uses criminal force on any woman, intending to outrage her modesty or knowing it likely that he will thereby outrage her modesty, shall be punished with imprisonment for a term which may extend to two years, or with fine, or with both.

    Section 509 (*Word, gesture or act intended to insult the modesty of a woman*) is included in Chapter 22 entitled 'Of Criminal Intimidation, Insult and Annoyance', and is cognisable, bailable and triable by any magistrate. It holds: 'Whoever, intending to insult the modesty of a woman, utters any word, makes any sound or gesture, or exhibits any object, intending that such word or sound shall be heard, or that such gesture is seen by such woman, or intrudes upon the privacy of such woman, shall be punished with simple imprisonment for a term which may extend to one year, or with fine, or with both.'

10. Delhi, Prohibition of Eve Teasing Bill, reported in Women's International Network News, Summer, vol. 0, No. 3, 1984./ as reported in Report of UN Rapporteur on Violence Against Women.

11. Chapter 5: 'Crimes Against Women', NCRB REPORT 2007.

12. Collaborative initiative of the Delhi government, UNIFEM, Jagori and UN Habitat.

13. Report available on www.jagori.org.

14. See Burton et al. (2000) for a detailed discussion.

15. Cited in 'Violence Against Women Factsheet: State of the World Population 2005-UNFPA'. Available at http://www.unfpa.org/swp/2005/presskit/factsheet/facts_vaw.htm

16. One study by Mansingh and Ramphal (1993) estimated the direct costs of treating victims of IPV in Jamaica's Kingston Public Hospital in 1991 to be $454,000. Another study conducted by the Inter-American Development Bank in Chile and Nicaragua in 1999 (Morrison and Orlando 1999) examined the impact of IPV on earning capacity. In developed or industrialised countries that this type of analysis has been performed include Canada (Greaves et al. 1995); Australia (Australian Institute of Criminology 2002); British Columbia (Kerr and McLean 1996); Holland (Korf et al. 1997); Northern Territory (Office of Women's Policy 1996); Queensland (Blumel et al. 1993); Switzerland (Yodanis and Godenzi 1999); and the UK (Stanko et al. 1998). These studies are mentioned in WHO (2004).

17. National Crime Victimization Survey, Bureau of Justice Statistics, 2002, Tables 87, 89, as reported on Sexual Violence Fact sheet, www. ncvs.org.

18. The Morrison and Orlando study differentiated between moderate physical violence and severe physical violence. 'Moderate physical violence occurs when a women's partner slaps her, holds her against her will, or shoves her. These actions must have occurred fewer than five times in a year. If they occur more often, they fall into the next category. Severe physical violence occurs when a women suffers more than five acts of moderate physical violence in a year, if her partner has kicked her, hit her with an object, burned her intentionally, cut her with a knife, or choked her, or if her partner's violent behaviour causes her injuries such as body aches, broken bones, loss of consciousness, or any type of injury that requires medical attention' (Morrison and Orlando 1999: 53).

19. Available at http://www.health.state.mn.us/injury/pub/MN_brochure21 FINAL to Web.pdf

References

Australian Institute of Criminology (2002). *Australian Crime: Facts and Figures 2001*, Canberra: Australian Institute of Criminology.

Blumel et al., (1993). 'Who Pays? The Economic Costs of Violence Against Women', Queensland: Women's Policy Unit.

Burton B, N. Duvvury and N. Varia (2000). *Justice Change and Human Rights: International Research and Response to Domestic Violence*, Washington: International Centre for Research on Women and The Centre for Development and Population Activities.

Buvinic, M., A. Morrison and M. Shifter (1999). *Violence in Latin America and the Caribbean: A Framework for Action*, Technical Study, Washington DC: Inter-American Development Bank.

Centers for Disease Control (CDC) (2003). *Costs of Intimate Partner Violence against Women in the United States*', Atlanta, GA: Centers for Disease Control and Prevention & National Center for Injury Prevention and Control.

Duvvury, Nata, Caren Grown and Jennifer Redner (2004). *Costs of Intimate Partner Violence at Household and Community Levels--An Operational Framework for Developing Countries*, ICRW.

Greaves, L., O Hankivsky, et al. (1995). 'Selected Estimates of the Costs of Violence Against Women', London, Ontario: Centre of Research on Violence Against Women and Children.

Heise, L., M. Ellsberg and M. Gottemoeller (1999). *Ending Violence Against Women*. Population Reports, Series L, No. 11, Baltimore: Johns Hopkins University School of Public Health, Population Information Program, December.

IPPF EN. (2009). *Choices: Gender-based Violence in Europe*, November, Brussels: IPPF European Network.

Kerr, R. and J. McLean (1996). *Paying for Violence: Some of the Costs of Violence Against Women in B.C.*, Ministry of Women's Equality, British Colombia, Canada.

Korf, D.J. et al. (1997). *Economic Costs of Violence Against Women*, Utrecht, Netherlands: Dutch Foundation of Women's Shelters.

Mansingh, A. and P. Ramphal (1993), 'The Nature of Interpersonal Violence in Jamaica', *West Indian Medical Journal*, vol. 42, pp. 53–56.

Miller, Cohen, and Wiersama (1996). 'Victim Costs and Consequences: A New Look', Washington, DC: US Department of Justice, Office of Justice Programs, National Institute of Justice.

Morrison, A. R., and M. B. Orlando (1999). 'Social and Economic Costs of Domestic Violence: Chile and Nicaragua', in A. Morrison and L. Biehl (eds), *Too Close to Home: Domestic Violence in Latin America*, Washington, D.C.: Inter- American Development Bank.

Morrison, Andrew R. and Maria Beatriz Orlando (2004). 'The Costs and Impacts of Gender-based Violence in Developing Countries: Methodological Considerations and New Evidence', World Bank Working Paper Series, Washington, DC: World Bank.

International Institute for Population Sciences (IIPS) and Macro International (2007). *National Family Health Survey (NFHS-3) 2005-06: Volume I*, Mumbai: IIPS.

Office of Women's Policy (1996). 'The Financial and Economic Costs of Domestic Violence in the Northern Territory', Northern Territory: KPMG.

Stanko A. et al. (1998). 'Counting the Costs: Estimating the Impact of Domestic Violence in the London Borough of Hackney', London: Crime Concern.

World Bank (1993). *World Development Report 1993. Investing in Health*. New York: World Bank.

World Health Organization (WHO) (2004). *The Economic Dimensions of Interpersonal Violence*, Geneva: World Health Organization, Deptartment of Injuries and Violence Prevention.

——— (2005). *Addressing Violence Against Women and Achieving the Millennium Development Goals*, Department of Gender, Women and Health, Family and Community Health, World Health Organization.

Yodanis, C., and A. Godenzi (1999). *Report on the Economic Costs of Violence against Women*, Fribourg, Switzerland: University of Fribourg.

Women and Homelessness

SHIVANI CHAUDHRY, AMITA JOSEPH,
INDU PRAKASH SINGH

Introduction

Homelessness is one of the worst forms of urban poverty and social vulnerability. It is a glaring indicator of the failure of governance and the state's commitment to the welfare of its citizens. In our view, it is both tragic and unacceptable in a civilised society and in independent India that a large percentage of our poor are homeless. No one is homeless by choice. Homelessness, like endemic poverty, is a situation people are forced into.[1]

We are not talking here about what Peter Berger described as a 'homeless mind', a state where, with the disappearance of the sacred canopy, the western mind lost its moorings, and 'segmentalisation' and 'compartmentalisation' became the order of the day. Rather, the homelessness we describe is about people losing meaning and connectivity in life; about people being totally isolated and neglected. Such homelessness is not specific to a country, it exists across the world, in rich and poor countries alike. Here in India, you see it in Delhi, Patna, Kolkata, Mumbai, Chennai, Hyderabad, Bangalore, Pune, Ahmedabad, Jaipur, Guwahati, Bhubaneshwar, and other cities, where the homeless are persons considered *non grata*. The homelessness we address here is a human construct, a state that is unjust, discriminatory, non-inclusive, dehumanising, debilitating, a state that sharpens economic, social and political divides.

The problems faced by homeless citizens are not merely in the nature of *being*: ontological, teleological, or phenomenological. They are existential. As Simone de Beauvoir said in *The Second Sex*, "One is not born a woman, but becomes a woman." Similarly one largely becomes homeless, primarily due to factors beyond one's control. The truth of being homeless is thus not just in the *being* of homeless, but rather in the *becoming* of homeless. And the greatest contributors to the creation of this illegal, inhuman and undignified condition are governments and policy-makers: central and state/federal; past and present.

Among the constituency of the homeless, women are one of the worst affected. While the phenomenon of homelessness violates the most basic of human rights for all populations, women who do not have access to secure housing and are forced to live on the streets suffer the most severe kinds of abuse and gender-based violence. Yet this significant section of the poor continues to be ignored, omitted from state poverty reduction schemes and programmes, and denied a voice in policy-making, both in urban and rural areas. State response to the needs of homeless women in India is grossly inadequate; the majority of homeless women are left to fend for themselves and suffer a daily onslaught on their human rights.

This essay attempts to draw attention to the plight of homeless women in India; identify the causes and characteristics of homelessness, discuss the nature of violence faced by them, identify gaps in policy and state response, document positive initiatives in other countries and finally make recommendations to address the crisis of homelessness at various levels. It is our hope that our essay will highlight the suffering and human rights violations of one of our society's most economically, socially and politically marginalised constituencies, while also urging the local, state and central governments to take concerted action to protect their human rights and prevent further abuse and discrimination.

Background

The problem of homelessness is not unique to India, but exists across the world, even in highly industrialised nations like Canada, Australia, and the United States of America.[2] It is estimated that over 800,000 people are homeless on any given night in the United States, and as many as 3.5 million people experience homelessness annually, living in shelters, transitional housing, or public places. Including those who have lost their own homes and live with family or friends, the number reaches 4.5 million. In India, in 2003 the total homeless population in the country was estimated to be 78 million.[3] The number is likely to be much higher today.

The causes of homelessness are manifold and complex, and may vary across regions and nations. But the primary reason that people find themselves homeless in any country is because of the lack of available affordable housing options. While homelessness is a phenomenon that exists in both rural and urban areas, its magnitude and extent is much more prevalent and extensive in urban areas. Rural homelessness is integrally linked to landlessness and distressed housing, and to growing displacement due to ostensible 'development' and projects, conflict, and disasters. While many continue to live under conditions of homelessness or near-homelessness in villages, large numbers of the rural homeless migrate to urban areas with the hope of finding better living conditions, but in the absence of low cost housing for the poor, tragically find themselves subjected to even worse forms of homelessness and precarious living conditions.

In order to understand the issue of homelessness and develop adequate responses to it, it is important to first provide a comprehensive definition. The only official definition in India is that of the Census of India, which defines 'houseless people' as persons who are not living in 'census houses.' The latter refers to 'a structure with roof.' Homelessness thus refers to those who are inadequately housed—without even basic shelter over their head, not even a *kutcha* (unfinished/temporary) slum or shanty house.

The United Nations (UN) in 1999 interpreted the homeless as including "those sleeping without shelter, in constructions not meant for habitation and in welfare institutions." The majority of homeless in India are found living in places such as roadsides, pavements, drainage pipes, under staircases, or in the open, temple-*mandaps*, platforms and the like (Census of India, 1991: 64).

A more encompassing definition of homelessness has been provided in Australian law,[4] which states that a person is homeless if, and only if, he or she has *inadequate access to safe and secure housing*, which means if the only housing to which the person has access:

- damages, or is likely to damage, the person's health; or
- threatens the person's safety; or
- marginalises the person through failing to provide access to:
  o adequate personal amenities; or
  o the economic and social supports that a home normally affords; or
- places the person in circumstances which threaten or adversely affect the adequacy, safety, security and affordability of that housing.

The former UN Special Rapporteur on adequate housing has reiterated that homelessness carries implications of belonging nowhere rather than simply having nowhere to sleep.[5] He also reiterated that reaching an agreed definition of homelessness that includes a deep understanding of the systemic causes of homelessness is the first step to address the issue, and is of crucial importance to draw efficient and cost-effective programmes.[6]

Homelessness is also of two types: direct homelessness and concealed homelessness. An increasing number of people who lose their homes move in with relatives, friends, or live in hostels and other forms of temporary shelters, and hence are not clearly visible; nor are they counted as part of the homeless population. The UN Special Rapporteur on adequate housing has called upon the US government to expand the definition of homelessness to include those living with family or friends due to economic hardship. The definition of homelessness globally should also include these people.

Homelessness is essentially a violation of the right to a life with dignity. Living on the streets, on railway platforms, under flyovers, in pipes/tents, and in precarious and exposed conditions can result in a plethora of problems including extreme distress, depression, humiliation, fear, insecurity, violence, and grave and chronic physical, mental, emotional, psychological and physical health disorders. The issue of identity is critical for all groups of homeless people. The absence of a permanent place to stay and a recognised address prevents the homeless from establishing proof of residence and denies them access to schemes, services, and rights guaranteed to all other citizens.

Homeless people are viewed by the rest of society at best with sympathy, and at worst, with disdain, distrust and contempt. It is a common tendency of the middle and upper classes and also of government officials to label them as 'beggars' and unproductive citizens. In reality, however, the majority of the homeless are engaged in productive work and contribute to the nation's economy with their subsidised services and labour. Instead of recognising their contributions and treating them as equal citizens entitled to equal access to services and protection of their legal rights, governments tend to discriminate against the homeless and systematically exclude and deny them their entitlements and rights. Legal systems across the world do little to protect homeless and landless people. Worse still is the existence and rampant use of laws and policies that criminalise the poor and homeless, and fuel cycles of violence against them.

The homeless population is not a homogenous group but consists of a range of communities, all of whom are homeless for different reasons. Their needs have to be addressed accordingly, as do the causes of their becoming homeless. The major homeless groups in India include: seasonal and migrant labourers, children, the mentally ill, unsupported senior citizens, victims of crime, post-imprisonment convicts, rickshaw pullers, head loaders, hand cart pullers, nomadic tribes, social outcasts, victims of substance abuse and violence (including domestic violence), and displaced persons. Amongst each category of the homeless, women and girls suffer disproportionate impacts and face greater discrimination on account of their gender.

The problem of homelessness is an ongoing and critical one, and measures need to be continuously put in place to protect and guarantee the human rights of the homeless, especially their legal and constitutional rights to adequate housing, food, livelihood/work, security of the person, and freedom to move and reside anywhere within the territory of India. Dealing with homelessness also requires fundamental structural changes in the way urban and rural development planning is undertaken and in the way economic policies are framed and implemented.

Homelessness and the Human Right to Adequate Housing

Homelessness is one of the most fundamental violations of the human right to an adequate standard of living, especially that of adequate housing. It has been well established in international human rights law and its interpretation that adequate housing is not merely a desired goal; it is a basic human right of all human beings. This has been affirmed by the Universal Declaration of Human Rights in 1948, which recognises the right to adequate housing as an integral component of the human right to an adequate standard of living.[7]

The Universal Declaration of Human Rights (UDHR) states under Article 25 (1) that, "*Everyone* has the right to a standard of living adequate for the health and well being of himself and his family, including food, clothing, housing, medical care and necessary social services, and the right to security in the event of unemployment, sickness, disability, widowhood, old age or other lack of livelihood in circumstances beyond his control." On the basis of the provisions established in the UDHR, the right to adequate housing was elaborated and reaffirmed in 1996 by the International Covenant on Economic, Social and Cultural Rights (ICESR), which in Article 11.1 declares that, "The State Parties to the present Covenant recognize the right of everyone to an adequate standard of living for himself and his family, including adequate food, clothing and housing, and to the continuous improvement of living conditions." Other international treaties that provide legal protection for the right to adequate housing, include, *inter alia*, the Convention on the Rights of the Child, the Convention on the Elimination of All Forms of Discrimination against Women and the International Convention on the Elimination of All Forms of Racial Discrimination.

According to General Comment 4, on the right to adequate housing adopted in 1991 by the United Nations Committee on Economic, Social and Cultural Rights, housing is more than just a physical structure of four roofs and a wall. It encompasses various material and non-material elements of adequacy, which are necessary to create a safe living space. General Comment 4 states that in order for housing to be adequate it must, at a minimum, include the following elements: security of tenure, affordability, adequacy, accessibility, proximity to services, availability of infrastructure and cultural adequacy.

General Comment 4 also makes direct reference to homelessness by noting that while the problems are often particularly acute in some developing countries which confront major resource and other constraints, "significant problems of homelessness and inadequate housing also exist in some of the most economically developed societies." Among the steps to be taken immediately towards the full realisation of the right to adequate housing, regardless of the status of available resources in a given country, the Committee mentions the adoption of a national housing strategy, which "should reflect extensive genuine consultation with, and participation by, all of those affected, including the homeless, the inadequately housed and their representatives." In General Comment 7 on forced evictions, adopted in 1997, the Committee emphasised the obligation of states to ensure that "(e)victions should not result in individuals being rendered homeless or vulnerable to the violation of other human rights." Agenda 21, adopted by the United Nations Conference on Environment and Development in 1992, states that "[a]s a first step towards the goal of providing adequate shelter for all, all countries should take immediate measures to provide shelter to their homeless poor."[8]

In the Constitution of India, Article 21—the right to life—has also been interpreted to recognise the right to shelter while Article 14 guarantees equality before the law. Article 15 prohibits discrimination; and Article 19 guarantees the right of all citizens to freedom of movement and freedom to reside and settle in any part of the territory of India. Several judgments of the Supreme Court of India and High Courts have also upheld the right to housing as an integral component of the right to life.

The former UN Special Rapporteur on adequate housing provided an inclusive definition of the human right to adequate housing: "The right of every woman, man, youth and child to gain and sustain a safe and secure home and community in which to live in peace and dignity."[9] Women's right to adequate housing, as an inalienable, integral and indivisible part of all human rights, has also been recognised, implicitly and explicitly in a range of international and regional human rights instruments. The Istanbul Declaration and the Habitat Agenda, adopted at the second United Nations Conference on Human Settlements in 1996, commit governments to providing legal security of tenure and equal access to land to all people, including women and those living in poverty.

It is thus the legal responsibility of the state to respect, promote and fulfil the human right to adequate housing for all its citizens, including women, as guaranteed in both national and international law. Though India has ratified several international human rights instruments and is also bound by national case law, the human right to adequate housing still eludes a large number of Indians, especially the homeless, who face the worst consequences of denial of this right.

Causes of Homelessness

Factors which result in homelessness are diverse and multiple; and people often find themselves rendered homeless because of a conjunction of causes and an interplay of various factors. Critical factors that result in homelessness, including of women, are:

1. *Landlessness:* The phenomenon of landlessness in rural areas is integrally linked to homelessness. Landlessness gives rise to interrelated problems such as inadequate housing, lack of livelihood options, poor health, hunger and food insecurity, and acute poverty. When families lose their land, they also tend to lose their homes.

2. *Rural Displacement:* Ostensible 'development' and large infrastructure projects such as mining projects, environmental conservation programmes, Special Economic Zones, and disasters, contribute to rural homelessness, especially when displaced families move to other rural areas or continue to live close to their original habitats for livelihood and subsistence purposes. Families also lose their homes due to rural indebtedness and inability to repay loans.

3. *Social/ communal/ ethnic conflict* as well as state-sponsored violence and destruction of homes also results in families being rendered homeless, in both rural and urban areas. Religious minorities (such as Muslims in Gujarat and Christians in Kandhamal) and discriminated groups (such as Dalits) face targeted violence and burning of their homes and lands, which often results in them becoming homeless/landless.

4. *Forced migration from rural areas due to distress conditions:* A multitude of factors such as natural disasters including floods, cyclones, and

drought; rural indebtedness; agrarian crises and loss of subsistence due to lack of adequate support for agriculture and agrarian reform; inadequate rural development; forceful land acquisition and conversion of agricultural land to industrial uses such as large infrastructure projects and Special Economic Zones, all tend to force rural communities to leave their homes and habitats. In the absence of any avenues for redress and human rights-based rehabilitation, the displaced are forced to move to cities with their families in search of employment and survival options. Migration to urban areas is generally a last resort, with women bearing the worst brunt. The burden of moving with children in the absence of any security or a safety net is much greater for women. Rural migrants comprise a significant percentage of the urban homeless population, as they are unable to afford housing in cities and towns.

Contrary to what bureaucrats and economists are wont to think, people from rural areas do not migrate to cities because they are attracted by the glamour and abundant opportunities. Homeless citizens, on the other hand, repeatedly affirm that they are in cities primarily because they were compelled to leave their villages. The migration is generally not of their volition. It is largely due to 'push' rather than 'pull' factors. Strong structural and systemic processes of destitution and distress are responsible for forcing people to move to urban areas; factors which are beyond the control of most vulnerable communities in rural areas.

5. *Lack of affordable and low-cost housing:* One of the most glaring failures of urban development is the absence of public and low-cost housing in cities and towns. Most cities, especially in India, have not planned to accommodate the growing population or to meet the needs of migrants. Despite the existence of Master Plans which mandate the need to plan for urban expansion in equitable ways, and to reserve housing for Low Income Groups, there is no implementation of these plans, neither is there any political will to develop low-cost and affordable housing options. Growth of cities is accompanied with increased demands for labour. Very often, labour, especially for construction purposes,

is brought into cities from rural areas (as in the case of the Delhi 2010 Commonwealth Games) but no provisions are made for their housing.

The absence of state subsidies and schemes for housing and basic services is further compounded by the backlog in the shortage of urban housing. At the end of the tenth five-year plan, the urban housing shortage in India was 24.7 million dwelling units while for the eleventh five-year plan period, the shortage was estimated at 26.3 million units, of which 99 per cent pertained to the Economically Weaker Sections and Low Income Groups. In the capital city of Delhi, the housing shortage was estimated at 1.13 million dwelling units at the end of the tenth plan. Despite this huge backlog, no comprehensive rights-based housing policy is being implemented in the country. While the *National Urban Housing and Habitat Policy 2007* lists, as one of its primary objectives, the provision of affordable housing, no measures have been taken to realise this objective. Even much acclaimed schemes such as the heavily funded Jawaharlal Nehru National Urban Renewal Mission, have focused on urban infrastructure rather than on providing housing and basic services for the urban poor.

Across the world, state funding for housing has seen drastic setbacks and cuts over the last decade. In the US for example, federal funding for low-income housing has been cut over the past decades, leading to a reduced stock and quality of subsidized housing.[10]

6. *Real estate speculation and growth of the land mafia:* Excessive speculation on land, housing and property results in spiralling prices of housing, including of rental housing. This also contributes to making housing unaffordable for the majority. A large percentage of families have to spend a substantial part of their income just to retain their housing. Those who are unable to afford the escalating prices are often forced onto the streets. In Australia, it is estimated that up to 35 per cent of low-income people experience "housing stress," while almost 10 per cent experience "extreme housing stress" meaning that they are required to spend more than 50 per cent of their income on rent to avoid homelessness.[11]

7.   *Globalisation, neoliberal economic policies and privatisation*

The current prevalent paradigm of development is largely based on neoliberalism and is driven by market forces rather than human rights consideration. The growth of neoliberal policies combined with the impacts of indiscriminate economic globalization have contributed to an increase in housing prices, in the privatization of basic services like water, healthcare and electricity as well as housing, and the dismantling of welfare schemes for the poor. Urbanization processes which result in "gentrification" of cities and creation of exclusive housing enclaves for the rich, further push low-income families into precarious situations, including homelessness.

This development paradigm has also resulted in an increase in social inequality, exclusion, and poverty. Studies on homelessness in Delhi in 2000 and 2008 have shown that most of the people are homeless because of systemic and persistent poverty and unemployment.

Solutions to the housing crisis are also sought from the private sector with governments encouraging public-private partnerships in housing, which are not aimed at providing housing to low income groups. A predominant reliance on the market and market-based options is also responsible for fuelling the homelessness crisis. A recent report of the UN Special Rapporteur on adequate housing identifies the economic crisis and significantly increasing numbers of foreclosures for driving up homelessness rates across the US.[12]

8.   *Slum demolitions and forced evictions without rehabilitation:* Forced evictions and demolition of informal settlements and slums, often accompanied with violence, are rapidly intensifying and increasing across India. Many of these are carried out under the guise of 'urban renewal' and 'city beautification' and the mission of governments to create 'world class cities' and 'slum free cities', which instead of improving housing conditions are actually resulting in the obliteration of slums and banishing of the poor from urban spaces.

Large events such as mega sports events like the 2010 Commonwealth Games held in Delhi also result in forced evictions that contribute to rising homelessness. A study by the Housing and Land Rights Network estimates that over 200,000 people were forcibly evicted and lost their homes in Delhi because of the Commonwealth Games.[13]

Women and children suffer disproportionately from the impacts of forced evictions and destruction of their homes. In the absence of adequate rehabilitation, thousands are rendered homeless and forced to eke out an existence on the streets. Even in the approximately 20 per cent of cases where rehabilitation is provided in Indian cities, living conditions in resettlement sites are abysmal. Most of the resettlement sites are located at the periphery of the city and do not provide adequate housing and essential civic services such as water, sanitation, electricity and transport. This makes it impossible for families to continue with their livelihoods and access education and healthcare from remote locations of resettlement sites. Many of the relocated families opt to live on the streets in order to continue working and supporting their families. Studies in the resettlement site of Bawana, Delhi, highlight that women suffer the most due to failed resettlement, and in particular have lost their livelihoods as a result of inadequate rehabilitation.[14]

9.   *Domestic Violence:* Domestic violence can greatly increase women's vulnerability to homelessness, especially when there is a lack of protection by law enforcement officials, or by the legal system itself. Many women who do manage to leave their homes become vulnerable to homelessness and consequently may suffer further violence. Across the world, a large proportion of homeless women are those who have escaped domestic violence. Reportedly, domestic violence is a major factor contributing to homelessness in Australia, particularly for women. In Indian cities too, domestic violence is one of the reasons for homelessness of women. On the other hand, the associated fear of homelessness can lead some women to stay in abusive and dangerous situations, or return to them if they have attempted to leave.[15]

Though India's *Protection of Women from Domestic Violence Act 2005* contains a provision securing women's rights to remain in their place of domicile, improper implementation of the Act continues to result in victims of domestic violence being thrown out of their homes or being forced to leave situations of violence. In the US, the *Violence against Women Act 2005* (VAWA) prohibits evictions by requiring public housing authorities to use leases which stipulate that domestic violence is not a cause for eviction of victims of such violence. It also prohibits public housing authorities from denying housing admission based on an applicant being the victim of domestic or dating violence, or stalking. Despite the presence of VAWA, women victims of domestic violence continue to experience discrimination.[16]

10. *Breakdown of Family and Partnership/Marriage*: Abandonment by husbands, eviction from homes after the death of the husband, fear, desertion, husbands or fathers remarrying, and mental illness also result in women being thrown out of their homes and onto the streets.[17] In settings where there is stigma associated with the perceived "breakdown" of marriage or domestic partnership, informal networks of care and support may disintegrate and further expose women to the risk of homelessness. Women also find themselves thrown out of their homes when their partner dies of HIV/AIDS, or if they are found to have HIV/AIDS. In the absence of adequate health services, schemes and short-stay / care homes and institutions that they can access, many such women find themselves on the streets.

11. *Inequitable Planning and Land Use:* Across urban India, land use planning is extremely inequitable and favours a development paradigm aimed at benefiting the upper classes and elite. A United Nations Development Programme (UNDP) concept note prepared in 2003, stated that 95 per cent of legal urban space was used and kept for the benefit of the most privileged five per cent of the city's population. Separate spaces for women are not factored into planning processes, neither are women consulted in the development of city and master plans. Housing and settlement planning is not gendered and city spaces are increasingly becoming more and more unsafe for women. The failure to reserve land for low-cost housing, the inability to implement master plans calling for mixed use neighbourhoods, and the lack of compliance with land-use legislation; contribute to homelessness.

12. *Inadequacy of the Law:* The absence of progressive laws which protect the human rights to adequate housing for women, minimise forced

evictions, and promote rights-based rehabilitation is a serious problem in India. This is compounded by the continued use of archaic and anti-people laws such as the *Land Acquisition Act 1894*, which enables the state to acquire land for 'public purpose'—a term that is largely undefined and subject to rampant misuse. The existence of discriminatory laws and anti-poor legislation such as the *Bombay Prevention of Begging Act 1959* (applicable in 18 states of India) also results in women finding themselves increasingly vulnerable to homelessness and violence in urban areas.

13. *Absence of Options to Escape Homelessness:* The responsibility of the state should be to ensure that housing as a human right is progressively realised. This includes providing solutions along a continuum, the first stage of which is to enable the homeless to access secure and adequate shelters and subsequently to access permanent low cost housing. In the absence of political will and budgetary allocations to developing and providing permanent housing solutions, and in the absence of options available for the homeless, in many cases transitional accommodations tend to become permanent structures and subsequently de facto inadequate housing structures.[18] In India, there also exists a shortage of temporary housing options such as hostels for working men and women, short-stay homes, rehabilitation centres, and options for seasonal migrants, who are then forced to become homeless.

14. Other factors contributing to homelessness, especially of women are: lack of legal security of tenure; patriarchal inheritance laws and land and housing titling practices; lack of information about women's human rights; lack of access to affordable social services, credit and housing subsidies; bureaucratic barriers preventing access to housing programmes; rising poverty and unemployment; and discriminatory cultural and traditional practices.

The former Special Rapporteur on adequate housing noted that a state's obligation to eliminate gender discrimination is one *of immediate effect* and failure to do so in itself constitutes a human rights violation.[19]

Violence against Women and the Right to Adequate Housing

The interlinkage between violence against women and women's right to adequate housing is well established around the world. Lack of adequate housing can make women more vulnerable to various forms of violence and, conversely, violence against women can lead to the violation of women's rights to adequate housing. The former Special Rapporteur on adequate housing presented a series of reports on women and housing to the UN Commission on Human Rights and the UN Human Rights Council.[20] The reports highlighted that the widespread prevalence of gender-based violence is a central thread in the fabric of human rights violations faced by women, including in violations of the right to adequate housing and land. Women also suffer more from forced evictions and homelessness as both situations subject them to greater violence as well as violation of personal dignity and health.[21] Persistent poverty which results in women being forced to live in inadequate and insecure housing and living conditions, also exposes them to forms of gender-based violence, and arguably is itself a form of violence.[22]

Homelessness and Women in India

The majority of the urban poor and the homeless are from excluded and marginalised sections, including minorities and dalits. In a survey done by HUDCO in Bodhgaya, over 67 per cent of the urban poor consisted of scheduled castes while 31 per cent were from other backward classes.

A study by Indo Global Social Service Society (IGSSS) in 2008 counted 88,410 homeless citizens in the capital city of Delhi.[23] Of the homeless surveyed, 37.41 per cent were Muslims while 4.7 per cent were women. The number of homeless women is, however, likely to be higher since many of the homeless sleep with their faces covered, making it difficult for the enumerators to gauge their gender and categorise them correctly. For every one homeless counted, however, it is established that at least one is missed (either at work, hidden in a shelter or temporarily relocated). The number of homeless citizens in Delhi is thus around 150,000, of which at least 10,000 are women, even by conservative estimates.

No national disaggregated data exists on the number of homeless women in India. The absence of accurate data greatly impedes adequate planning and budget allocations for the homeless. Accurate documentation of the number of homeless people in a city, state and country is integral to developing comprehensive policies to address their concerns and protect their rights. In 2000 Ashray Adhikar Abhiyan counted 52,765 homeless citizens in Delhi. But according to the 2001 Census, Delhi had just 24,966 homeless. The Census of India for the homeless in 2001 and again in 2011 was fraught with grave inadequacies, inappropriate methodology, lack of political will and commitment to counting the homeless, and hence presents a gross underestimation of the number of homeless people in the country.[24] This has serious ramifications on urban poverty planning and budgetary allocations and development of schemes, shelters and solutions for the homeless.

Kinds of Violence Faced by Homeless Women

While all homeless women suffer multiple forms of abuse, gender-based violence and discrimination, there are certain groups within homeless women who are even more vulnerable. These include: women with disabilities and mental health problems; single women and single homeless mothers; widows; women living with HIV/AIDS; chemically dependent women and victims of substance abuse; pregnant and lactating women; Dalit women, adivasi/tribal women, Muslim women and women of other religious minorities, migrant women, sex workers, lesbian and transgender women, and girls and adolescents. Women experiencing homelessness are subject to unique violations of their rights and multiple forms of discrimination and gender-based violence. It is reported that homeless women are 10 times more vulnerable than homeless men. The different kinds of violence experienced by homeless women, include:

Verbal and Physical Abuse

Homeless women across India encounter abuse of several kinds, including foul language, verbal abuses by police and passersby; violence from male police who slap and physically abuse women, even when they are sleeping at night; and abuse from other men on the streets. They are often called derogatory names and insulted by other locals. Even homeless men exploit homeless women. Repeated police harassment is a common complaint of homeless women across the country. Women are supposed to be dealt with by women police officers and constables, but more often than not it is men constables who handle their issues. Hardly any cases of abuse against homeless women are reported, let alone any action being taken against the perpetrators.

In Delhi, homeless women stated that their husbands often behave abusively towards them as a result of factors such as: unwashed clothes; poorly cooked food; meals not prepared on time; or misbehaviour of the children.[25] Where women in the community are in control of the family earnings and responsible for expenditure on family essentials, the issue sometimes leads to conflict, when the husband feels that he has not been given adequate money for his needs.[26]

Sexual Violence and Exploitation

Homeless women, particularly young women are vulnerable to sexual exploitation and violence, trafficking, and drug abuse. Adolescent girls are among the most vulnerable to sexual abuse and also face the risk of being trafficked. Instances of rape, molestation, and mothers spending sleepless nights watching over their adolescent daughters, are common among homeless women. In Bangalore, a recent study reported indications of sexual exploitation of women under duress and blackmail. If the women do not give in to these pressures they face threats that their tents will be set on fire. Several homeless women reported of miscreants teasing and harassing women and girls of the homeless community.

In most urban areas, homeless women find it difficult to get sustained employment. They are often exploited sexually with promises of jobs. This sometimes leads to the women being forced by circumstances to take up sex work to survive.[27] In Canada, a study found that one in five homeless women interviewed reported having been sexually assaulted while on the streets or homeless.

Even homeless shelters are not the safest places for women. Locations for night shelters are often decided without the participation of the homeless and do not always have security arrangements for women.

Lack of Basic Services and Risks to Security and Personal Safety

Essential services required to sustain life, such as clean water and sanitation, are largely beyond the reach of the homeless. Facilities such as toilets, bathrooms, and potable water are not easily accessible to the homeless. Each service that a homeless person needs has to be paid for, and that too in cash. Inability to pay coupled with the lack of access to secure toilets and bathing areas often means that the homeless must relieve themselves in the open, bathe less frequently or in the open/behind plastic covers, and access unclean water through public taps and leaking pipelines. This is most difficult for women, rendering them vulnerable to multiple forms of violence and abuse. The lack of a secure place to undress and change clothes, and bathing in public spaces also makes women vulnerable to gender-based violence.

Inadequate Living Conditions and Risks to Health

The World Health Organization defines health as "not being the absence of illness, but a state of complete physical, mental, cultural and spiritual well-being." Culturally some of the most private spheres of life such as bathing and sanitation are intrinsically linked to the feeling of well-being and dignity. For homeless women, however, these basic requirements are not met.

The World Health Organization's Health Principles of Housing (1989) clearly establish that housing is intimately related to health. They acknowledge that, "the structure, location, facilities, environment and uses of human shelter have a strong impact on the state of physical, mental and social well-being." And that, "poor housing conditions and uses may provide weak defences against death, disease, and injury or even increase vulnerability to them. The heavy impact of inadequate housing and homelessness on health and life has been globally well documented. The UN Human Rights Committee, in 1999, expressed concern that homelessness had led to serious health problems and even to death in Canada.[28]

A study on homelessness in Bangalore revealed that while water for washing is sometimes available, it is not fit for drinking. Homeless people, however, have to use this water for washing clothes and utensils. This has serious repercussions on their health, thus making them vulnerable to various kinds of contamination, diseases and infections.[29] Homeless women suffer from several diseases and illnesses due to unsanitary living conditions and extreme weather conditions. They are vulnerable to excess heat, rain and cold, and often have insufficient clothes and blankets during winter months. The harsh living conditions also cause homeless women to age rapidly. In most instances, illnesses go untreated or are detected too late, making the women more susceptible to infection. Malnutrition is a common problem among homeless women, affecting especially pregnant and lactating homeless women.

In order to protect themselves, homeless women, especially single women and those without families, have to sleep in obscure places, which are hidden from the public view. Many of these spots due to their remote locations are not always clean and well ventilated, and hence adversely impact their health. Research studies also indicate a direct correlation in increase in mental health and psychiatric disorders among homeless women, especially those who are abandoned.[30] The poor sanitary conditions and lack of privacy in most shelters for the homeless, also pose health risks for women.

The custodial nature of women's homes and beggar's homes is also a major problem threatening the security of homeless women. These institutions rather than creating a safe environment for women to live in dignity, treat homeless women as criminals, and subject them to mental and psychological stress.

Difficulty in Accessing Healthcare

Accessing healthcare, in particular hospitals, is a tremendous challenge for homeless people, especially women. There are countless incidents of women being denied treatment and turned away from hospitals, including a shocking case of a 32-year old mentally ill woman Poonam Das in 2002.[31] Most hospitals refuse to admit homeless women, often making them run from pillar to post, before they are able to receive any medical aid. In July 2010, a homeless woman died while giving birth on the street in Shankar Market, Delhi, reflecting a situation of criminal negligence by the state. In Bangalore, pregnant homeless women reported fear of visiting hospitals since doctors sometimes physically or verbally abused patients who shouted when they were in labour.[32] This is also reportedly the case in several government hospitals in Delhi.

Lack of Access to Government Schemes and Livelihood Opportunities

As mentioned above, most government schemes are not accessible to the homeless, especially homeless women. State response to address the specific needs and concerns of homeless women has been largely absent. The number of women-specific shelters for homeless women across the country is woefully inadequate. Cities such as Mumbai, Bangalore, Kolkata, Guwahati, Dispur, and Pune, have no shelters for the homeless. In cities such as Patna, Lucknow, Varanasi and Allahabad, where shelters do exist, there are only night shelters for men. While Chennai has one shelter for homeless families, Hyderabad has a few family shelters. In the capital Delhi, there exists only one shelter for the city's 10,000 homeless women. The New Delhi Municipal Council (NDMC), which is one of the richest municipal bodies in Asia, has not one homeless shelter in its precinct and has abdicated its responsibility of, "construction and maintenance of rest-houses, poor houses, infirmaries,... shelters for destitute and disabled" (u/s 12:h-z of *The New Delhi Municipal Council Act, 1994*).

Due to the stigma attached to being homeless, homeless women do not get jobs as housemaids or in shops. In contrast to homeless men, the women face more difficulty in getting jobs as most have small children to take care of and most employers consider this a handicap. Yet the responsibility to purchase food and rations for their families generally rests with women, making them more vulnerable to exploitation, stress, and other psychological disorders.

Destruction of Possessions and Livelihood Means

The homeless are among the poorest of the poor, and own few possessions. Yet, these are routinely destroyed by the police. Women in Pul Mithai, Delhi, reported that MCD officials remove and confiscate their wares when they try to sell them on pavements. In particular, on Saturdays these authorities usually destroy such objects, which results in residents working under conditions of constant fear. Homeless women also consistently talk about destruction and theft of property by the police, even of their *tripal* (protective plastic or canvas sheets), dishes, food, and other property.[33] In some areas homeless women report that they find it difficult to go to work for fear that their meagre belongings will be stolen or confiscated by the police.

Hunger as Violence

Malnourishment and hunger among homeless women is common. In Pul Mithai, Delhi, homeless citizens stated that local police only allow residents to cook at night, which has significantly limited their food intake. If the women try to prepare a meal during the day, police confiscate or destroy their utensils and food items. As a result, families are only able to eat one daily meal at night. If food remains from the night before, the women serve the leftovers the next morning, else the family remains hungry. However, the women typically purchase food from the outside market for their children, adding further economic strain.Not all homeless shelters permit residents to cook, which means that the residents have to buy food, which is often unaffordable. In the run up to the Commonwealth Games in Delhi, the government prohibited homeless people from selling items and carrying out their livelihoods, forcing many into hunger. This most severely affected children and women, especially pregnant and lactating women. Aap Ki Rasoi, a scheme for free food distribution by the Delhi government was suspended for two weeks during the Games, resulting in extreme hunger for the homeless citizens. When homeless citizens are prevented from working and when their wares are confiscated, they are unable to earn their daily wage, which forces them to go hungry due to their inability to buy food.

Police Brutality

One of the most serious threats faced by homeless women in urban spaces is harassment by the police. It is no secret that police personnel, who are officially meant to protect ordinary citizens of the country, are often the biggest threats to their security. The homeless are particularly vulnerable in this regard, and are routinely victimized by the police. A series of Participatory Action and Reflection (PRA) discussions with the homeless, organised by Indo-Global Social Service Society (IGSSS) in April 2011, reveal that a common problem faced by almost all homeless people is false charges of theft levelled against them by the police. That very few of them are educated and fewer still have access to legal advice, adds to their woes.

Homeless women at Pusa Roundabout (Rachna Golchakkar) in Delhi reported that not only are they often beaten up and falsely implicated in cases of theft by the police, but they are also not allowed to earn a living—with their husbands' cycle rickshaws being deflated on the beat officer's whim, and items of sale being confiscated or thrown away every now and then. In a horrifying disclosure, a woman mentioned that police officers had even, at times, demanded 'young, healthy women' for sexual favours from the homeless community in the area. On being asked why the homeless community was beaten up by the police, the women said that it was a way to stop them from selling balloons at the crossing, and thereby force them to leave the area. The homeless are almost defenceless against the police, which for them, represents the state. Since they have no access to legal advice and no means to protest or fight, their only option is to give in to the demands of corrupt police officials.

Criminalisation and Arbitrary Arrests and Detention

The existence of anti-poor and anti-vagrancy legislation such as the *Bombay Prevention of Begging Act 1959* are routinely used to criminalise and arrest the homeless across India. The Act defines a "beggar" as anyone "soliciting alms" and who has "no visible means of subsistence", including those who sell goods and articles at traffic lights and other public places.

When penalised, beggars or homeless persons have to face hearings at a special court and may be sent to an institution, or can bail themselves out by paying money. Most homeless people, however, are not beggars. A 2003 Action Aid study found that only 28 per cent of the homeless live on mendicancy.[34]

Women who are arrested under the Act are often separated from their children, who are left on the streets to fend for themselves or taken to child welfare homes. The "home" for women in Delhi is located in Nirmal Chhaya, in the Tihar Jail complex and is nothing better than a jail. The living conditions are deplorable, with no hygiene, sanitation, or adequate food. The conditions are so bad that Ratnabai Kale, a 50-year old woman detained in Nirmal Chhaya, attempted suicide twice by trying to hang herself with her own sari in 2009.

The detained homeless women have no access to legal remedy in the form of a lawyer or other judicial redress, and often ending up serving a sentence from anywhere between one to ten years.

Across the world, anti-vagrancy laws target the homeless and criminalize them. In every urban centre in Australia, laws exist which either criminalize essential human activities, such as sleeping, or create "move on" powers that authorise policing authorities to continuously displace people who occupy and live in public spaces. For example, some people are forced to live in public places, yet local council by-laws make it illegal for a person to fall asleep in a public place between sunset and sunrise. These laws disproportionately affect people who are homeless, and indigenous people.[35] In London, even the public benches where the homeless used to sit are wetted down or removed. Germany, Hungary, Italy, Luxemburg, Slovenia and Sweden are some of the countries where both private and public security services have been accused of violence and harassment against the homeless. In a 2008 survey, the United States Conference of Mayors found that criminalizing homelessness appeared to be a growing trend.[36]

Death

The lack of access to adequate healthcare and medical services, and the social stigma associated with being homelessness, results in many women suffering silently on the streets, many of them of serious health issues and disorders. Deaths of homeless women, such as that of the woman who died during childbirth in Delhi, are not uncommon, but continue to be mostly unaccounted for. A study in Canada found that homeless women aged 18 to 44 years old were 10 times more likely to die than women of the same age group in the general population of Toronto.[37]

The Homeless Girl Child

India has the largest number of street children in the world. According to Indian Embassy figures, there are 314,700 children living on the streets of Mumbai, Kolkata, Chennai, Bengaluru, Kanpur and Hyderabad, while another 100,000 live in New Delhi. However, these numbers may not reflect the true picture, as accurate census information is difficult to access.

Street children face a daily violation of their rights to education, secure housing, and participation, as guaranteed by the United Nations Convention on the Rights of the Child. For instance, the recently passed Right to Education Act (2010) in India does scant little for ensuring that homeless children are able to access their fundamental right to education. Street children, in particular girls, find it difficult to go to school and are not able to access many government schemes, including Integrated Child Development Services (ICDS). The uncertainty of tenure of stay at any place, fear of eviction, and not having any identity proof that gives them a sense of 'existence' and 'belonging', and above all the need for survival, has made education a distant dream for street children. Though Sarva Shiksha Abhiyan has several schemes, nowhere have efforts been made by the education department to promote street children's education.[38] Often forced evictions take place on the eve of exams forcing first generation learners to drop out or lose a school year.

When homeless children in Bangalore were asked about the greatest problem they faced, the majority of them answered that it was the non-availability of drinking water. Often children have to queue up at public taps to collect drinking water due to which they lose out on their recreation/study time. The children also expressed that older people took advantage of them and often destroyed their plastic pots. This led to the children being abused and beaten up, even at home.[39] Girl children living on the streets are especially vulnerable to victimisation, exploitation, and sexual abuse. Recently, a six-year old girl in Pusa Roundabout, Delhi, was gang-raped in a car, and is suffering from multiple injuries and disorders, including psychological trauma.

Inadequacy of State Response

The few schemes available for the urban poor in India also remain largely beyond the reach of the urban homeless. The Ministry of Housing and Urban Poverty Alleviation lists the following initiatives and schemes for the urban poor: National Urban Housing and Habitat Policy 2007, National Policy on Street Vendors 2009, JNNURM basic services for the urban poor (BSUP), JNNURM integrated housing and slum development programme (IHSDP), Rajiv Awas Yojana (RAY), Swarna Jayanti Shahari Rozgar Yojana (SJSRY), interest subsidy scheme for housing the urban poor (ISHUP), integrated low-cost sanitation scheme (ILCS), Urban statistics for HR and assessments (USHA). None of these schemes, however, reaches the urban homeless because of a lack of political will, failure at the implementation level, and lack of need-based planning and research on the urban homeless and their specific concerns and needs, as distinct from those of slum dwellers and other urban poor groups.

The Government of Delhi's Mission Convergence attempts to address issues related specifically to the homeless through its Homeless Resource Centres (HRCs), which are run by selected non-government organizations (NGOs), and are responsible for surveying the homeless, collecting data, and delivering services to them. At present, there are four NGOs running HRCs in different parts of Delhi, under the Mother NGO (MNGO) – St. Stephen's Hospital (Community Medicine Department), which started functioning in August 2009.

While the services offered and programme objectives of the Mission sound positive, there is a huge gap between the stated goals and the ground reality. The Mission has made some headway in directly addressing the concerns of the homeless, including provision of shelters, but much of this has been achieved only in response to the directions of the Honourable

Supreme Court of India and the Honourable High Court of Delhi. It is safe to assume that had the Courts not intervened, government bodies and bureaucrats would not, of their own accord, have addressed the problems of the homeless. The major reason for this is that the homeless do not form a political constituency, and the majority of them are not on the electoral rolls and do not have voter identity cards. For the longest time, they have either remained invisible to the state or, worse, have been treated as non-citizens.

The role of the MNGO and HRCs has so far been limited to conducting a survey of the homeless and providing provisional identity cards to them (*Beghar Cards*). While service delivery, too, is a stated objective of the programme, it will depend on the findings of and follow-up to the homeless survey. It is difficult to say how far it will be successful without the continued vigilance of civil society and support of the Delhi High Court.

Role of the Judiciary

Over the past few years, the judiciary's role in recognising and addressing homelessness-related issues, and creating pressure on the state to deliver, has been significant. As mentioned above, much of the progress that has been made in setting up more shelters and establishing new institutions to work with the homeless, is a direct result of court orders. On December 22, 2009, the Municipal Corporation of Delhi (MCD) pulled down a temporary tent shelter for the homeless at Rachna Golchakkar (Pusa Roundabout). Shortly thereafter, it was reported that two of the evicted persons died due to the cold. Following their deaths, on January 4, 2010, a coalition of groups working on homelessness in Delhi—Shahri Adhikar Manch: Begharon Ke Liye (SAM:BKL—Urban Rights Forum: For the Homeless) organised a press conference on the human rights violations of the homeless. The story received extensive media coverage, and on January 6, 2010, the former Chief Justice of the High Court of Delhi issued a notice, *suo moto*, to the MCD and Delhi Government, seeking an explanation for the demolition of the shelter (W.P. (C) 29 / 2010).

After the High Court took up the matter, the Supreme Court of India Commissioners in the Right to Food case (I.A. No. 94 in writ petition (civil)

No. 196 of 2001), sent a letter to the apex court explaining the vulnerability of homeless citizens to the extreme cold, the increase in starvation-related deaths in winter and the negligence by the Government of Delhi. It proposed the setting up of 100 temporary shelters and 500 community kitchens in the city within a week, and 140 permanent shelters by the end of December 2010. Finally, on January 20, 2010, the Supreme Court of India ordered the Delhi government to provide both shelter and food to the city's homeless immediately. A week later, the apex court issued notices to all state governments in the country to provide information on the facilities for the homeless in their respective states. According to the order, all state governments are required to build at least one well-equipped shelter per one lakh population. These shelters are supposed to be functional throughout the year on a 24-hour basis.

In the winter of 2010-11, as a result of continued pressure from civil society and subsequent court orders, the concerned government bodies agreed to the setting up of 89 temporary tent shelters in Delhi. There are also 64 permanent building shelters in the city, though many of these are unused because they are located in areas where the concentration of the homeless is extremely low, or are inaccessible.

Shelters can only be a temporary solution to the problem of homelessness. What is really needed is affordable housing for all, which will not sound as far-fetched as it does if the state makes sincere efforts to address the housing deficit in the country, particularly for the Economically Weaker Sections (EWS). Existing shelters, too, are not equipped with adequate facilities, as directed by the courts. Most shelter authorities neither have any provisions to distribute or sell food to residents nor do they allow the homeless to cook their own food. There are also other problems like inadequate or no sanitation facilities, absence of drinking water and delayed release of funds for shelter maintenance. That the number of shelters has grown, however, is a step in the right direction in so far as it acknowledges homelessness as a real concern that needs to be addressed on a priority basis.

The High Court of Delhi on Pregnant and Lactating Homeless Women

In August 2010, the Delhi High Court initiated a *suo moto* action, on the basis of a report published in the *Hindustan Times* on August 29, 2011 about Laxmi, a destitute woman, who died four days after childbirth in Shankar Market, New Delhi. Laxmi was a homeless woman living on the footsteps of Mohan Singh building, adjacent to Shankar market. She had earlier been married to a man in Bihar and was a victim of severe domestic violence. Her husband's family had even tried to kill her by setting her on fire, but she escaped and came to Delhi. In the Shankar Market area, where she lived, and it was here that an autorickshaw driver had sexually abused her.

She received no pre-natal care during pregnancy, and survived on discarded food. On the day of the delivery, she was helped only by another homeless couple after she crawled to them for help. At 2:30 am on July 25, 2010, she delivered a baby girl on the Shankar Market pavement. She was given no medical guidance before, during or after the delivery. Her placenta was not removed, and she and her baby lay on the footpath without food or any kind of assistance for four days. On August 1, 2010, Laxmi died of septicemia (from the report of the fact-finding mission of the death of Laxmi, in Delhi by Human Rights Law Network) on the same footpath.

On October 20, 2010, the Delhi High Court issued the following directions (W.P. (C) 5913/2010) in the Shankar Market case:

1. Government of Delhi to demarcate five secured shelter homes exclusively meant for destitute women, pregnant and lactating women so that apposite care can be taken and no destitute women would be compelled to give birth on the footpath.

2. The availability of the facilities in such shelter homes shall be monitored by the helplines handled by professionally trained people.

3. In the aforesaid shelter homes, food and medical facility shall be available for 24 hours as such facilities are imperative for the cases of the present nature.

4. Despite various schemes being framed by the state government, as the people are not aware of the same, especially due to illiteracy, there

would be dissemination of information by radio as well as television in Hindi.

5. There should be awareness camps in the areas or cluster of areas by professionally trained people every fortnight.
6. The state government shall provide a mobile medical unit so that the people, especially who are living in slum areas can be taken to the shelter homes or to the hospital as the case may be.
7. The state government shall make endeavours to involve genuine NGOs so that they can also work for getting the scheme fortified as such an activity has to flow from the top to the ground reality level."

Efforts to Address Homelessness in Other Countries

The Indian government could benefit by undertaking research on, and learn from, state-sponsored initiatives in other countries to address homelessness, in particular the specific problems and violations of rights of homeless women. Some of these efforts are mentioned below.

In the US, homelessness of women is a major issue, and is accelerating at an increasing rate. Major reasons for homelessness of women are not just poverty but also factors such as divorce, domestic abuse, violence, abandonment, and lack of affordable housing. There are six national level ongoing programmes on homelessness, and approximately 50 in 44 cities mainly focusing on homelessness and health issues. Many schemes that are designed to assist the homeless population have incorporated some type of housing programme for their clients. Whether it is a transitional, permanent or even emergency housing programme, the assistance is often provided for a very low cost and maybe even free. In the United States each year, there are around 3.5 million people who live their lives without shelter or a stable occupation. Volunteers of America is an agency that believes that preventing family homelessness is a critical part of their organization. Through them, transitional housing and emergency shelters are available to those who are in need, including women. Housing First is a relatively recent innovation that has met with success in providing housing to homeless people with substance abuse problems or mental health issues. Housing First allows homeless men and women to be taken directly off the street into private community-based apartments, without requiring treatment first. This allows the homeless to return to some sense of normalcy, from which it is believed that they are better poised to tackle their addictions or sicknesses. The relapse rate through these types of programmes is lower than that of conventional homeless programmes. It was initiated by the federal government's Interagency Council on Homelessness. It asks cities to come up with a plan to end chronic homelessness. In this direction, there is the belief that if homeless people are given independent housing to start off with, with some proper social support, then there would be no need for emergency homeless shelters.

In Canada, in 1999, the federal government created the National Homelessness Initiative (NHI) to fund transitional housing and a range of services for homeless people in more than 60 communities across the country. Some provincial authorities have tried to find innovative solutions to address inadequate housing and homelessness. For instance, the city of Montreal supported the creation of a legal clinic and a special prosecutor at Municipal Court in charge of problems linked to homelessness. The Special Rapporteur on adequate housing commended Canada's housing system's concept of "housing continuum", while noting the complexity that can result from the role played by multiple agencies. This approach responds to different housing needs and preferences with a range of options, from temporary housing to permanent forms of accommodation, including homeownership.[40]

Australia has around 42,000 homeless women (2001 Census). Homeless women are exceptionally harder to count than men. Because of the risk factors associated with women sleeping on the streets, those that are homeless stay out of sight. For the same security reasons, women are more likely than males to come to a homeless shelter for help. Between 2005 and 2006, over 62,000 women sought help from Supported Accommodation Assistance Programs (SAAP). Of those women, the majority were aged between 15 to 19. SAAP is a joint Commonwealth and state government programme which provides funding for more than 1,200 organizations which are aimed at assisting homeless people or those in danger of becoming homeless, as well as women and children escaping domestic violence. They provide accommodation such as refuges, shelters and half-way houses, and also offer a range of supported services.

In the UK, there are a number of women facing homelessness; the reasons for their homelessness include sexual abuse, neglect, abandonment, reproductive health issues, and violence. The UK government has ensured that all local authorities have a legal duty to provide 24-hour advice to homeless people, including women or those who are at risk of becoming homeless within 28 days. A local authority must accept an application for assistance from a person seeking homelessness assistance if they have reason to believe that the person may be homeless or threatened with homelessness. They are then duty bound to make inquiries into that person's circumstances in order to decide whether a legal duty to provide accommodation and assistance is owed. "Interim accommodation" must be provided to those that may be eligible for permanent assistance pending a final decision. If the local authority decides that a person is homeless but does not fall into a priority need category, or became homeless intentionally, then a lesser duty shall be owed which does not extend to the provision of temporary accommodation. The local authority shall still however be lawfully obliged to offer advice and assistance.

In Bangladesh, homelessness of poverty stricken women is not uncommon. They basically gravitate towards the *mazar*—a mystical Muslim site, because it has a public restroom to wash in. One of the projects (Girls Off the Street) was established in March 2008 to meet the needs of homeless women living in Dhaka. Before initiating this project, homeless women were interviewed at bus stations and in the *mazar*. Incidents such as giving birth on the streets by women led to recognition of the issue. Pregnant women were informed about clinics that they could access. The idea of the project is basically to discourage prostitution and is currently using training courses put together by an NGO which focuses on giving women self worth by looking at God's view of them and supporting healing. The project is for girls and young women and includes various knowledge-based and other classes aimed at providing livelihood opportunities. The project also opened a night shelter for homeless women in 2010.

While the socio-economic context in Bangladesh is closest to India, the Indian government needs to incorporate the component on housing strategy from programmes in other countries, especially since India has an excessive backlog on housing for low income groups and economically weaker sections. In India, Mission Convergence in Delhi, is one of the few initiatives to address issues of homelessness. But as mentioned above, this needs greater integration and improvement as well as stronger political will to bring about real improvement in the lives of the city's homeless. What is worth commending in Delhi is the mobilisation and organisation of the homeless to form the Beghar Mazdoor Sangharsh Samiti, which is a grassroots movement led by the homeless themselves, and aimed at promoting and protecting their rights.

Conclusion

In order to address the needs of homeless women and protect and guarantee their human rights, it is important to have a clear understanding of the reasons for them becoming homeless as well as their problems in finding employment and safety concerns. As emphasized by the former UN Special Rapporteur on adequate housing, addressing the problem of women's vulnerability to homelessness must first address their access, or lack thereof, to the skills, resources and place in the community that allow for the securing of adequate housing. A combination of a humanitarian and a human rights approach is needed to address both the immediate and the long-term need of homeless women and communities. Immediate relief in the form of more and improved shelters is first needed, but efforts must be focused on addressing the structural causes of homelessness and on developing solutions to end the crisis by providing adequate, affordable and permanent housing for all.

Homeless women face multiple forms of discrimination on grounds including class, caste, health, disability, sexual orientation, and other factors. An intersectional approach to gender discrimination is essential to address such multiple forms of discrimination faced by women along with the adoption of an indivisibility-of-rights approach to promoting women's rights to adequate housing. The Indian government should adopt a comprehensive definition of homelessness and collect reliable and disaggregated data in order to develop a coherent and concerted solution to homelessness.

As a first step, permanent 24-hour shelters for homeless women need to be urgently set up in all cities and towns, as homelessness is a perennial year-round problem, not limited just to the winter. Separate shelters should be created for single women, for women with children, for women with mental illness and disabilities, and for women and their families. These need to be long-stay homes with facilities for treatment and rehabilitation. The shelters should be based on human rights standards of adequate housing and should be set up close to sources of livelihood. The plans for long-term care, shelters/shelter homes, and where required, treatment and rehabilitation (for those with mental illness, disabilities, and other health concerns), of these groups need to be developed in close consultation with experts and NGOs specialised in working in these areas. Special care, treatment and rehabilitation is also required for chemically dependent persons and victims of substance abuse. The government should consult civil society organizations and homeless people at all stages of the process, as well as in the development of all plans for the homeless—short-term and long-term. Information must be provided to all shelter residents on nearest hospital, police station, ration shop, and all other available government schemes and services. Cities should set up a 24-hour emergency response system, including a help line and nodal point for homeless women. Hospital facilities (including beds in private hospitals) should be made available for homeless women. Community Health Departments of hospitals need to also ensure that services are provided for homeless women. Special schemes should be made available for easy loans/subsidies for entrepreneurship by homeless women, including skill development and livelihood support.

Laws such as the Bombay Prevention of Begging Act 1959 that criminalise homelessness need to be repealed and replaced with laws and policies that recognize the right to adequate housing for the homeless. The state must follow and implement orders of the Supreme Court of India and High Courts that relate to homelessness and adequate housing. The High Court of Delhi has passed several interim orders calling for rehabilitation of evicted homeless communities and the need for developing a short-term and long-term plan to address homelessness in the city, but these orders are routinely violated by the Delhi government. A mechanism to report periodically to the Court on progress in implementation of court orders/ judgments should be set up. States should set up independent monitoring committees consisting of experts, including representatives of civil society and the homeless to look at brutality by state actors, such as police, against the homeless. State-sponsored violence and police brutality against the homeless must be urgently checked and those responsible for offences must be brought to justice.[41]

Adequate attention and efforts must be devoted to addressing the root causes of homelessness, including investing in agrarian reform and rural development, preventing forced evictions and displacement, reviewing urban planning and development policies, rejecting the neoliberal paradigm and adopting more equitable policies.

The state should ensure access to affordable utilities such as water, electricity and heating, as well as access to education, employment and health facilities. Women should have equal access to avenues of legal redress for violations of their right to adequate housing.[42] Patriarchal and discriminatory laws and practices related to inheritance and ownership of housing, land and property should be systematically repealed.

Legislation against domestic violence must recognize the link with the human right to adequate housing and contain legal protections for women to realize this right, while ensuring the provision of alternative adequate housing for victims of domestic violence and abuse. It should also protect women's right to be free from violent offenders. The government must introduce low-cost housing and public housing schemes for the poor with special incentives for women, including single women and women-headed households to access housing. Access to affordable rental housing is central to addressing women's homelessness. Gender-sensitive housing policies and laws need to be developed and implemented. These should make special provisions for women who are even more vulnerable to homelessness and other housing rights violations—victims of domestic violence, widows, women-headed households, women victims of forced evictions, minorities, and indigenous women.

A coordinated national strategy for reduction of homelessness should be adopted that links short-term measures (such as temporary shelters for the homeless) with long-term measures (to ensure the availability of permanent, affordable housing, along with income and employment support). The realization of the human right to adequate housing should be viewed along a continuum with the ultimate goal of providing affordable, safe, and adequate permanent housing to every woman, man, youth and child in the country. This should be carried out in conjunction with a comprehensive and coordinated national poverty reduction strategy. National laws and policies must ensure compliance with international human rights law and the Indian government must work towards meeting its international legal obligations.

It is the legal and moral responsibility of the Indian government to ensure that the human rights of all citizens, especially the most marginalized, of which homeless women constitute an important category, are respected, promoted and fulfilled. A state that continues to violate the rights of the poor and fails to provide them with respect, dignity, protection of livelihood, health, adequate living conditions, security, and freedom from violence, is failing in both its international and national legal commitments.

Notes

1. In Savi Sawarkar & Lokesh Jain. (Curator & Editor) 2010. Voice for Voiceless. indu prakash singh *Kanglistan's Homeless Citizens*, New Delhi: MF Hussain Art Gallery, Jamia Millia, p. 118 (117 - 127). In Sabir Ali. 2007. Poverty and Deprivation in Urban India. indu prakash singh *The Indian Urban Morass – Today's Preference.*, New Delhi: Bookwell (Council for Social Development). Pp. 117 – 152.

2. See reports of the UN Special Rapporteurs on adequate housing at: http://www.ohchr.org/EN/Issues/Housing/Pages/CountryVisits.aspx.

3. "Study of the Homeless," ActionAid India, (2003) Also see, Aashray Adhikar Abhiyan (2001), "The Capital's Homeless".

4. Supported Accommodation Assistance Program Act (1994) Australia.

5. Report of the UN Special Rapporteur on adequate housing, Miloon Kothari, E/CN.4/2005/48, 3 March 2005.

6. Ibid.

7.   See, *Handbook on UN Basic Principles and Guidelines on Development-based Evictions and Displacement*, available at: www.hic-sarp.org.

8.   *See*, Report of the Special Rapporteur on adequate housing, Miloon Kothari, E/CN.4/2005/48, 3 March 2005.

9.   Report of the Special Rapporteur on adequate housing, Miloon Kothari, E/CN.4/2006/41, 21 March 2006.

10. Report of UN Special Rapporteur on adequate housing, Raquel Rolnick, Mission to the United States of America, A/HRC/13/20/Add.4, 12 February 2010.

11. Report of the UN Special Rapporteur on adequate housing, Miloon Kothari, Mission to Australia, A/HRC/4/18/Add.2, 11 May 2007.

12. Report of UN Special Rapporteur on adequate housing, Raquel Rolnick, Mission to the United States of America, A/HRC/13/20/Add.4, 12 February 2010.

13. *See* "Planned Dispossession: Forced Evictions and the 2010 Commonwealth Games", Housing and Land Rights Network, Delhi: 2011. Available at: www.hic-sarp.org

14. See Kalyani Menon Sen and Gautam Bhan (2008) *Swept Off the Map*, New Delhi: Yoda Press.

15. Report on 'women and adequate housing' by the UN Special Rapporteur on adequate on housing, E/CN.4/2005/43, 25 February 2005.

16. Report of UN Special Rapporteur on adequate housing, Raquel Rolnick, Mission to the United States of America, A/HRC/13/20/Add.4, 12 February 2010.

17. The 2008 IGSSS study on homelessness in Delhi revealed that of the homeless women surveyed in Delhi, 28.57 per cent left home due to the ill treatment meted out to them; 18 per cent were deserted by their husbands; 25 per cent were forcibly thrown out by their relatives. It is also found that some of the women had mental health issues, which could also be the reason for homelessness.

18. Also see Report of the UN Special Rapporteur on adequate housing, Miloon Kothari, Mission to Australia, A/HRC/4/18/Add.2, 11 May 2007.

19. Report on 'Women and Adequate Housing' by the UN Special Rapporteur on adequate on housing, E/CN.4/2005/43, 25 February 2005.

20. Reports of the Special Rapporteur on women and housing available at: http://www.ohchr.org/EN/Issues/Housing/Pages/WomenAndHousing.aspx

21. Ruzbeh N. Bharucha (2006) *Yamuna Gently Weeps: A Journey into the Yamuna Pushta Slum Demolitions*. New Delhi: Sainathann Communications.

22. Report of the UN Special Rapporteur on adequate housing, Miloon Kothari, E/CN.4/2005/48, 3 March 2005.

23. "Study of the Homeless in Delhi," Indo Global Social Service Society, 2008. Used by the Supreme Court of India. Forthcoming publication.

24. See, Indu Prakash Singh. (2001April). "Census of the Homeless: A Painful Farce and an Assault". New Delhi: *First City*.

25. Findings from a PRA exercise conducted by IGSSS and Praxis with homeless residents of the Pul Mithai community, located in the area of Old Delhi, in close proximity to the Old Delhi Railway Station, June 2010.

26. Idem.

27. "Invisible City-Makers: An Action Research on Homelessness in Bangalore City," 2010. Bangalore: Bangalore Based NGOs and IGSSS

28. Report of the UN Special Rapporteur on adequate housing, Miloon Kothari, Mission to Canada, A/HRC/10/7/Add.3, 17 February 2009.

29. "Invisible City-Makers: An Action Research on Homelessness in Bangalore City," 2010. Bangalore: Bangalore Based NGOs and IGSSS.

30. For example, see, Housing, Health and Mental Health, http://www.cmha.ca/ data/1/rec_docs/549_CMHA_Housing_EN.pdf, Also see Wellesley Institute for more studies on homeless women in Canada: www.wellesleyinstitute. com

31. See article by Indu Prakash Singh, "And the Night Never Seemed to End."

32. "Invisible City-Makers: An Action Research on Homelessness in Bangalore City," 2010. . Bangalore: Bangalore Based NGOs and IGSSS.

33. Findings from a PRA exercise conducted by IGSSS and Praxis with homeless residents of the Pul Mithai community, located in the area of Old Delhi, in close proximity to the Old Delhi Railway Station, June 2010.

34. Study of the Homelessness and Beggary, Action Aid, 2003.

35. Report of the UN Special Rapporteur on adequate housing, Miloon Kothari, Mission to Australia, A/HRC/4/18/Add.2, 11 May 2007.

36. Miloon Kothari and Shivani Chaudhry, 'Unequal Cities Mean Unequal Lives,' *Urban World*, Volume 1, Issue 5 (December 2009–January 2010).

37. See Wellesley Institute: www.wellesleyinstitute.com.

38. Ibid.

39. "Invisible City-Makers: An Action Research on Homelessness in Bangalore City," 2010.

40. Report of the UN Special Rapporteur on adequate housing, Miloon Kothari, Mission to Canada, A/HRC/10/7/Add.3, 17 February 2009.
41. Report on 'women and adequate housing' by the UN Special Rapporteur on adequate on housing, E/CN.4/2005/43, 25 February 2005.
42. Report on 'women and adequate housing' by the UN Special Rapporteur on adequate on housing, E/CN.4/2006/118, 27 February 2006.

Role of Media in Addressing Gender-based Violence in Public Spaces

MOHUYA CHAUDHURI

❊❖❊

Introduction

When the world slid into the 21st century, women had grown out of their skins in many ways. They had access to better education, a gamut of employment opportunities, financial independence and the power to decide. Yet, some things remained stubbornly the same. Violence, both within the home and beyond its walls, was one of them. In some instances, it took on different hues, the protagonist and the methodology changing but the intensity of pain and scarring remained the same. Convictions in these cases were very low, so justice was denied to most victims of violence.

As women began to step out of their homes in search of an identity beyond what was prescribed to them, the established order was challenged. Dialogue and negotiation worked in some instances but if you were poor and marginalised, the response was extreme violence. In the last decade, crimes against women have risen sharply and they extend from the womb to the tomb.

Despite the insecurities and the ambiguity surrounding their lives, the last decade was an exciting period for women. India was opening up to the idea of globalisation, embracing the path of liberalisation in a big way. There was a sudden rush of green field projects in the services sector, throwing open opportunities which women grabbed unapologetically. So, the workplace witnessed a transition with men reporting to women, couples taking home dual incomes and daughters financially supporting families. Socially and culturally, however, the idea of a woman remained in stasis. A majority of women perceived that despite the economic transformation, the space that they inhabited did not change in any significant manner.

Stepping out, Cinderella-like, into the world, they never really felt safe. Whether walking on the streets after dark, waiting at a bus stop or travelling by public transport, a woman wore fear like a cloak. She was alert and aware at all times and watched her back. From sexual harassment in offices—a hand on the shoulder, tasteless, sexually overt comments—to groping in buses and lurid comments in public spaces, all of these were routine.

Daylight offered no security either. On the streets, women have been molested, chased by men in cars and even gang raped inside moving cars. Inside university campuses, the bastions of higher education, women have been harassed publicly for dressing in a particular manner and some have even been driven to death by politically-backed youth gangs.

Coming of age for many girls has been at a price. In the last decade, women have had to struggle with newer, excessively brutal forms of violence. Young adolescents have been stalked, and those who refused overtures from ardent lovers faced the threat of having acid poured on their faces. Single, independent women are used to sexual harassment, whether in a pub or shopping mall, while dealing with landlords or travelling alone in a taxi. And, in states like Haryana, if women dare to marry against social norms—for instance, within the same *gotra* or clan—they end up being hacked to death or hanged from trees before the eyes of the community. These decrees are passed by *khap* panchayats, the self-styled custodians of society who control large parts of rural Haryana and western Uttar Pradesh.

Many of these violent crimes would have remained invisible or ignored except for the media. Till a couple of decades ago, most cases of crimes against women went unreported. Families, especially economically well off ones, preferred to keep these dark incidents locked away inside the walls of their homes to prevent the family's name from getting tainted. But crimes unfailingly draw the reader and the viewer, and so newspapers and television channels have always followed crime like hounds. Initially, the only cases of violence that got reported in the press were those related to dowry and rape. But this has since changed.

Bhanwari Devi, a development worker in Bhateri village in Rajasthan, was gang raped for trying to stop child marriage. Her story was picked up by the local Hindi dailies and then the national dailies. Women's groups came forward to help her fight for justice in court. So also with the case of Maya Tyagi, a six-month pregnant woman, who was stripped and paraded naked on the streets of Baghpat in Uttar Pradesh by policemen and then raped mercilessly.

These incidents hit the headlines and grabbed public attention. However, the attention span of the media was short. Even in cases like those of Bhanwari Devi and Maya Tyagi, where there was genuine public outrage, after the initial shock and anger, the media moved on. Stories related to them would surface only when the court case came up or queries were raised in Parliament, but once the court ruled in favour of the culprits, denying Bhanwari Devi and Maya Tyagi justice, their stories received a quiet burial.

Media in the New Millennium: The Problem of Plenty

The new millennium witnessed a complete transformation of the media. Private television channels were given licenses and the market boomed. The multiplicity of television channels, both for entertainment and news and current affairs, split the skies wide open. Radio, too, began to shape urban consciousness in a big way. FM channels, though not permitted to air news, navigated intelligently to raise social issues. Crimes against women, their safety in public spaces, were given priority. Niche channels, both in radio and television, were launched exclusively for women.

But a slew of channels meant steep competition. Ratings began to dictate the content. Crime emerged as a popular genre, fetching higher Television Rating Points (TRP) than even political stories. Once that happened, every crime, even the most innocuous ones, began to be featured in a sensationalised fashion. Anchors screamed into the cameras building atmosphere, explicit graphics were used to reconstruct the event and judgments were passed live on air. Reportage hovered on the thin line between fiction and reality. Facts flew into the wind, identities of victims of violence were revealed, microphones were shoved into their faces and inappropriate questions were asked, further traumatising them, all in the name of news. Even minors were not spared. Over 70 per cent of girls who were raped were below eighteen years of age. Their faces were morphed but every possible detail was revealed in contravention of the Juvenile Justice Act. Since the police was a major source, with junior officers trading confidential information to cub journalists to grab their share of the limelight, no one rapped reporters for these transgressions. Stories were often one-sided and editorial guidelines seemed to be forgotten.

Competition became so stiff that most news was ungoverned. In the race to be first with the news, television newsrooms would put out images and content without vetting them. There were many challenges. As channels grew exponentially, there was an acute shortage of news. Every source was tapped, to fill the 24x7 news wheel. But there weren't enough trained scribes. Newspapers suddenly faced a massive exodus with journalists leaving for better pay packages that TV offered but even that did not meet the demands of the ever-hungry TV channels. Local journalists in smaller towns were hired piecemeal to feed news. Earlier, they were used as basic sources of information, an informal postmaster, but now with the pressures of time, their copy and the visuals hit the air without any checks. Even senior journalists, against their better judgement, became part of this rush. File first, withdraw later. No one would remember a mistake in the volume of news what was churned out endlessly.

Things became progressively worse. Viewers complained about how news was becoming perverse and failing in its mandate, yet they remained glued to their televisions. Newspapers, much more conservative than news channels, were influenced as well. Print journalists positioned stories keeping in mind what was played out through the day. The tone of the stories and the manner in which stories were told began to get tinged by the same hyperventilation that marked TV news. The earlier cut and polish, the sober tone and in-depth factual reporting that newspapers were generally known for were losing some of the sheen. It was as if the reporter had become a participant in the news, like a 'third eye'. At times, personal biases began to creep in.

Behind the hyperbole, news was turning offensive when dealing with violence against women. In the last decade, trafficking of women and girls has emerged as a massive, organised crime. Millions of girls are lured, kidnapped, bought and sold into various forms of exploitation, within India as well as across its borders. During a year-long campaign that New Delhi Television (NDTV) had launched, critical facts about the media's role emerged.

First, the campaign made the word 'trafficking' a household word. It captured the trend and the factors that drove the trade. News reports linked the skewed sex ratio in states like Haryana, Punjab, Gujarat and Rajasthan to the forced sale of girls. It was a heady mix of crime, women and sexuality—a perfect cocktail for the media. Almost daily, one newspaper or the other or some network would travel to some village, *moffusil* town or second rung city to film or write about the rescue of girls, mostly minors. The stories remained as grisly as ever—about girls, barely in their teens, being abused and battered by men dozens of years their senior. Though the reports exposed the existence of trafficking as an organised crime on one hand, on the other they also revealed how shoddily the media treated the same victims. Images of beheaded girls, faces of victims of multiple rapes marked in red circles, and their details were freely put out. MMS, pictures taken on mobile phones, began to reach the newsrooms. There was public discomfort but journalists themselves, who shared this sense of disquiet, did not push for steps to be taken to right this wrong. A few responsible channels, leaders in the business, adhered strictly to the universal ethical guidelines, but in most cases the sensational value of a news story came before the subject.

Then came the dreaded age of 'sting journalism', India's version of the West's 'paparazzi' culture, with cheap invasive technology as its backbone. The market was flooded with eye-popping, innovative cameras and gadgets that made snooping frightfully easy. A miniscule camera could now be fitted into a pen, a shirt button, a purse, a cap or a belt. No one could detect its presence. Suddenly, channels began to be flooded with images of women being exploited, facing different kinds of violence. In some instances, it even spawned its own version of violence. Take the case of Uma Khurana, a government schoolteacher who was stripped in public by angry parents because she reportedly lured her students into prostitution. It was dubious from the start. The visuals were created with the help of a hidden camera. There were no gatekeepers to verify the story. The teacher was beaten and shamed in public, her clothes nearly ripped off, her reputation in shreds and her job hanging in the balance. But the media was relentless. Her images were looped, played over and over again, creating a monster. Her denials did not get equal space. The Delhi government, on the back-foot, ordered an inquiry. It later transpired that the reporter who had done the sting operation had set it up to grab eyeballs. The story was false. The girl in the clips was reportedly paid by the journalist to accuse Khurana. No one bothered to check what happened to the teacher or what her students felt towards her after the episode. The journalist was penalised but reinstated.

It, therefore, became difficult to draw the line between the private and the public. The most problematic part of this kind of reportage was that a woman had no choice in the matter—whether she wanted to go public or not about what she went through. Also, the manner in which she was represented left her more violated. So, the media was also becoming a perpetrator in a sense and the decision-maker as well. Matters of consent did not really come up in these instances.

In the new world order, the image has replaced truth. What you see is what it is. Reality can be constructed through crafty use of images. One simple principle that most channels use is to loop images. There is always a crunch of visuals so the same shots are stitched together and played over and over again. What would be a multi-layered story earlier with different voices providing depth and nuance to an issue is now reduced to just one or two images playing repeatedly. So, when the shot of a young boy being slapped by a cop for stealing bread is looped, it begins to look like a bigger crime than it is. This applies to reportage on violence against women in public as well. The victims are even more victimised by the media.

Take the case of two young women in Mumbai who were molested as they emerged from a hotel on New Year's Eve in 2008. Grainy images of a mob of about seventy men groping them in up-market Juhu appeared on every channel. Some channels circled the girls in red thus revealing their identities. In the race to get the first images, an individual's rights are constantly compromised. Media ethics is becoming the first casualty in the 24x7 news wheel. In possibly every newsroom, there are manuals with guidelines on how to represent women in the media, especially when it comes to violence such as rape, molestation, sexual harassment and other forms of abuse. Names, faces, identities must be safeguarded and explicit images must be avoided. Instead, it is these images that are shown on channels. Whether it is an MMS of an underage girl being forced into a sexual act or a woman being exploited by very senior bureaucrats, these images easily find space on channels, playing ceaselessly. The camera is now a voyeur and crimes against women entertainment.

However, there is a silver lining. In the midst of this bedlam, where reportage had become such an ethical nightmare, the 24-hour format and the higher viewership for crime also provided an opportunity to look at issues that would otherwise not find space in the news. In the process, television uncovered several newer forms of violence, which continue to jeopardize the safety of women. So, if there was an acid attack, it was not just a crime but also an indicator of the emergence of a new social deviant, created by the changing attitudes of women. They were taking independent decisions, stepping out to study in colleges or going out to work. The image of woman was clearly changing. She was a power woman now, wrestling her way into male territories. Women rode bikes and cars, flew aircraft, and even took up jobs as mechanics in villages. The fashion industry, too, made a big difference to young women, who now dressed differently. The tagline for a scooter ad (Hero Honda's Pleasure), which said 'Why should boys have all the fun', encapsulates this transformation. The media, always hungry for something new, mapped this makeover through news reports and long format documentaries. Papers carried news reports on the changing face of India, often showcasing a single woman or a working woman navigating the challenges of life with grit and determination.

While there was a sense of celebration, there was a sense of disquiet as well. The modification of social and cultural patterns of behaviour of women was causing pressure points to build up, within and without their homes, leading to conflict. However, while women fought hard to gain access to previously barred spaces, they were not prepared to face the violence that was unleashed at several levels, beginning at home and ending at the workplace. Some newspapers and TV channels did capture this dilemma, but curiously more in the mega-cities than smaller towns.

In a report published by *Tehelka* magazine (9 February 2008), Anupama Rao, a researcher at Barnard College, Columbia University, is thus quoted:

In these globalising times, what might be worth noticing are new formations of anti-women violence and new sites for its enactments. For instance, consumer culture, advertising, and the putative opening up of public spaces to women have produced yet more surreptitious forms of gender violence. These include everything from sexual harassment on the job to new forms of psychic violence that target female bodies through conceptions of beauty, desirability, etc.

Along with physical violence, there was a great degree of emotional violence as well. Parents and brothers resented a girl getting a job in place of her brother, male colleagues abused women because they got promoted faster, and husbands and partners brutally beat up women for breaking out of their straitjacket roles. What made the scars cut deeper was the fact that women knew that what was happening was wrong, yet they realised that the law was ineffective and would inevitably fail to deliver justice. Such social transitions were well mapped by the media, both in print and television, which provided a context to the violence. However, the images could not capture all the nuances of the crisis. Print articles faced the same challenge since brevity for want of space is common to both media.

Acid Attacks: The Vicious New Weapon of Dominance

One of the new modes of violence against women that emerged on the cusp of the new millennium was acid throwing. It was a disturbing social anomaly that pointed to a breakdown in the social order. Thousands of women have been burnt to death or disfigured in the name of dowry, but acid throwing took mutilation to a different level altogether. Such an assault left a woman indelibly crippled for life, a permanent reminder of the gruesome act.

The first known cases were reported by the media. The maximum number of cases of acid attacks was from Karnataka, Andhra Pradesh and

Kashmir. In 2009, there were several reports of women suffering acid burns in Andhra Pradesh. In most of these cases, a spurned lover was involved. The scale of injuries on an average was very grave, the scarring lifelong. Most of the women who have been attacked can never regain their lives. The case that got most prominence in the media were that of nineteen-year-old Haseena Hussain in Karnataka who had 2 litres of sulphuric acid poured on her by her former boss because she changed her job. Her mutilated face appeared on every newspaper and television channel, her cry for justice found resonance across the country.

Following her case, in the last ten years, the scale of these assaults has only risen and spilled into smaller cities. Women, mostly young, continue to get accosted by angry wannabe suitors, or simply because they could not be controlled. The attacker is often in denial and cannot accept rejection and is driven by the need for revenge. Acid attacks are an extreme form of violence against women who dare to stand up against men.

These assaults have been reported widely in all media. The victims were followed and their tales told poignantly. Channels like NDTV, Aak Taj, Zee and CNN-IBN have reported extensively on the issue. So have newspapers like *The Times of India*, which campaigned for nineteen-year-old Laxmi, who went to court in 2006, for enhancement of punishment for acid attacks. She had been assaulted for turning down a marriage proposal. The attack was so brutal that she was left disfigured horribly for life. A combination of courage on the part of victims and media reportage led to the National Commission for Women (NCW) and the Law Commission demanding that the laws be made more stringent in order to ensure deterrence. The Supreme Court, in response to her petition, said the perpetrators must be punished with an iron hand. It wanted to ban over-the-counter sale of acid and asked states for their opinion. Unfortunately, none of the pressure tactics worked on the government. In April 2010, *The Times of India* reported that the government not only refused to increase the punishment against acid throwing, even though it is pre-mediated, it also refused to ban the free sale of acid on the grounds that it was used for household purposes. So, the sale of acid continues without any restrictions making it one the most potent weapons of violence against women today.

Woman: A Commodity

Many of these crimes, social scientists say, have become part of the social landscape because of the gender imbalance in the country. The sex ratio is skewed in states like Haryana, Rajasthan and Punjab and so it comes as no surprise that trafficking, too, is highest in these same states. The issue was picked up in a big way by a cross-section of the media. All leading dailies, including *The Times of India, Hindustan Times, The Telegraph*, Hindi dailies such as *Dainik Jagran* and *Hindustan*, papers of the northeast (*Asomiya Pratidin, Assam Tribune, Khobor*) as well as magazines like *The Week* and *Outlook*, almost went on a mission mode establishing how rampant female foeticide in the above mentioned states was a form of violence against women that had a ripple effect, engendering even more violent forms of violence.

More girls killed in the womb meant that the number of women dwindled sharply, so men of middling age with money in these economically forward states were turning to poorer regions like Jharkhand, Bengal, Assam and Orissa when they needed a bride. These were not formal marriages so women faced unlimited violence of all forms. Some bought their brides, some resold them into sex work or even killed them when the women no longer met their needs.

As the commodification of women got almost institutionalised, so did the violence. Women were butchered in public, like the eighteen-year-old Adivasi girl from Jharkhand, Triphala, who was taken to the fields by her husband, Ajmer Singh, a Jat, and beheaded because she refused to have sexual relations with his brother who could not find a bride for himself.[1] Singh was arrested but let out without punishment. In Jharkhand, from where a large number of girls are trafficked annually, there was a deafening silence. Leading newspapers like *Prabhat Khabar* reported extensively but the state government remained unmoved.

The savagery was not limited to individual families. The skewed sex ratio was also responsible for the meteoric rise in street crimes and greater harassment of women in public places. Just as in China, the media has consistently raised the issue of gender imbalance leading to crimes but the government has been unable to take criminal or civil action against female foeticide. Even the amendments to the law are still in waiting.

While reporting on crimes against women, especially in public places, a point that bothers most journalists is the absence of community support. In fact, there are clear instances where the community itself participates actively in the crime. Whether it is a *khap* panchayat or witch hunting or the practice of sati, the community stands up to preserve a custom and is willing to pay any cost. Clearly, while new forms of violence are emerging, violence against women also remains trans-historical in many instances.

Sati: Commerce in the Garb of Tradition

The first ever case of extreme violence against a woman in public that the media picked up in a big way in recent memory was that of Roop Kanwar in 1987. The nation was shocked to learn that the eighteen-year-old was burned on her husband's pyre in the name of sati. Newspapers launched a campaign seeking justice for Roop Kanwar, even though the press itself was divided. While some journalists, though not in favour of the murder of a young woman, found it difficult to question practices they themselves believed in, the months following her tragic death saw national publications pursue her case relentlessly.

During this period, it also became clear that in districts like Jhunjhunu in Rajasthan, sati was not an unusual phenomenon. Several villages have small shrines dedicated to women who gave up their lives after their husbands died. None of these ever became public. Many believed that the practice of sati had died out over time. But once Roop's story of being drugged and then taken to the pyre before the entire village broke, investigative journalists found that she was not the only woman forced to die a violent death in recent times. In Jhunjhunu district, in the years before and after her death, other widows had faced the same end; they were driven to immolate themselves.

As late as the mid-1990s, temples were being built in the memory of women who had sacrificed their lives in the name of sati; all them large revenue earners for both the family and the community. During a closed door meeting with the members of the Rani Sati Temple Trust, the biggest shrine in the name of 'sacrifice, motherhood and bravery' as their website puts it, I understood that the underpinnings of the tradition was commerce, though no one would obviously admit it openly. The idea of a woman setting herself on fire still found sanction because it raked in billions of rupees from devotees. Besides, a school, an annual Rani Sati festival and merchandise were additional spin-offs. During the annual festival, the temple made crores of rupees selling the notion of a 'pure' woman who gave up her life to prove her chastity. Once the report was aired, several irate callers, most of them well-educated professionals, questioned such treatment of an ancient tradition. Clearly, knowledge does not necessarily change mindsets.

But there were positive outcomes as well. The heat generated by the media after Roop Kanwar's death and the activists' demand for a law banning sati resulted in the passing of the Commission of Sati (Prevention) Act, the first ever law to punish widow immolation. The law also made inciting and abetting the act of sati punishable. Anyone who indulged in such action would get life imprisonment or even death. It was a significant step forward in the fight to end violence against women.

Those were the days when newspapers ruled. So there was no loud posturing or cacophony created around crimes against women in public spaces. The reportage was muted. The only television channel that existed was Doordarshan and the station with widespread reach was All India Radio (AIR). But neither of them, being government owned, was in a position to challenge the government.

Women's groups and the media did fight for the victim's rights in each of these crimes, placing them under the spotlight, exposing the lapses of the system and the betrayal by the judiciary. The media provided the platform for public outrage at such bestiality. However, as the newsworthiness of the story, called the 'peg', began to be lost, fresh stories replaced the older ones, pushing them to the inside pages, before going on to dismiss them completely.

Roop Kanwar died in 1987. Though her story faded away with time after the courts let the perpetrators go free, it became clear that her tragic death was not an aberration. This ancient form of violence against a woman's right to life continues even today despite the law because society still condones it silently. The reportage around Roop Kanwar's death set in motion a cycle of stories on widow immolation. It was found that sati cases may not be common today but the practice hasn't been wiped out. Women continue to be immolated in some parts of north India because of money. Since most take place in rural India with the silent backing of the entire community, they are rarely reported. Here too the media is the only tool that exposes this cruel, inhuman tradition. For many years after Roop Kanwar died and the law was enacted, many believed that the heinous practice was more or less wiped out. But they were wrong.

In August 2002, sixty-five-year-old Kattu Bai immolated herself on her husband's pyre as a mob of 1,000 people stood around her, inciting her to burn herself in Patna Tamoli village in Panna district in Madhya Pradesh. Two of her sons were present for their father's cremation but they did nothing to stop her. In fact, villagers put coconuts and garlands at her feet chanting loudly. A couple of policemen did try and drag Kattu Bai away from the pyre but were beaten back by villagers with sticks and driven away. No one would have known about the incident except for the fact that a photographer from *Navbharat Times*, a Hindi daily, was there and witnessed the immolation. He captured images of Kattu Bai on the pyre and published them. The state government, headed by former Chief Minister Digvijay Singh, took stern action against the village since not only had everyone participated in the event, they had actively abetted the crime. The evidence was enough for the administration to arrest the Sarpanch, seventeen villagers and both the sons. The story was picked up by the international press, including the BBC, perhaps because of its "quaint" value. Following sustained media coverage, the government felt it needed to send out a warning that such incidents would not be tolerated. All development funds for Patna Tamoli village were stopped.

Clearly, persistent and well-rounded coverage of such events does put pressure on the government to act. But the Panna case was unique. Most often, the government takes immediate action but once the media noise dies out, the administration's attention wavers as well. In general, there is no effort to send a strong, unequivocal message that such practices will not be tolerated. The cause lies deeply embedded in the social ethos of north

India. A woman is sacrificed in the name of sati because of property and also because the family immediately rises in stature in the community. In order to legitimise the crime, it is shrouded in ritual and religion. At the Rani Sati temple, secret rituals are conducted, as reported by *The Times of India*, August 2009, glorifying sati. The message that goes out to women in states like Rajasthan and Madhya Pradesh, where widow immolation is still attempted, is that sati is a divine act and not a form of violence.

The state, too, in a sense, is a perpetrator, since it refuses to intervene despite being aware of these practices. Those who represent it, such as the police, often see no wrong in the tradition and therefore end up condoning the act. Those in power—the politicians themselves visit these temples—refuse to take a stand against their own beliefs. Therefore, it is left to the media to create an uproar to push the administration to take action, but it is invariably inadequate.

It is hard to find data on how many people have actually been convicted for inciting and then committing sati. In the Panna case, the sons got life imprisonment but the rest of the villagers who were equally guilty were set free. The case itself is forgotten. With no punishment, the practice continues, locked away in the underbelly of rural India.

Witch Hunting: A Saga of Inequalities[2]

Old traditions die hard. Unlike metropolises, where women are learning to deal with neo-aggression, in rural India, crimes against women are still embedded in feudalism, caste inequalities and custom. A woman's life is not worth much in these parts.

One of the worst forms of extreme force used against Adivasi and Dalit women in at least six states in India is witch hunting. All victims of this vicious violence are poor, vulnerable women, usually widows or women abandoned by their families. The state with a terrible report card is Jharkhand. In fact, 30 per cent of all witchcraft related cases that took place in 2007–8 in the country were reported from Jharkhand. The state government's own data shows that at least 249 women were killed and 1,200 women branded as witches and tortured in public in the state during 2001–9. Women have been tonsured, tortured, beaten up, paraded naked and forced to eat excreta because they were labelled witches. Gladson Dung Dung[3] in his article "Hunting Witches or Hunting Women" says that the practice of witch hunting in the Adivasi community has been shaped through tradition and culture and is extremely deep rooted. But along with the Adivasi's belief in ghosts and spirits, a key reason why women, especially older women and widows, are particularly chosen as witches by their own relatives is because of property, money or land. In Adivasi communities like the Santhals, women and widows are given property rights. And as land holdings shrink and get divided, such attacks are on the rise.

However, in all this, the role of tradition cannot be completely ruled out either. Publications like the non-mainstream *Jharkhand Mirror* reported the blood chilling story of two women, sixty-year-old Somri Hansda (a widow) and forty-year-old Vahamay Kiskoo of Mahuwasol village, who were beaten to death by sixty villagers because a nine-year-old child had dreamt that they were eating her father's heart. The entire village watched them die slowly and then they were burnt to ashes. Their deaths were celebrated through the night.

Another key issue that has come up several times in media reports, both national dailies as well as the international press, is the link between healthcare and witchcraft. Every time someone falls sick in the village and does not recover with the help of the traditional healer, the *ojha*, the blame is shifted to someone, usually a woman who is marginalised in the village. So the government's failure to deliver healthcare to people propels them to depend on *ojhas* who are nothing better than quacks. And, invariably, to shift the blame for the loss of life, a witch is created, who in turn often pays with her own life. This is documented by the media. However, the media also perpetuates these myths by showing agitated women having fits on air. A woman's off key, agitated behaviour becomes a signal of witchcraft.[4]

Unlike sati though, very few stories on witch hunting find space in national newspapers or television channels since it usually happens in some of the remotest areas among the poorest communities. Apart from some sporadic stories, so far the media has never chased the phenomenon of witch hunting the way it ought to. International media has focussed on the subject once in a while. Though the reports are detailed and present a grim picture, no major human rights campaign has ever been launched to tackle witch hunting.

Like every other tradition which targets women, witch hunting shows no signs of dying out because the state has no interest in intervening. An article on the issue by *India Today* profiles some cases in which the relatives and neighbours have taken the lives of scores of people in the name of sorcery. On the night of 2 January 2010, fourteen-year-old Pinki Khakha's parents and sister were hacked to death by three of their relatives who believed they were practising witchcraft in Sauda village, very close to Jharkhand's capital Ranchi. Pinki managed to hide and so she survived but she now watches every step she takes. The danger is far from over. The men who wiped out her family were not punished and live close by.

Jharkhand is one of the two states with a law—Prevention of Witch Practices Act, passed in 2001—banning the practice of witch hunting. Sadly, the law remains unimplemented. As seen in the case of Pinki Khakha, despite evidence against the culprits, no one was punished. With almost negligible conviction rates, women have no choice but to suffer inconceivable brutalities in silence. Look at the state's track record when it comes to convictions. Despite the law, National Crime Records Bureau (NCRB) figures show that convictions for culpable homicide cases in the last decade, which are low across the country at less than 35 per cent, is at a shocking 17 per cent in Jharkhand, which has the largest number of witch hunting murders.

And now the poison is spreading. Haryana, with its abysmal history of abuse against women, is emerging as the new hub of black magic. After female foeticide, trafficking of women and 'honour' killings, witch hunting has now emerged as the new form of violence women have to contend with in the state. Once again, this trend was discovered by the media. The *India Today* report, January 2010 mentions that during 2005–8, 117 women were branded and killed as witches. Apart from buying women from poorer states like Jharkhand, Haryana is now also importing some of their cruel, primitive customs as well. This is particularly worrisome because the community at the village level in the state is a power unto themselves. The state allows the existence of *khap* panchayats, an extra-constitutional authority that decides the course of social behaviour.

Khap Panchayat: Media and the Medieval Rule of Law

A panchayat is the representative of the government at the village level. Its primary responsibility is to ensure that the Constitution and the laws enshrined in it are implemented thereby ending social inequities. The 73rd Amendment devolved power to the village level to allow for self-governance, giving back power to the people. However, in Haryana, some parts of Rajasthan and western Uttar Pradesh, the word 'panchayat' has diabolical connotations. In this region, a group of elders drawn from the same clan or *gotra*, from a cluster of geographically contiguous villages, form a 'khap' or caste panchayat. Families of the same *khap*, usually from the Jat community, must follow their writ. Going back to the 14th century, the *khap* panchayat's ultimate aim is to control the lives of the community, especially that of young girls. Their stand is: *gotras* are sacred and their sanctity cannot be breached by marrying within the same clan, since, according to custom, the man and woman belong to the same lineage and therefore are siblings. And that's not all. Couples cannot marry within the same village either, even if they belong to a different clan. It is of little significance if they share a bloodline or not. If anyone dares to defy *khap* rules, which basically means if couples dare to fall in love and decide to marry on their own, they have to pay a steep price, often with their lives. It is a dangerous cocktail of gender and caste, where a woman comes off worse every time.

Khap panchayats are not new and their repressive acts continue without any censure because the elected panchayats do not intervene or rein them in, despite knowing well that their orders have no legal validity. The community of same *gotra* families also do not question the *khap*'s decrees, no matter how illegal or unjust, because many who approach these caste panchayats are relatives, including parents and brothers. Also, many families choose to follow the community's decision, even to the extent of killing their own children, for fear of losing everything. *Khap* panchayats are known to drive those who break their diktats out of the village. In order to retain whatever little property, land and prestige they have in society, they are forced to sacrifice their own kin. A report in a website run by Azad Foundation says how it is well known that parents feed their daughters pesticide pills and then dispose off their bodies by burning them. It is evident that for believers, the village, community and family honour resides in the girl. A boy can, at times, be forgiven his trespass but not a girl.

The list of those punished remorselessly because they broke social norms is endless. In 2009 alone, several couples faced the *khap*'s wrath. In June, Anita and Sonu, who married without consent, were lured back to their village in Rohtak by the promise of reconciliation. But once they entered the village, they were stabbed to death by *khap* members in public in the presence of policemen.[5] A month later, twenty-three-year-old Ved Pal Mor was lynched by the villagers of Singhwal where his wife, Sonia, lived. They were both from the same *gotra* but the court had validated their marriage. He had returned with that order to take her back with him and was accompanied by a court officer as well as policemen for his safety. But no one could stop him being killed.

Another couple, once again in Haryana, Ravinder (a gehlot) and Shilpa (a kadyan), were given the death punishment on 24 July 2009 because Shilpa's extended family lived in Ravinder's village and therefore the *khap*, in a bizarre twist, declared them relatives. Unable to take the pressure, Ravinder tried to commit suicide but failed. Consequently, the *khap* commuted the punishment and banished the couple and Ravinder's family from the village. His relatives had to pay huge fines. While investigating the case, newspapers like *The Times of India* reported that the family had 100 *bigha* of land which provided strong evidence that *khap* panchayats were not just the protectors of their clan but also of the socially and economically dominant groups in these areas.

Cutting across the span of media platforms, whether print, TV, radio or the internet, there has been a deluge of stories documenting the blatant, vicious public murders of couples. These barbaric acts of the *khap* panchayats have also been likened to those of the Taliban, a militant group that has enforced its social order through extreme violence. In a world dominated by cutting edge technology and broadening opportunities of education and employment, where India has sent its own craft to the moon, such medieval practices, which are clearly unlawful, continue to flourish. The contrast couldn't be greater, the message more stark.

As case after case became public, a significant amount of space was given by newspapers and air time by TV channels to 'honour' killings. Chat shows and special reports showcased different opinions from both sides, keeping the debate alive. Gradually, apart from highlighting the inhuman practice, these discussions helped to give 'honour' killings strong political hues as well. But instead of going on the defensive, various versions of *khap* panchayat groups—'*Maha khap*', '*Sarva khap*' and '*Maha Sarv khap*'—all stepped forward to argue aggressively the relevance and purpose of such entities. They spoke of the problems of inbreeding and the importance of maintaining the brotherhood. None of their representatives admitted that these so-called caste councils were extra-constitutional and what they practised was nothing short of homicide.

And no matter how much the media pushed for the need for extraordinary action to prevent such atrocious crimes against women, the pressure did not yield much. The political superstructure remained a passive spectator. Within the government, there was a clear division. While the home ministry and agencies like the NCW did demand action against the perpetrators and a law banning *khap* panchayats, they could do little since law and order is a state subject. On its part, the Haryana government thwarted all such moves in the public domain.

In fact, Chief Minister Bhoopinder Singh Hooda defended the existence of *khap* panchayats claiming that they were not responsible for honour killings. In a report on NDTV, he said marriages within the same *gotra* were not part of the state's tradition. However, he forgot to mention that in his own state there are many villages where the *khap* writ does not apply and couples do marry within the same caste and the same village as well. Clearly, it was a political gambit. Hooda, a Jat himself, did not want to alienate his constituency and vote bank by taking stringent actions against *khap* panchayats. He described them as non-government organisations (NGOs) that were doing social work and that they had a life of their own.[6] Following in his footsteps, even future leaders with promise—young, educated MPs like Navin Jindal, who are in Parliament for the first time and want to prove themselves—backed the idea that drives such *khaps*.

With so much political support, a *khap mahapanchayat*, a massive congregation of caste panchayats from the three states, was called in April 2010, in an attempt to strengthen their position. Held at Kurukshetra, the *mahapanchayat* issued fresh warnings in public against couples who married within the same *gotra*. As if it were not enough that hundreds of couples had been savagely killed contravening every law, and the huge media pressure, the Jat community now wanted legal sanction. So they demanded that the Hindu Marriage Act (1955) be amended to ban same *gotra* marriages. Each and every element in this complex play of caste and politics was drawn out by media reports but the voice of tradition drowned out the voice of reason.

But the *khap* conglomerate's arrogance and invincibility got a jolt when the District and Sessions Court in Karnal, Haryana, gave a landmark judgement in the case of Manoj and Babli Banwala in March 2010. Manoj (twenty-three years old) and Babli (nineteen years old), lived in the same village, Kaithal, and belonged to the same *gotra*. They eloped and married in 2007, breaching the *khap* panchayat's rules. A case was filed against Manoj. To prevent his family from getting harassed further, both he and Babli came out of hiding and testified in court that she had married him willingly. On their way back from the court, despite an escort, they were kidnapped by Babli's relatives—her brother, two cousins, two uncles and a powerful, well connected village elder. It is believed they were forced to drink pesticide. Manoj was also strangulated and thrown away. The court found all six guilty of murder and gave them life imprisonment.

Manoj and Babli's families have tasted justice but for hundreds of others justice is an impossible dream. Even today, courts have piles of pending petitions asking for the liberty to marry a person of their own choice. So has the media. Every other day, couples ring in with their horror stories. But unless there is political support and some amount of judicial activism along with social change, this savage system will continue to make couples, especially women, pay for wanting to live life on their own terms.

Moral Policing: Terror in the Name of Tradition

This is India's duality today. On the one hand, the government boasts of becoming an economic superpower, yet deep within society there is a great deal of regression. Patriarchy views women through the same old prism, refusing to accept that the old order has changed. Therefore, the social quotient against violence committed on women is extremely low. In this neo-liberal age of consumerism, women have become commodities and no one showcases that better than the media.

The last decade has also seen the media promote the idea that India is part of the global village, where women enjoy equal rights. That society is far more permissive than before. Products endorsed through the media sell this notion of a liberal and progressive India of the youth. Therefore, colleges are full of young girls flaunting not just 'modern' attire (read jeans and shorts, figure hugging dresses) but they are not afraid to walk the talk. They demand freedom to be who they are.

But this has fuelled the anger of right-wing groups cross the country. In Chennai, Kanpur, Mumbai, Delhi, Agra, Meerut, Bangalore and Mangalore, girls have been attacked and traumatised for breaking 'traditional Indian values'. Women were beaten up because they wore jeans, smoked, drank or stayed out late without supervision. Today's big brother is not the family but the so-called upholders of tradition and morality.

No city reflects this dichotomy better than Bangalore. It is an IT nerve centre, with a rainbow mix of powerhouse professionals from all across the country. Some of the biggest multinational corporations have set up bases here. It was the country's first city to herald in the pub culture in a big way. A string of pubs came up in a short period, each filled with smoke and song. The city of gardens was shrugging off its sleepy town image and turning into an upwardly mobile global city, buzzing with possibilities; but not for long.

The city's transition depended on who was in power. Once the Bharatiya Janta Party (BJP) took over, the storm troopers of the Sangh Parivar took on a new life. The Rashtriya Swayam Sevak Sangh (RSS), Vishva Hindu Parishad (VHP) and Bajrang Dal have a strong base in the state and have programmed several attacks on Christians and Muslims. And now there were no restrictions on their activities. It was a matter of time before their presence began to be felt. Bangalore became the hub of moral police squads. Women were harassed in every possible way. Goons riding on bikes would attack women on the street, hurling obscenities. Single women were targeted especially in the name of 'protecting society'.

In 2009, at least eighty cases of moral policing were reported in six months alone. Two women killed themselves after facing such humiliation. Both had been attacked by Bajrang Dal activists. Newspapers, FM radio stations and television channels reported these crimes but no action was taken. For the police, moral police squads are not vigilante groups on the prowl. Many in khaki actually support such subversive behaviour, not seeing any violation of the law or harassment of women in their acts.

Take the case of Operation Majnu, a drive against obscenity undertaken by the Meerut police in December 2005, which turned ugly. Mysteriously, the plan was to prevent couples from getting intimate in public. But that day, at Company Gardens, a large public park where couples usually met, women cops unleashed an unprovoked physical assault on unsuspecting couples. Girls were viciously slapped, their hair pulled and some were called filthy names. One girl was kicked in the chest and slapped several times before being dragged to the police vehicles to be taken away to the police station along with the others. Two siblings were beaten up as well. The men didn't fare any better as the violence was indiscriminate. Significantly, there appeared to be an element of premeditation in this exercise.

The media had already been informed about Operation Majnu and so camera persons and journalists were close at hand, capturing every moment. But once the images played out on TV screens, protests broke out all across Meerut city. Students and the general public demanded that instant action be taken against the guilty women cops. Effigies were burnt and pressure was built up by the press as well. Some couples, caught on camera, were so terrified of their family's reaction, they went missing. The din got so loud that the chief of police admitted that the operation had gone wrong. He ordered an internal enquiry and suspended the cops at fault.

It isn't unusual for the police in any part of the country to harass couples in public spaces. The woman often faces greater ostracism since she is seen as the transgressor. The Meerut case was highlighted by the media, albeit with no bona fide intentions, but in the end it did become a platform to raise vital questions about the mindset of law enforcers and the urgent need for reform. Moral policing cannot continue without the support of agencies like the police and political backing. This was clear from the Mangalore case, which has now become a landmark in the history of moral policing.

In February 2009, a mob of forty men from the right wing Sri Ram Sene entered Amnesia-The Lounge, a pub in Mangalore, at night and brutally beat up the girls present there, dragging them out of the club. They threatened to get the couples married. They were told that their 'behaviour' was an aberration and tarnished Indian values. The women did not get a chance to defend themselves. Inside the pub, there was a sense of paralysis. No one intervened when the women were being attacked. It was evident that women were not free to go anywhere or be independent since the moral brigade would shadow them wherever they went. A woman was simply not safe in public places.

Those who were witnesses to the anarchy and rage that night at the pub say some media houses had already been informed of the plan. A few broadcast reporters had reportedly travelled with the Sene members. So, if the attack was orchestrated and the journalists were in the know, does that not make them accomplices as well? The line between journalism and reality television is becoming increasingly blurred. Media becomes both a spectator as well as a participant, jettisoning objectivity. In these instances, there appears to be collusion between those who generate news and those who consume and sell it. So, the question was: Were the images of the attack that shocked the nation manufactured? Were the women abused to send out a message? Did the over-active, hungry press facilitate that? Clearly, the media needs to introspect urgently about its own role.

Despite the media pressure, the state government, led by the BJP, did not take stern action against the Sri Ram Sene. To save face, twenty-seven men were arrested but were let out on bail. The chief of this motley group of moral watchdogs, Pramod Muthalik, was arrested only because of the media. National news channels and newspapers made it their headline for days. Along with the mainstream press, the internet was funnelling some of the rage that young people felt towards such self-righteous messiahs of Indian culture and morality. Bloggers were furious, and campaigns were launched on popular social networking websites like Facebook and Orkut, ripping apart Muthalik and his gang of rowdies.

But since there was tacit support from the government (Chief Minister Yeduyirappa refused to ban the Sri Ram Sene and Rajasthan Chief Minister Ashok Gehlot also declared that he was opposed to the pub culture), the Sriram Sene did not stop with the attack. Their moral policing only got worse. From behind bars, Muthalik kept up his tirade. He threatened to attack those who celebrated Valentine's Day. In return, the 'pink chaddi' campaign was launched by a group of women, who promised to send pink underwear to Sene members, pink being the colour of Valentine's Day. Undaunted, Muthalik promised to send them 1,000 sarees as a reminder of who they were and where they belonged. Even the caustic remarks made by the then minister of women and child development, Renuka Chowdhary, did not deter Muthalik.

The reason is out there. Sri Ram Sene, an off-shoot of the Sangh Parivar, was created so that Muthalik and men like him could carry on arson on Muslim and Christian shrines with impunity. Sene represents the violent face of the Parivar and has sanction of the highest possible authorities. In the case of moral policing, the notion of preserving culture is used as a tool for violence, a mechanism of control. Many couples are usually attacked and humiliated on Valentine's Day for no reason.

In many parts of the country, where smaller towns are heaving to join the metropolitan cities, attitudes are clashing with change. Within colleges, youth gangs, usually affiliated to some political party, are driving the institution's policies, of what a student can wear to maintain propriety. In the event they are not complied with, like the Kanpur case, where women wore jeans to college, well planned attacks are unleashed on unsuspecting youngsters. Many colleges now no longer allow women to wear western wear like jeans. The media has raised the flag of moral policing regularly, critiquing it and demanding that women be free to make their own choices. But since these groups are politically strong, no real action can be taken against them. This is a case where politics segues into culture.

Rape and Molestation

One of the oldest methods used to control a woman is rape. There are multiple dimensions to this crime in India. Caste, class, gender, business rivalry, family feuds or simply revenge. In the end, it is an act to make a woman submit through brute force. Reportage on rape has been extensive in India. National dailies, vernacular press, regional newspapers, television channels, radio stations and now the internet, have all discussed the phenomenon of rape down to every point—the gross violation of a woman, her self-esteem and her identity; the role of the police, who are often the perpetrators; the unending victimisation of rape survivors; the lacunae in the law; the poor conviction rates; the absence of rehabilitation.

But how have these women who have suffered the ordeal of rape been represented in the media, especially now that the media has exploded to form tentacles of its own? First, let us look at the good news. Looking back, the bulk of reportage on various forms of rape in public spaces resulted in a review of the antiquated rape laws. Amendments were made in 1983 and now a new draft bill, The Criminal Law (Amendment Bill) 2010, is pending with the home ministry.

The bad news is that most of the demands made by feminists and lawyers are still outside the realm of the anti-rape law. The media, fed with brand new forms of violence daily, is no longer interested in covering rape cases. Crime shows on TV and metro pages are the only spaces where rape cases are reported. There is a sense of fatigue and ennui when it comes to rape. Even sexual harassment cases do not set the editorial in motion. The attitude is: been there, done that. It's as if there is no news value left to these issues, except perhaps, if it is a celebrity like Shiny Ahuja.

In these times of sensation and mind-numbing noise, rape cases, if featured, are hyped beyond measure. But are lines crossed? Well, almost every time. In Shiny Ahuja's case, the maid's name was revealed. Her desperate attempts to hide her face as flashbulbs went off incessantly were foiled by some channels. She was identified. Her uncle who accompanied here was pursued as well. Some reporters even followed her to her home, interviewing her neighbours and relatives, which is a complete breach of privacy, since the anonymity and confidentiality of a rape victim must be maintained. The same goes for the accused. In the absence of a clear shot of Ahuja, a red circle was made on a grainy image to prove to the viewer they were not being cheated. The media has turned into such a crusader that it has stopped questioning its role in passing the verdict even before the courts do so. Ahuja's family, too, found itself in the media glare. Though not guilty of the crime herself, his wife struggled to retain her composure in the midst of this onslaught.

Media: Messiah or Monster?

In its anxiety to ensure justice for the wronged, the media has begun to overstep its bounds without taking into account the impact such infringement of privacy can have on the victim herself. Society still does not accept women who have been sexually abused. There is a systemic denial of the rights of the person. Best friends turn away, families ill-treat them, marriages break up and some get thrown out of their jobs. And yet, these guidelines are regularly flouted by the press.

There is a long-term impact of poor reporting as well. After a young Mizo girl, a student of Delhi University, was gang raped in a moving car in May 2007, the media hounded her to such an extent that she left the city. Following the incident, the principal of Kirori Mal College in Delhi asked girls from the northeast to wear salwar kameez to college thus sending a strong message that the victim herself may have been responsible for the crime that was inflicted on her. In addition, the entire student population from the northeast got categorised as well.

Some sections of the media, too, sent out similar veiled hints that perhaps girls from the northeast were too liberal for a regressive city like Delhi; that taking a walk in Delhi at night had greater connotations here than back home. None of the channels or papers criticised the government for not ensuring safety for single women at night, that Delhi's streets were dangerous for women. So, while the girl had to give up her dreams of higher education, the government continues to turn a blind eye at non-functional street lamps for long stretches that leave roads dark and frightening, at unlit bus stops where women are forced to huddle together, and at non-existent patrolling by the police. A call to 100 or 112, both emergency numbers, is a lesson in itself. Women have found to their dismay, when being stalked on the streets or chased by cars, the response time is long enough to let perpetrators of violence walk away untouched.

The arrival of a number of television channels has made the reportage on gender violence in public spaces significantly worse. Continuous airing of looped images of women who have faced violence—minor girls who are victims of trafficking, girls who have been raped on the streets, or girls who have had acid thrown on them—and of their faces as they were paraded before the camera in the name of justice has trivialized the crimes and transformed them into bizarre forms of entertainment. The anger and the demand for punishment against those who committed the crimes have been replaced with a curious interest in the details of the incident itself. The viewer, regardless, is now an accomplice. As a result, the media's role in pushing for justice is now getting diluted and the victim ends up getting more victimised. Clearly, the media has failed to drive home the message where it matters most. Safety of women is not high priority on the list of what makes news today. And so the government remains nonchalant as well.

Moreover, media ethics has become even harder to regulate since there is a plethora of publications and channels, both radio and TV, and in Indian languages as well. The Press Council cannot take action against biased reporting which violates a victim's fundamental rights unless it is brought to their notice. Going by the assumption that the audience is always on the lookout for infotainment (news as entertainment), even regional papers and channels, who have significant reach and clout, dress up their stories with the right kind of frills to draw eyeballs.

An Assamese weekly, *Sadin*, was sued in 2003 for publishing an objectionable news item, identifying a rape victim. Not only was her photo printed but the entire timeline of the crime was written about. She was a minor as well, so several laws had been broken. It is a penal offence to publish these details but many reporters, especially the current crop, who often hit the ground running, forget what the law says.

Such sensationalisation is taking place across the entire spectrum of violence that women have to face both in public and in private. Whether it is sexual harassment or eve-teasing, women end up being more victimised. They end up as a commodity, once again up for sale. The woman's USP is her tragedy, her grief. The post-mortem done by the media in such cases often pushes victims to take drastic action. Like twenty-four-year-old Saujanya, who took her own life after the Mumbai police failed to act against those who sexually harassed her. The police failed her. So did the media.

Conclusion

That women of all ages face violence in public spaces is a grim reality. Addressing it will be a huge challenge since the matrix is complex. The issue is not just of law and order. The social order must change. The new woman must be accepted. Besides, cultural changes need to be initiated as well. But they cannot take place overnight. Women themselves must demand change and demand security for themselves. There is greater awareness of the responsibilities among women and they are willing to go that extra mile, if only they knew how. This is where the media, a mirror to society, comes in.

Media institutions need to do some serious spring cleaning. Both top management as well as reporters on the ground must reflect on and assess the quality and standard of their work. The crucial aspect of ethics must be raised with the editorial. Gatekeepers must be put in place to review and cross-check how stories are played and guidelines of ethical reporting formulated.

Second, a continuous process of dialogue is required. Investing in the media has enormous spin-offs. There's a buy-in. Once reporters understand the impact of their work on people, they will pursue rights-based sensitive journalism. The media must be treated as a partner and not an adversary. A partnership makes news organisations much more responsible. Right now, each entity is in its separate, isolated space. If the government, media and civil society are brought together to discuss how best to prevent violence against women in public spaces, change is possible.

The media must continue to highlight the risks women face even today. To strengthen this effort, women's organisations and other civil society groups need to move beyond critiquing the media and work closely with members of the media without aiming to push any agenda. Information is always at a premium, and fact-based unbiased data inevitably buttresses news reports. NGOs (including international agencies) must move beyond news conferences and invest in journalists. Civil society organisations must play the role of facilitators. Once the media understands the nuances of a problem, the issue will begin to find space through various ways, including campaigns. For that, de-branding is crucial. If the media is not restricted by any agenda, the quality and depth of reporting on gender violence improves vastly.

Third, in order to ramp up the quality of reportage, journalists must receive training through interactive methods such as workshops, field trips and meetings. Once a reporter is exposed to a variety of material and is mentored by experienced trainers, the person is transformed. Learning about what causes violence, how to interview a victim and how to decipher the law can shore up a journalist's ideating and reporting skills. It also ensures personal growth as well.

Fourth, there needs to be a monitoring mechanism that evaluates the media. There must also be a path to convey and correct the breaches that take place. This must be a voluntary, collaborative process with all stakeholders. Finally, much of today's debates and opinions are shaped in cyberspace. Blogs, diaries, websites, chat sites, online news portals, there are a vast number of platforms to raise the issue of violence. However, the internet itself has thrown up its own forms of violence against women.

Cyber-stalking, verbal abuse and sexual exploitation of women by misusing images, (morphing of faces, MMS clips) all make a woman extremely vulnerable in the age of the internet. The woman is not in control and lies can easily become truth. Abuse on the net is a growing phenomenon. Children too are under attack. Child pornography has grown exponentially. Today, the media uses the internet extensively. Websites like Youtube are used for images, Google and Yahoo for searching, while Twitter and Facebook have become a key source of information and social networking. Many developing news stories—like the Lalit Modi case or Shashi Tharoor's many gaffes—are followed on Twitter. Today, lead actors in news do not give quotes of sound bytes, they just post messages on websites or social networking sites.

While reporters find this avenue attractive because access has become easy, there are risks attached. If a woman is publicly abused on the internet, she is unable to fight it. Take the case of a woman who worked in a BPO office, who found intimate pictures of herself posted on the net by a rebuffed colleague. She went to the police and the pictures were removed. But the humiliation and trauma forced her to leave the job. Punishment is that much harder for internet crimes. Since the net is not regulated and ban on websites can be circumvented, users themselves must define their own guidelines and the government must develop laws to prevent this new age violence on women.

However, the government can play a key role in curbing virtual violence. As in countries like Brazil, United States and the UK, India, too, must have clear laws on violence against women that takes place on the internet. Internet Service Providers (ISPs) can be asked to play a proactive role and women themselves encouraged to report such crimes so that perpetrators can be punished. Special support systems can be made within the policing system to actively track down cyber criminals. Currently, laws do exist but they need to be fine-tuned to the needs of women when it comes to virtual crimes.

Today, the Indian media is an aggressive creature. Despite agencies to regulate it in case it oversteps the line, so far issues like gender violence in public spaces are treated poorly in mainstream media as well as regional media. Norms are flouted easily and there is no recourse for those who fall victim to news voyeurism. Key stakeholders, such as women's organisations and agencies like the UN, need to work closely with the media to develop guidelines on how gender violence is reported along with a commitment that corrective action will be taken in case of violations.

However, despite challenges, the media is not a closed chapter. Change is bound to take place within its portals, albeit slowly. Transitions are always difficult and the Indian media is no different. Just like in politics, the media, too, depends heavily on people for its very existence. Through the 24x7 cycle, media managers are glued to TRPs and sale figures to track what is popular on news. No matter how much entertainment, sleaze and sports is fed to the reader and the viewer, once the threshold is crossed, people hit back. Television channels and newspapers have been known to soar and then flounder because they crossed the line or just didn't get the formula right. While numbers will continue to matter, what is emerging is that content that closely reflects the interests and demands of the public can make a difference to the image and ratings of news agencies. With a nudge in the right direction, especially from the public, which is today vocal, the media can be persuaded to incorporate gender violence in public spaces as a key issue. Only then can social transformation take place.

Notes on Contributors

❀✿❀

SARA PILOT is the Chairperson and co-founder of CEQUIN. She was previously associated with UNIFEM and has worked on gender issues for over eight years. She has a Master's degree in International Relations from the University of Kent, U.K.

LORA PRABHU is the Director and co-founder of CEQUIN. She has worked in the development sector and media, with a special focus on gender, for the last 16 years. She has a Master's degree in Modern Indian History from JNU, New Delhi.

URVASHI BUTALIA is the co-founder of Kali for Women, India's first feminist publishing house and is currently, Director, Zubaan, an imprint of Kali. She is an independent researcher and writer who has been active in the women's movement in India for over three decades. Among her publications are: *Women and the Hindu Right: A Collection of Essays* (co-edited, 1995), *Speaking Peace: Women's Voices from Kashmir* (edited, 2000) and the award-winning history of the Partition of India, *The Other Side of Silence: Voices from the Partition of India* (1998), winner of the Oral History Book Association award and the Nikkei Asia Award for Culture.

SANJAY SRIVASTAVA is currently Professor of Sociology at the Institute of Economic Growth, Delhi. His research focuses on masculinity, sexuality and the body in contemporary India, as well as on urban spaces (locality, neighbourhood and the transnational) and modernity and etiquette training. He has been associated with several universities and academic institutions, including the Centre for the Study of Developing Societies, Delhi and the International Institute for Asian Studies, University of Leiden, Leiden, The Netherlands. He has published widely in books and journals in India and abroad. Among his key publications are: *Passionate Modernity: Sexuality, Gender, Consumption and Class in India* (2007), *Entangled Spaces: Slum, Gated Community and Shopping Mall in 'Global' Delhi* (2011) and *The Sexualities Reader* (edited, 2011).

SHILPA PHADKE is a sociologist, researcher, writer and pedagogue. She is Assistant Professor at the Centre for Media and Cultural Studies at the Tata Institute of Social Sciences, Mumbai. She has been educated at St. Xavier's College, Mumbai, SNDT University and the University of Cambridge, UK. She conceptualised and led the Gender & Space Project at PUKAR from September 2003 to September 2006 and has co-authored a book (*Why Loiter: Women and Risk on Mumbai's Streets*) based on this research. She publishes in academic journals and in the popular print media. Her areas of concern include gender and the politics of space, the middle classes, sexuality and the body, feminist politics among young women and pedagogic practices. She loves the chaotic city of Mumbai and fantasizes that it will one day have a very large park.

FLAVIA AGNES is a women's rights advocate and a legal scholar. A pioneer of the women's movement, she has worked consistently on issues of gender and law reforms. Her widely published writings have provided a vital context for feminist jurisprudence, human rights law and gender studies in India. Her publications include *Law & Gender Inequality – The Politics of Personal Laws in India* (1997), *Women and Law* (co-edited (2004)) and *Family Law: A Text Book on Personal Laws, Constitution and Matrimonial Litigation* (. 2 vols, 2011). Her autobiographical essay on domestic violence titled, `*My Story Our Story ... Of Rebuilding Broken Lives*' is an important marker of the Indian women's movement and has been translated into several languages. She is the co-founder of MAJLIS, and director of its legal centre.

RUKMINI SEN is Associate Professor at Ambedkar University, Delhi. She holds a Phd in Sociology from the University of Calcutta, Kolkata and her doctoral work explores the existence of a culture of silence among Bengali women. She has been associated as Senior Lecturer with the Centre for Women's Development Studies Delhi and has taught at the West Bengal National University of Juridical Sciences, as well as at the universities of Jadavpur, Calcutta and Burdwan, and has been a Visiting Fellow at the School of Law, University of Keele. Her academic essays have appeared in several journals including the *Indian Journal of Gender Studies, Economic and Political Weekly, Voice of Dalit* as well as on the internet.

PRITI A. PRABHUGHATE is currently Research Director, Humsafar Trust. She has a Phd from the Jane Addams College of Social Work at the University of Illinois at Chicago, and a Masters in Philosophy in Psychiatric Social Work from NIMHANS, the National Institute of Mental Health and Neuro Sciences. Her work has focused on mental health and sexual minorities and she has focused on couselling, capacity building, skill training, documentation and research.

ERNEST NORONHA is Programme Officer, Sexual Minorities with the United Nations Development Programme (UNDP) India. He has previously worked with a number of national and international organisations in the areas of HIV/AIDs, MSM and Sexual Minorities. He studied at the universities of Allahabad and Mumbai and has a long involvement in the management of projects and provision of technical support to non-profit and community based organisations. His work includes advocacy and research, as well as policy interventions. He has also worked with corporates, focusing on sensitisation in order to initiate workplace interventions and CSR activity and research. He was the principal investigator for a baseline study of female sex workers in Bhandup Sonapur area.

ALKA NARANG is Assistant Country Director (HIV and Development) with the United Nations Development Programme (UNDP) India. She has previously worked with the UNDP in Manila, the Philippines where she initiated the National UN Volunteer Programme, and has also worked in the USA and Switzerland. She is a Fulbright scholar with a Masters degree in Social Work from Delhi University. She studied HIV/AIDS management in the workplace from Stellenbosch University, South Africa and Development Management from Jones University, U.S.A. She is especially interested in understanding and advocating the causal factors of HIV and its social and economic impact on human development. Apart from her long experience in the development sector, she has taught graduate students of social work and has been actively involved in training officers from the nationalized banks in leadership, strategic planning and motivation. She has several publications to her name on issues of mental health, disability, education, training and development.

PREM CHOWDHRY is an independent researcher and historian. She has been a fellow at the Nehru Memorial Museum and Library in New Delhi.. Among her many publications are: *Political Economy of Production and Reproduction: Caste, Custom and Community in North India* (2011); *Contentious Marriages, Eloping Couples: Gender, Caste and Patriarchy in Northern India* (2007); *Colonial India and the Making of Empire Cinema: Image, Ideology and Identity* (2000); *The Veiled Women: Shifting Gender Equations in Rural Haryana, 1880–1990* (1994) and *Punjab Politics* (1984). She has recently edited *Understanding Politics and Society, 1910–1997* (2010); *Gender Discriminatioan in Land Onwership* (2009) and has also written a number of research articles on politics, society, popular culture and gender both in colonial and contemporary India, in edited works and reputed national and international journals.

NANDITA BHATLA is a senior Gender and Development Specialist with the International Centre for Research on Women. She has been closely associated with the development sector for several years and has conducted research, evalutations and programming on issues of gender, empowerment and violence. Her particular focus has been on domestic violence and its links to other development concerns. Through her work with community based organisations, she has focused on designing and implementing need-based and gender-integrated programmes in an effort to bridge the gap between field realities and policy planning. She has also worked on developing educational curricula, editing news-feature magazines, planning programmes. She has previously worked with groups like Sama and Nirantar in Delhi, focusing on health, education and gender.

MOHUYA CHAUDHURI currently heads the Health desk in NDTV. She has over two decades of experience in journalism and is a specialist in health, gender and conflict. She has reported from across India on a wide range of issues including gender violence, trafficking and cutting edge science. Many of her reports have had great impact and led to policy change. Mohuya has won several national and international awards for her films. These include the EU-India Award for Excellence in HIV Reporting, the UNAIDS Civil Society Award for Best Social Awareness film on HIV AIDS, Commonwealth Broadcasting Association (CBA) award for Best Conflict Reporting as well as the National Television (NT) awards for the Best Current Affairs Programme.

INDU PRAKASH SINGH works with the Indo-Global Social Service Society (IGSSS) as Technical Advisor, CityMakers Programme, focusing on homelessness and urban poverty. He has been associated with the development sector and the women's movement for several decades and has published a number of books and essays, key among which are: Women's Oppression, Men Responsible; Women, law and Social Change in India; Indian Women: The Captured Beings and Indian Women: The Power Trapped. He is coauthor of Delhi: A Tale of Two Cities. A student of Philosophy, and Sociology, Indu Prakash Singh has won many awards including the CNN-IBN Citizen Journalist Award in 2010 for his film, 'No Shelters for Homeless Women in Delhi'. He is currently a member of several organisations that work on issues of homelessness.

AMITA JOSEPH studied Law, Management and Human Rights. She has worked for over two decades in die legal, corporate and development sectors, both at the grassroots level, and more broadly at the national and regional levels. Her interests cover fair trade, migration, poverty, trafficking and disability. Amita was part of the core group that started work on homelessness a decade ago, and she has also worked on public interest litigation. Currently she writes and lectures on corporate responsibility and is associated with BCF, a non profit civil society organisation working to promote accountability

SHIVANI CHAUDHRY is Associate Director of the South Asia Regional Programme of the Habitat International Coalition's Housing and Land Rights Network (HLRN), New Delhi, where she has been working since 2004. Prior to this, she worked at the Center for International Environmental Law (CIEL) in Washington, DC, for five years. She has worked in the field of human rights for over 12 years and has prepared material and conducted training sessions and held workshops for grassroots communities, civil society actors and students.